MW00657692

THE SEVEN SECRETS OF GERMANY

The Seven Secrets of Germany

ECONOMIC RESILIENCE IN AN ERA OF GLOBAL TURBULENCE

David B. Audretsch
and Erik E. Lehmann

OXFORD
UNIVERSITY PRESS

Oxford University Press is a department of the University of Oxford.
It furthers the University's objective of excellence in research, scholarship,
and education by publishing worldwide. Oxford is a registered trade mark
of Oxford University Press in the UK and in certain other countries

Published in the United States of America by Oxford University Press
198 Madison Avenue, New York, NY 10016, United States of America

Cataloging-in-Publication Data is on file at the Library of Congress

9780190258696

9 8 7 6 5 4 3 2 1

Printed in the United States of America on acid-free paper

This book is dedicated to our children – Hannah, Christopher, James, and Alexander

Contents

Preface

WHEN WE MET up in Jena in November 2003, Germany was at the depths of economic stagnation, worrisome unemployment, growing self-doubt, and angst that was on the verge of entering its second decade. Ever since the euphoria triggered by the fall of the Berlin Wall on November 9, 1989, and the subsequent reunification on October 3, 1990, economic growth had stalled, leading Germans on both sides of the once-divided country to wonder what exactly they had accomplished. In the west, resentment of the *Solidaritätszuschlag*, or solidarity tax, grew. In the east, *Ostologie*, or a new nostalgia for the quality of life under the stable and predictable communist regime, resonated, especially with the older generation.

Our mandate came from Professor Dr. Peter Gruss, who as president of the Max Planck Society tasked us with creating and directing the newly established Division on Entrepreneurship, Growth and Public Policy of the Max Planck Institute of Economics, which was located in Jena. When colleagues asked why we did not come up with a German title for our new division, the answer was as striking as it was disturbing. There was no word for entrepreneurship in German. The closest concept, *Unternehmertum*, typically refers to a high-level manager of a company.

In a country that did not seem to have a place for entrepreneurs, where would we ever find talented, but also highly trained and motivated, scholars to embark on a research agenda identifying how Germany and other countries could best ignite the creative and innovative spirit of entrepreneurship? Staring at the corridor of empty offices that cold, dark November day, it was hard to imagine that such young scholars might actually exist.

But find them we did. Thanks to the generosity and professionalism of the Max Planck Society and its stellar world-class reputation in both the natural sciences and the social sciences, they found us. The three-hour train ride from Berlin or Frankfurt did not deter an inspired and determined group of young scholars from joining us from destinations as diverse and heterogeneous as China, Japan, Italy, Spain, Germany, Sweden, the United States, India, the Netherlands, Canada, Australia, Colombia, and Portugal. These young scholars spanning a broad spectrum of scholarly and national backgrounds descended upon Jena and coalesced to tackle not only what exactly influences the extent of entrepreneurship and innovation, but also how exactly those twin forces could best be harnessed to promote society in general and *Wohlstand*, or economic prosperity, in particular.

We are of course grateful to all of these young scholars for all that we learned from their intellectual endeavors as well as from their inspiration, spirit, and optimism. Some of the most important ideas contained in this book have their origins in the long and heated discussions and debates with our young colleagues back in Jena.

Jena was not the beginning of our work leading to this book. David came to Berlin in 1985, where he served first as research fellow and later as acting director and research professor until 1997 at the Wissenschaftszentrum Berlin für Sozialforschung (Social Science Research Center Berlin). This provided an extraordinary opportunity to observe and even participate in Germany's transition from a country divided by the Berlin Wall and Cold War, to a reunified and autonomous country, and finally to a leading economic engine of Europe in the context of a globalized economy.

While we met during this time, we did not begin working together until Erik spent a year at the Institute of Development Strategies at Indiana University in 2002 to complete his habilitation. Our growing research collaboration gained momentum as we assumed the director and assistant director positions of the Max Planck Institute of Economics in 2003 and continued even as Erik accepted the appointment as professor of business economics at the University of Augsburg in 2005. In fact, the work of our research team at the Max Planck Institute of Economics led to the discovery that Germany was rapidly becoming an entrepreneurially driven economy, which was documented and explained in our book with our friend and colleague Max Keilbach, *Entrepreneurship and Economic Growth*, published by Oxford University Press in 2006.

Our research identifying what seemed to be working and not working in Germany extended beyond David's departure from the Max Planck Institute of Economics in 2009, and increasingly pointed to a number of key elements that, when taken together, seemed to provide Germany with an economic resilience in an era of global turbulence. The purpose of this book is to share what we and our colleagues at the Max Planck Institute of Economics learned about the high degree of economic resilience exhibited by Germany and why and how this might be insightful and instructive for other countries and contexts.

We would like to express our gratitude to a number of colleagues who have contributed to this book, either directly or indirectly. First and foremost, we would like to express our deep thanks to our colleagues at the Max Planck Institute of Economics as well as the broader community of scholars who participated and devoted their ideas, inspiration, energy and efforts to taking a fresh perspective on what factors and forces influence the *Wohlstand* of a country or place. We are grateful to the careful and meticulous help and support of Chemain Nanney, Aileen Richardson, and Sara Cockerham of the Institute of Development Strategies at Indiana University and Cornelia Noglinski of the Department of Business and Economics at Augsburg University at virtually every stage of this manuscript. Their effort and contributions to this book are invaluable and greatly appreciated. We would also like to thank several owners and managers from traditional Mittelstand companies for their valuable inputs, in particular Alexander Starnecker, Manfred Starnecker and David R. Eisenbeiss.

Finally, we are particularly grateful to Scott Parris, who is the executive editor of economics and finance at Oxford University Press and Cathryn Vaulman, who serves as his assistant editor, for their determined support of this book. We very much appreciate their enthusiasm, encouragement, and commitment to high-quality scholarship and publications, along with their care, effort, and wisdom in guiding the writing process from inception to initial drafts and finally to publication.

THE SEVEN SECRETS OF GERMANY

1 Introduction

WHY GERMANY? SIMPLY look to its neighbors. Europe has been suffering its worst and most prolonged economic crisis since World War II. Growth has been stagnant throughout the continent, as unemployment ratchets ever higher. Unemployment in the euro zone is well into double digits. Countries like Spain and Greece have suffered unemployment rates exceeding 20 percent and youth unemployment rates of over 50 percent. While the economic disaster in Greece may have grabbed the most headlines, *The Atlantic* points out that "Spain Is Beyond Doomed."[1] In France, Portugal, and Italy it is barely better as sluggish growth and troubling rates of unemployment trigger political and social instability. The former secretary of the Treasury, Larry Summers, warns that "Europe is at risk of secular stagnation," leading the *New York Times* to the alarming conclusion that "Europe is facing a fresh downturn, with few new ideas on the table for reigniting growth and deepening political divisions of the austerity policies that many blame for worsening the malaise."[2]

And this is not just happening in Europe. Organization for Economic Cooperation and Development (OECD) countries outside of Europe, including the United States, have also struggled in the wake of the Great Recession, the worst economic calamity since World War II.

But not Germany. While much of Europe has suffered from either putrid or no economic growth and rising unemployment, Germany has enjoyed a second *Wirtschaftswunder*, or economic miracle. As of 2014, growth in Germany had been robust enough to drive unemployment to less than 6 percent, while the country enjoys record levels of employment and the lowest levels of unemployment in decades. The crisis in the euro zone wiped out some 3.8 million jobs between 2007 and 2014, but Germany never faltered in continuing to create new jobs.[3] In some Länder, or states, such as Bavaria and Baden-Württemberg, unemployment has virtually disappeared, with unemployment rates approaching just 3 percent.[4] Exports are also at record levels, as Germany has emerged as the export leader, not just in Europe, but in the world.[5] In July 2014, Germany reached a new monthly record with exports exceeding 101 billion euros, which represented an 8.5 percent increase from the previous year and a 4.7 percent increase from the previous month.[6]

Just as the economic crisis in the rest of Europe spooked financial markets, driving interest rates on ten-year government bonds in some countries, such as Greece, Spain, and Italy, to nearly double digits, those same markets recognize the fundamental economic strength of Germany. Interest rates in Germany have been driven down to remarkably low levels, approaching less than 1 percent.[7] The market knows what everyone else also knows—in a sea of economic despondence and despair, the German economy is a welcome island of dynamism, optimism, and success.

While this is not the first Wirtschaftswunder experienced by Germany, what makes this current economic miracle all the more remarkable is that the country has bucked the trend exhibited by most of its neighbors on the continent, indeed throughout the OECD. In the first, and original, Wirtschaftswunder of the 1950s and early 1960s, all of Europe, in fact, the entire developed world, enjoyed a surge in economic growth and diminished unemployment, almost to the point of wiping out unemployment, as all boats were lifted by the rising tide of postwar economic growth. This economic euphoria was even more prevalent in Germany. In May 1945, Hitler was dead and National Socialism had been defeated. After months of allied bombing and door-to-door combat and bombardments, little remained of the once majestic medieval cities and architecture along with the mighty plants and factories that had fueled two world wars. Germany had been reduced to ashes.

But by 1946, the eminent British newspaper *The Times* characterized the unexpected rapid recovery that was well underway as the *Wirtschaftswunder*, or economic miracle—a term that has stuck to this day.[8] The miracle was the rebirth of a Germany that was not just recovering but booming.[9] Germany was vigorously rising from the ashes of defeat from two world wars. And what a miracle it was! Industrial production, which was the locomotive for economic growth during that era, grew by an astounding 25.0 percent in 1950 and 18.1 percent the following year. These stunningly high rates of growth continued throughout the remainder of the decade, so that by 1960 industrial production had increased by more than two and half times. The German Wirtschaftswunder fueled a corresponding rise in gross domestic product (GDP) by two-thirds, while employment rose from 13.8 million in 1950 to 19.8 million in 1960. Over 10 percent of the workforce was unemployed at the beginning of the decade, but by its end, the unemployment rate had been reduced to a microscopic 1.2 percent.[10] Unemployment was virtually wiped out by the Wirtschaftswunder.

Although the growth rates, levels of employment, and drop in unemployment may not have been quite as spectacular elsewhere in Europe and throughout the OECD as compared to Germany during those heady years following World War II, they were still impressive, certainly by today's standards. After all, this is generally considered to be a "golden age" for American economic growth and performance. The US unemployment rate reached a remarkable 2.9 percent in 1953, and in only one year of that decade did unemployment exceed 5.5 percent. Similarly, in the United Kingdom, the unemployment rate barely rose above 2 percent during that same decade. In fact, the rate of unemployment averaged around 2 percent, not just in countries like France and Italy, but for all of Western Europe.

Thus, while Germany may have enjoyed its postwar Wirtschaftswunder, so, too, did the rest of the developed world. What is different, and even more striking about contemporary Germany, is that its economic performance is not simply being lifted, perhaps a little more, by the same rising tide that is lifting economic performance everywhere in the developed world. Rather, in its astounding economic performance, Germany is swimming against a current, or perhaps seen through the eyes of some of its European neighbors, a tidal wave of economic despair and angst. More amazingly, it is doing so while much or even most of Europe is bogged down in economic gloom and despair; yet economic confidence and optimism reign supreme in Germany.

However, things were not always so rosy for Germany. First there was *Stunde Null*, or hour zero, as those fortunate enough to have survived the horrors of the Third Reich began to clear away the rubble of what remained from the devastation of World War II to make a fresh start. Then there was the deepening economic stagnation and pessimism accompanying the upward ratcheting of unemployment following reunification in the 1990s. As the unemployment rate entered into double digits and economic growth stalled at the end of the last century, the German outlook was indeed gloomy.

Germany was falling behind. The per capita GDP of France pulled sharply ahead of Germany by the end of the century, and perhaps even more alarming, Italy's almost reached parity with Germany. *The Economist* branded Germany as "The Sick Man of Europe."[11] Germans wondered, "Are We Still in the Champions League?"

When exactly Germany's Wirtschaftswunder stopped being a *Wunder* is subject to considerable debate. But there was no doubt that what the president of the influential Kiel Institute for the World Economy, Herbert Giersch, and his two colleagues, Karl-Heinz Paqué and Holger Schmieding, characterized as *The Fading Miracle* had indeed taken place.[12] Much of the public sentiment, policy and business leaders, and even scholars attributed the demise of the Wirtschaftswunder to the fall of the Berlin Wall on November 9, 1989, and German reunification on October 3, 1990. Right before the Berlin Wall fell, (West) German growth had been a vigorous 6 percent in 1987 and 5 percent in 1988. But by 1993, growth had stalled and the economy actually shrank by 1 percent. Growth rates remained negligible, never rising above 2 percent, for the remainder of the decade. Meanwhile, unemployment continued to skyrocket. While the unemployment rate was around 7 percent as the Berlin Wall fell, it subsequently jumped to alarmingly high levels of double digits, climbing to well over 12 percent by the middle of the decade. The army of unemployed workers seemed to grow relentlessly, rising from around two and half million at the time of German reunification, to nearly five million people toward the end of the decade. The miracle had indeed faded.

Explanations for the demise of the Wirtschaftswunder were many and varied. The team of scholars led by Herbert Giersch pointed to the dual rise of labor unit costs and the value of the currency on international exchange markets.[13] According to the careful and meticulous analyses of Giersch, Paqué, and Schmieding, the economic growth miracle had been fueled largely by a growth in labor unit costs that remained less than the overall growth of productivity. Combined with low currency value of the Deutschmark, German goods became highly competitive in international markets, triggering an explosion of exports.[14] However, as the standard of living and wages began to rise faster than productivity growth, German competitiveness began to sag. By 1994, the mean manufacturing employee compensation, which includes social insurance and other employee benefits, was considerably higher in Germany, at $25.71 per hour, than in the United States, where it was only $16.73, or in Japan, at $19.01.[15]

Germany, perhaps even more than other countries, had anticipated that the end of the Cold War, triggered by the fall of the Berlin Wall, would usher in a welcome peace dividend. Resources previously allocated toward fighting the Cold War and preserving the viability of a country under constant threat from its one-time enemies on the other side of the eastern borders could now be diverted away from financing national security and instead be invested for productive purposes.

But the widely anticipated economic boom accruing from the peace dividend never materialized. The Wirtschaftswunder had succeeded because of German competitiveness vis-à-vis the Western Allies. However, along with the end of the Cold War came new competition from a different direction—from the East, in both Europe and Asia. For example, the daily earning of labor in 1992, just after the country was reunified, was only $6.14 in Poland, $6.45 in the Czech Republic, $1.53 in China, $2.46 in India, and $1.25 in Sri Lanka, in comparison to $78.34 in the European Union.[16]

Labor cost differentials can, of course, be offset through productivity increases and through the substitution of technology for labor. Germany, like every country, was being subjected to competition in the new globalized economy. However, unlike any other country at that time, Germany had just absorbed 18 million people who worked at substantially lower levels of productivity.[17] Estimates of East German productivity relative to that in West Germany ranged between 40 and 70 percent.[18] This drag on productivity precisely at a time when the country was exposed to new global competition had a drastic impact on competitiveness.

The twin forces of globalization and reunification seemed to be impacting Germany more severely than other countries. However, economic decline was not the only response to the new era of globalization. When policy and business leaders looked to the other side of the Atlantic, they saw a United States that was prospering during the decade of the 1990s.[19] It wasn't that America had avoided plant closings and downsizings. Mass layoffs were prevalent in the news media at that time. Still, economic growth ratcheted to ever-higher levels toward the end of the century, and unemployment virtually disappeared.

The two sides of the Atlantic were clearly on divergent trajectories. At the beginning of the decade, in 1991, per capita GDP was only $2,000 higher in the United States than in Germany. A decade later, this gap in the standard of living had exploded to $12,000. Germany was clearly going in the wrong direction.[20] But how had America managed to go in the right direction?

The answer lies in the shifting source of competitive advantage. If large plants and factories, or what the economists term as physical capital, drove economic prosperity in the post–World War II era, globalization shifted the comparative advantage in capital-intensive industries to the lower-cost countries of Asia and Eastern and Central Europe.[21] The world, of course, still had a huge demand for such products, but with globalization, the geography of competitive production shifted away from the high-cost countries of North America and Western Europe to the new entrants in the global economy in Asia and Eastern and Central Europe. This was the decade when the high technology and innovative industries in the United States, such as personal computers, software, and semiconductors, exploded, driving up economic performance and driving down levels of unemployment. New companies, such as Apple and Microsoft, spearheaded by bold entrepreneurs like Steve Jobs and Bill Gates were leading the way to unprecedented American prosperity and wealth through innovation and entrepreneurship.[22]

The view from the other side of the Atlantic, in Germany, was bleak. Joschka Fischer, a member of the Green Party, who would subsequently serve as minister of foreign affairs under Chancellor Gerhard Schröder, lamented in 1995 that "a company like Microsoft would never have a chance in Germany."[23]

But it wasn't just the newly founded entrepreneurial companies that proved to be so elusive to Germany. It was also the capacity for those new start-ups to grow into global competitors, such as Intel, Microsoft, and Apple, leading the dean of the Sloan School of Management at MIT, Lester Thurow, to highlight Germany's vulnerability, pointing out that it "is falling behind because it doesn't build the new big firms of the future."[24]

Thurow was not alone in his concern. One of the leading weekly magazines in Germany, *Der Spiegel*, warned, "Global structural change has had an impact on the German economy that only a short time ago would have been unimaginable. Many of its products, such as automobiles, machinery, chemicals, and steel, are no longer competitive in global markets. And in the industries of the future, like biotechnology and electronics, German companies are barely participating."[25]

The *Wall Street Journal* looked at Germany and reached a similar conclusion: "If you look at the chip industry, it's a disaster. And the computer industry has been for many years. Energy technology as such is a disaster."[26] One of the leading politicians of Germany, Lothar Späth, who had served as minister president of the *Bundesland*, or state, of Baden-Württemberg, teamed up with the chairman of McKinsey & Co. Germany, Herbert A. Henzler, in their best-selling book,[27] *Countdown für Deutschland: Start in die neue Zeit?* (*Countdown for Germany: Start in the New Era?*) to warn that Germany's "greatest structural crisis in the postwar period has been the result of missing the boat on cutting edge technologies."[28] Hans-Werner Sinn, one of Germany's leading economists, who serves as president of the influential IFO Institute in Munich, put it even more bluntly in the title of his best-selling book, *Can Germany Still Be Saved*?[29]

Fast-forwarding to today, all this seems distant in a long-forgotten past, as if it were from a different era. Germany has emerged as *the* bright spot in an economically distressed Europe, and even among leading developed countries. As Jochen Bittner, political editor for the prestigious weekly newspaper *Die Zeit*, explains, "My country has made a remarkable journey from being labeled the 'sick man of Europe' just 10 years ago. Since then, it managed to bring down unemployment by almost half. In the past five years our economy has grown by 8 percent—a fantastic rate for such a developed country. And only last month, the federal government announced that it aimed to implement a budget with zero new debt in 2015. All this has been achieved despite a worldwide financial crisis and the near-collapse of the euro."[30]

Germany has managed not only to transform and upgrade its economic performance, but has done so precisely during an era when most of its neighbors on the continent, and even other partners in the developed world, are struggling against economic stagnation and despair. For example, as the *New York Times* warns, "France, which has in modern times been Germany's indispensable partner in European crisis management, is now in near revolt."[31] Invoking the great Russian novelist Leo Tolstoy, the *New York Times* observes, "Unhappy economies, it turns out, are all unhappy in the same way."[32]

But not Germany. How did Germany not only turn around its economy, from being the sick man of Europe and perhaps being downgraded out of the Champions League of high-performing developed economies in Europe and elsewhere?

The purpose of this book is to answer that very question. We do so by highlighting seven particular areas, or dimensions, of Germany that seem to be unique and distinct from not just its European neighbors, but from any other country in the world. And they matter. We refer to them as "secrets," not so much because they are actually unknown or unarticulated in Germany, or even elsewhere, but for three other reasons. First, because until only very recently, the country was considered the sick man of Europe, Germany has not been a place to look for uncovering and deciphering any secrets concerning economic success. A minor literature has emerged responding to, and reflecting, a long era of German economic despair, not to mention a timidity reflecting a political and social hangover, natural remnants from the devastation wrought by National Socialism and two world wars.[33]

The second reason is that, when taken and considered together, these secrets constitute a much more holistic, integrated, and even structured and organized economic approach to generating a strong economic performance, or what is referred to in Germany as *Ordnungspolitik*, than exists in most other countries.

The third reason is that the striking turnaround in Germany's economic performance offers an important role model for countries in Europe and elsewhere, suggesting that there is a considerably more optimistic alternative to resignation accepting the inevitability of economic decline in the era of globalization. This book shows how Germany was able to accomplish a "jolt through society", as former Bundespräsident Roman Herzog called for in his famous "Berlin Speech" in April 1997. He boldly challenged Germany to overcome its well-known and deeply rooted angst, for Germans to become more self-sufficient instead of always relying on the state and the government to provide solutions, and to proactively harness the opportunities afforded by a globalized world. In particular, Bundespräsident Herzog called for the emergence of an innovative and courageous society, which places a premium not just on flexibility and mobility but also on solidarity with others, in order to play a responsible role and make a positive contribution to society.[34]

That Germany has been able to carve out success and resilience where some of its neighbors in Europe and partners in the OECD have not has caught the attention of influential thought leaders in policy and business. For example, Charles Wessner, the former director of the Board of Science, Technology and Economic Policy (STEP) at the National Research Council of the National Academies of Science and Engineering, responds to the seemingly inevitable continued erosion of manufacturing in the developed countries by pointing out that "one thing is clear. Countries that lose their manufacturing base risk losing their ability to innovate. Against the background of an economic environment which has seen the erosion and offshoring of traditional industries in the face of global competition, the German model, or some parts of it, warrants careful consideration. Above all, we have to pay attention to other countries' policies and programs and learn from them."[35]

It is important to emphasize that this book is in no way claiming that Germany has discovered a panacea neutralizing the inevitable economic slowdowns, downturns, and full-blown recessions wrought by the business cycle. Scholars and thought leaders in policy and business who should have known better had already deluded themselves into proclaiming "the end of the business cycle" during what the Nobel Prize–winning economist Joseph S. Stiglitz termed "the world's most prosperous decade" of "the roaring nineties" in the United States.[36] Germany, like all developed countries, continues to be subjected to the business cycle as it is integrated into the larger European and global economies.

What this book does suggest, however, is that there are three key differences exhibited by Germany in this young century. The first is the stunning and widely unpredicted and unanticipated resurgence from being Europe's sick man to ranking among the continent's most prosperous nations and serving as the unquestioned locomotive for economic prosperity. The second is a remarkable degree of economic buoyance, which while not immunizing the country against economic downturns and exogenous shocks enables Germany to rebound with considerable resilience.

The third is the unexpected emergence of a remarkable entrepreneurial society. This shift to an entrepreneurial society is reflected by educated and *weltoffen*, or globally aware, young Germans, who have triggered a wave of unexpected dynamism, flexibility and mobility, and ultimately underlies the impressive surge in the German economic performance.

Everything comes to an end. So too it was with America's soaring economic ascension during Stiglitz's "roaring nineties." But even after the euphoria was long past, key lessons, insights, and takeaways about the fundamental forces driving economic prosperity and success were not lost on scholars and thought leaders in policy and business. In particular, what most of the world, including the Americans themselves, had learned by the end of that decade that they did not understand in any fundamental way at its beginning, was the crucial role played by knowledge and ideas along with entrepreneurship as a key to transforming that knowledge and ideas into innovation, growth, employment, and competitiveness in a rapidly globalizing economy.

In its widely heralded proclamation at the turn of the century, the European Council of Lisbon proclaimed both knowledge and entrepreneurship to be the cornerstones to ensuring sustained economic prosperity in Europe. By the time that the president of the European Union, Romano Prodi, echoed the Lisbon mandate in 2002, confirming, "Our lacunae in the field of entrepreneurship need to be taken seriously because there is mounting evidence that the key to economic growth and productivity improvements lies in the entrepreneurial capacity of an economy,"[37] no one needed convincing any more about the primacy of what would become known as the *entrepreneurial society*.[38]

At the beginning of the 1990s, almost no one would have pointed to knowledge and entrepreneurship as the key ingredients fueling economic growth, employment, and competiveness. By the end of that decade, it would have been difficult to find someone who did not think that they matter.

Driving downtown from the airport in Riyadh, one sees a large placard with the greeting "Welcome to the Kingdom of Saudi Arabia—The Knowledge Society." Even an underground ocean of oil pales in value in comparison to the riches buried in knowledge and ideas.[39]

The lessons from the America of the 1990s were not lost upon President Barack Obama, who emphasized the key role that innovation and entrepreneurship needed to play to reignite economic growth and prosperity in his proposed plan, *A Strategy for American Innovation: Securing Our Economic Growth and Prosperity*.[40] Similarly, in his 2011 State of the Union Address to the US Congress, President Obama emphasized that "America's economic growth and competitiveness depend on its people's capacity to innovate. We can create the jobs and industries of the future by doing what America does best – investing in the creativity and imagination of our people. To win the future, the U.S. must out-innovate, out-educate, and out-build the rest of the world. We have to make America the best place on earth to do business."[41]

Just as Stiglitz's "roaring nineties" in the United States came to an end, so too will the impressive German second Wirtschaftswunder. This too shall pass. But just as the lessons about the key fundamental forces driving the impressive American prosperity of that decade were not lost on policymakers and business leaders all around the world, what we characterize in this book as the *seven secrets of Germany* will also serve as a useful starting point for thinking about and deciphering the fundamental forces contributing to economic resilience for a particular country in a particular context.

Thanks to the breathtaking American economic dynamism over the last decade of the previous century, the policy mantra for this century has become knowledge and entrepreneurship. Thus, that is exactly the way we will start our exploration and analysis of Germany, with a focus on the singular role of German small business and entrepreneurship in chapter 2 and the particular role of knowledge in Germany in chapter 3.

It is certainly no secret that small firms and entrepreneurship are among the most important keys to a dynamic and innovative economy, so that *small is beautiful*, as the title of chapter 2 states. The difference in Germany is not that there are lots of small and medium-sized enterprises (SMEs). Rather, the qualitative and sufficiently significant difference, which underlies the secret, actually merits a particular German name distinguishing SMEs from their counterparts in other countries—the Mittelstand. There is certainly no paucity of examples highlighting the high-flying and breathtaking technology-based start-ups, particularly in information technologies and increasingly in the life sciences. But the main point of chapter 2 is that the German Mittelstand represents a kind of main street entrepreneurship, in that it is deeply embedded in local communities. Mittelstand companies are also governed differently. They tend to be family-owned businesses that take full advantage of strong linkages and ties to their communities, enabling them to access both highly skilled labor through the local apprentice programs along with key financial resources through local financial institutions. Not only is their governance different but they also exhibit a decidedly different economic performance—a better economic performance—than do their counterparts in other countries. A subset of the Mittelstand companies has performed so well that the business consultant Hermann Simon famously refers to them as *hidden champions*, in that they dominate their product niches in global markets.[42]

Germany has long been known as the *Land der Dichter und Denker*, or the country of poets and thinkers, reflecting a reverence for science, ideas, and art that is centuries old. How does this Old World country measure up in terms of the key institutions and mechanisms used to produce knowledge, such as universities and education? Not especially well when compared to its European neighbors and OECD trading partners, a fact that presents a curious paradox. Despite its unspectacular performance of higher education, Germany is able to generate highly skilled workers and high levels of human capital. The resolution to the paradox is the focus of chapter 3, "Poets and Thinkers," and lies in a rich array of key institutions, ranging from the apprentice and training system that creates skilled labor, to world-class research institutes.

As it became clear in the 1990s that knowledge and ideas were powerful economic forces, it seemed that the newly emerging Internet with its World Wide Web would render geographic location and proximity superfluous. Knowing the price of gold on

Wall Street or the value of stocks in Tokyo no longer required spatial proximity. As *The Economist* famously proclaimed in 1995, "The death of distance as a determinant of the cost of communications will probably be the single most important economic force shaping society in the first half of the next century."[43]

It took the giant of a scholar, Maryann P. Feldman, who is the Heninger Distinguished Professor of public policy at the University of North Carolina, Chapel Hill, meticulously building upon her Ph.D. thesis in her book *The Geography of Innovation,*[44] to explain that, like Mark Twain's famous demise, the death of distance may have been greatly exaggerated. Paul Romer, professor of economics at the University of California, Berkeley, had revolutionized thinking in the scholarly field of macroeconomics by showing that knowledge not only drives economic growth, but is particularly potent because of its propensity to spill over from the firm or organization where it is created for use by individuals and other firms.[45] But once knowledge and ideas spill over from the company or organization where they are created, why should they remain geographically localized? That is, why should knowledge and ideas stop spilling over just because they reach the border of a city, state, region, or country?

It took Feldman's important theory of localization to complement the theory of knowledge spillovers to fully explain and understand that rather than leading to the death of distance, globalization and the emergence of knowledge as the key factor of production were actually making location and local strategies more important, because the knowledge spillovers remain localized within close geographic proximity to their source. Feldman carefully and painstakingly developed a theory of localization that explained the key role played by face-to-face contact and human interactions in creating and transmitting new ideas and insights.

Chapter 4 of this book highlights the long tradition of people in Germany being deeply connected to their roots, or where they came from. While Americans have a history of mobility, Germans and their culture have a strong link to the place where a person is born. The title of chapter 4, "Roots and Wings," draws from the famous insight of Johann Wolfgang von Goethe celebrating the preeminence of roots in grounding a person. Perhaps even more important is the legal and institutional basis in Germany that provides for a greater degree of decision-making autonomy at the decentralized state and local levels than in many other countries. While this degree of decentralized decision-making and governance has been a part of Germany for decades, Feldman's important ideas about the role of geography and place in economics and innovation implies that just as location has become more important in the global era, so too has the German competitive advantage emanating from strong and autonomous decision-making and governance at the state and local levels.

The second part of the title of chapter 4—the wings—refers to the other aspect of Goethe's famous penetrating insight, which is the capacity to move beyond these invaluable, but also inevitably constraining and restrictive, roots. Germany has managed to do exactly that in nurturing and developing numerous capacities, institutions, and policies to look outward and beyond its own borders in identifying and discovering new economic opportunities.[46] Hermann Simon emphasizes this cultural orientation in Germany toward internationalization and global opportunities, which did not just fall from heaven but was created, nurtured, and developed. According to Simon, "The best language is the language of the customer."[47] In particular, Simon points out that, in terms of international orientation, Germany has become like a small country, such as Switzerland, the Netherlands, and Sweden.[48] Small countries such as Denmark have historically developed a culture and orientation that looks for opportunities beyond their own borders because the country itself was simply too small geographically to sustain growth and economic development. Rather, access to external markets was required in order to generate growth. Such access required an orientation toward learning about and understanding foreign cultures in order to successfully trade and integrate with them. Simon's point is that in recent years Germany has become more like a small country in that knowledge of foreign languages, especially English, which is widespread, and an orientation toward understanding and communicating with foreigners in other cultural contexts is emphasized and celebrated. It is no coincidence that, thanks to developing the wings enabling it to identify and create opportunities around the globe, German trade with, and foreign direct investment in, China has skyrocketed, while it has remained largely a dream for other European countries such as France and Italy.

Just as globalization and the Internet technologies might have seemingly rendered place and location irrelevant, so too would infrastructure seem to be less central in an economy where ideas and knowledge matter more than plants and factories. In fact, chapter 5 explains why exactly the opposite is true. Part of the reason is because infrastructure can play a crucial role in facilitating the spillover of knowledge and ideas by making it easier for people to interact with each other. This means that places, ranging from cities, regions, and states to entire countries, that have invested in a stout infrastructure will also be facilitating the spillover of knowledge and ideas, which is one of the keys to igniting and sustaining economic growth and prosperity.

This is where Germany comes in. For years Germany has invested in an impressive infrastructure that has few rivals anywhere in the world. Very recently, Germany's commitment to investing in that infrastructure has come under thoughtful and well-formulated criticism from Professor Dr. Marcel Fratzscher, who is president of the German Institute for Economic Research (DIW) in Berlin. In his widely acclaimed book *Die deutsche Illusion*, or *The German Illusion*, Professor Fratzscher warns that, in fact, the once-prized jewel of Germany, its infrastructure, is actually eroding and depreciating at a rapid rate.[49] Still, as Jochen Bittner responds, "It's not as if our autobahns and schools are falling apart just yet."[50]

The new alarm for Germany's infrastructure mirrors a similar alarm expressed by the German media and public following several close matches in the initial stages of the World Cup in June 2014. Anything close to challenging the public view that the German national *Mannschaft*, or team, must overwhelm each opponent was simply unacceptable. Numerous articles even appeared wondering whether "Jogi," as Joachim Löw is referred to by the press and public, was even the right head coach for team. That was before they beat up on one of the heavily favored teams, Brazil, winning by a margin of 7–1, and going on to win the World Cup. But even that didn't put an end to the angst. In November 2014 the German national team that beat an obviously overpowered national team from Gibraltar by a score of "only" 4–1 was subjected to considerable scorn.[51]

So too it may be with the infrastructure. As Jochen Bittner suggests ironically, "Whenever I travel between Hamburg and Berlin, Germany's two biggest cities, a big sticker on the high-speed train now informs me that it is running on '100 percent green energy.' Yet as soon as the train pulls away from Hamburg, my cellphone connection gets shaky, or breaks down completely. Much worse is that there still isn't free Wi-Fi on board."[52]

Our colleague Silvio Vismara, who is a professor of finance at the University of Bergamo in Italy, is quick to sympathize with those who perceive decay of the vaunted German infrastructure, but is also quick to make an offer: "Let's trade." The complicated public transportation system between Bergamo and Milan hardly compares to the glistening, high-speed trains, or one of the many alternatives, between Augsburg and Munich, or Wuppertal and Cologne. Not to mention transportation options available between Bloomington and Indianapolis.

We title chapter 5 "(Infra)Structure" to emphasize that infrastructure is only one type of structure, reflecting a more fundamental approach to providing structure and organization in Germany, embedded in *Ordnungspolitik*. The mandate for structure and organization in German is legal, cultural, and historically rooted. It provides a framework for making decisions that few other countries have. As the great German philosopher Oswald Spengler observed a century ago, "The secret of all victory lies in the organization of the non-obvious."[53]

With all its emphasis on structure and organization, Germany and flexibility have not traditionally appeared together in the same sentence. Yet, as chapter 6 explains, Germany has exhibited remarkable flexibility as the country and its policies and institutions evolve over time to meet the challenges of a particular *Zeitalter*, or moment of time. Most strikingly, Germany was able to accomplish something that eluded many of its European neighbors, including France, Italy, Spain, and Portugal—to fundamentally reform and modify not just the labor market, by inducing considerable more flexibility, but the orientation of the entire society and economy toward globalization, with all of its implications and ramifications. As the title of the chapter suggests, a place that is characterized by both laptops and lederhosen may create considerable cognitive dissonance but also exhibits a degree of flexibility that contradicts the more prevalent and pervasive stereotype of a rigid and stubborn culture, society and nation.

While the German flexibility highlighted in chapter 6 may contradict the premises of many readers, the focus on Germany's prominence in manufacturing in chapter 7 will not. Germany has invested mightily, carefully, and strategically to create the brand *made in Germany*. The chapter emphasizes how and why Germany has succeeded in thriving with a manufacturing-led economy, while most of its neighbors, and certainly the United States, have not. Rather than view the twin forces with which this book started—knowledge and entrepreneurship—as substitutes for manufacturing, as certainly has been the case for the United States, the German strategy has been to treat them as complements. Through carefully developed and meticulously layered institutions at all levels of government and governance, Germany has pragmatically funneled new science, technology, and knowledge into the manufacturing process, rending it among the most productive and competitive in the world, especially in terms of product quality.

Most of the chapters to come deal with deep and historically rooted institutions, policies, and traditions in Germany. What is not deeply rooted and is without precedent since 1945 is the focus of chapter 8. For decades it did not seem possible for anyone in the world to think about Germany without first thinking about the atrocities committed in two world wars and the regime of National Socialism under the leadership of Adolf Hitler. First and foremost, it was not possible for Germans not to think about them, anywhere and everywhere. Such an awareness, consciousness, and karma left an indelible imprint on economic life, indeed all aspects of life, for decades in Germany.

But no more. As the title of chapter 8, "It's Good to be German," suggests, something fundamental has shifted, both in the way Germans view themselves, their identity, and in how the rest of the world views Germans and Germany, their image. As Jochen Bittner reflects, "In historical terms, Germany has entered a comfort zone. We ended up here thanks to two simultaneous developments. The first is the experience of becoming Europe's indispensable nation, both politically and economically. The second is the growing biographical distance from a history that demanded remorse, reparation, and proof of tenacity. For the first time in their lives, the current generation of German leaders doesn't have to struggle for international approval; instead they struggle not to be bothered by too many wishes from abroad. European unification is more or less complete, we've offered billions in loan guarantees to the euro zone, and we have even won the World Cup. Time to lean back!"[54]

It is one thing to feel positive and have others feel positive about you. It is another thing to be able to capitalize on that new identity and image and leverage them into dividends in economic growth, employment, and competitiveness. As chapter 8 shows and analyzes, that is exactly what Germany has done.

The last chapter provides a conclusion along with a number of key reflections and takeaways from what has preceded it. This final chapter will highlight the insights emphasized, what the main lessons are, along with the main takeaways from the book. The most salient point of "Conclusions: The Right Zeitgeist for the *Zeitalter*" is to suggest that Germany has institutions, both formal and informal, that facilitate crucial underlying forces—knowledge, skilled labor, human capital, spillovers, and entrepreneurship—that are the keys to a strong economic performance in the contemporary global economy. In contrast to its European neighbors and most of its partners in the developed world, the German economy has proven to be remarkably buoyant and resilient. This book illuminates seven secrets, or key features, of Germany that have contributed significantly to this strong and striking economic performance at a time when such buoyance and economic resilience has eluded most of its European neighbors and trading partners within the OECD.

The concluding chapter also suggests an eighth and previously unmentioned secret, upon which the effectiveness of the previous seven is based. These key institutional characteristics work together in an integrated complementarity that is mutually reinforcing. In trying to gleam insights and lessons for other places, nations, and contexts, the interdependence and mutually reinforcing interaction of the secrets are emphasized. While each of the secrets may be more or less feasible for adaptation in a different national and institutional context, there are compelling reasons to believe that the real secret of Germany is that they are highly linked in a carefully crafted mosaic that, in the end, may come as close to defining the country as anything else. At the same time, the seven secrets surely highlight that if Germany can transform itself from the sick man of Europe into a stunning economic, political, and social success, there is no reason for any other country or place to abandon hope. There is no reason that other countries cannot create their own turnaround and transformation—through the same effort, determination, commitment, and follow-through. As the great British novelist George Eliot penned well over a century ago, "It will never rain roses: when we want / To have more roses, we must plant more trees."

2 Small Is Beautiful

IN THE GLOBAL economy, you've got to be big to make it, right? The American companies that have withstood, and even thrived under, the gale winds of global competition have been among the largest. Of course the high-technology giants are obvious, such as Apple Computer, Amazon, eBay, Microsoft, Google, and Facebook, but the old standbys, such as Coca-Cola, Disney, Walmart, General Motors, and Exxon still remain as symbols of imposing American might in a globalized economy.

And in Germany? The leading economy in Europe lists its share of global giants, such as Volkswagen, Siemens, Deutsche Telekom, Robert Bosch, Allianz, and Deutsche Bank. In this way, Germany resembles all countries, in that it has leading industrial giants inhabiting the economic landscape. Just as Sweden has Ericsson, Finland has Nokia, France has the Carrefour Group, the United Kingdom has the HSBC Group, Spain has Telefónica (TEF), and the Netherlands has Philips, so too Germany has its share of, name recognition global corporate leaders.

But Germany has something else, too. It has companies like Herrenknecht.[1] The company is the leading manufacturer in the world of drills used to construct tunnels through mountains. Herrenknecht is a family business. Martin Herrenknecht started the company in 1977, when he manufactured his first tunnel-boring machine. In October 2010, pictures from the breakthrough ceremony of the drilling operations in the eastern tunnel at the Gotthard Base Tunnel, the longest traffic tunnel in the world, measuring 57 km, were broadcast live on television. The superstars of this live show were not your typical high-profile television actors or personalities, but rather, Sissi and Heidi, the names affectionately given to two of the four tunnel-drilling machines from Herrenknecht.[2]

The family still owns and operates the company. And like Herrenknecht, numerous but typically unknown and hidden world market leaders in Germany demonstrate their competitive superiority through impressive high-quality products. Like Herrenknecht, these companies are small and have learned to compensate for their small scale in a highly competitive, globalized world economy by being nimble, especially in terms of productivity and innovation.

Although Herrenknecht has had to travel extensively throughout the world to identify business opportunities and work with customers at worksites and meet with potential clients, company headquarters remain in Herrenknecht's home town of Schwanau, which is a small village located in the *Bundesland*, or state, of Baden-Württemberg.

It's hard to spot the existence, let alone the impact, of a company like Herrenknecht in the official economic statistics of Germany. Seen through the thicket of data and statistics measuring economic activity, Germany looks more or less like any other leading developed country. Most companies, as elsewhere throughout the developed world, are small. In fact, in Germany, as in virtually every other developed country, including the United States, France, the Netherlands, and Japan, well over 95 percent of enterprises are classified as being small or medium sized, in that they have fewer than five hundred employees. Thus, from the macro perspective, it's hard to see how or why anything is different in Germany.

However, when viewed through the micro perspective, a different picture begins to emerge. It is not just the number of small firms, or even their share of economic activity, that makes the difference in Germany. Rather, it is a qualitative difference in the small firms that matters. This qualitative difference is so profound that Germans have a unique word and concept to describe their small and medium-sized enterprises—the Mittelstand.[3] While much of the world has embraced big is beautiful as a strategy for dealing with globalization, this secret in Germany is a matter of doing exactly the opposite. It is not just the Mittelstand that makes it clear, but also the recent entrepreneurial revolution in Germany, triggered by a wave of innovative policies and institutional reforms, that shows that, at least in the German context, small is not just beautiful but also one of the secrets to a strong and sustained economic performance and resilience.

The Mittelstand

There are actually two very distinct ways that Germans understand what the Mittelstand means or is all about. The first meaning refers to the size of the firm. Small may be beautiful, but it is far from obvious what actually constitutes a small firm or business. In fact, there is no singular consensus cross-country contexts defining a small firm and distinguishing it from big business. As table 2.1 shows, what is considered to constitute a small

TABLE 2.1

Small and Medium-Sized Enterprises Defined

	Number of employees	Sales in euros per year	Balance sheet in euros per year
German definition			
Small enterprises	Up to 9	Less than 1 million	
Medium enterprises	10 to 499	1 to 50 million	
Large enterprises	500 and more	More than 50 million	
European Union Definition			
Microenterprises	Up to 9	Less than 2 million	Up to 2 million
Small enterprises	10 to 49	Up to 10 million	Up to 10 million
Medium enterprises	50 to 249	Up to 50 million	Up to 43 million
Large enterprises	250 and more	More than 50 million	More than 43 million

firm in the national context of Germany is somewhat different from the rest of the European Union. According to the definition used in Germany, small and medium-sized enterprises have fewer than five hundred employees and sales of less than 50 million euros. Under this criterion and view, which is shown in figure 2.1, almost all firms belong to the Mittelstand—99.6 percent of all firms, which encompass 60 percent of employees and over one-third of sales.

The second sense conveyed in Germany by the Mittelstand is considerably more qualitative and nuanced in nature.[4] What constitutes a Mittelstand company is not necessarily any particular size criterion, but rather a common set of values, strategies, governance, finance, human resource practices, and orientation. Here the size of the firm is less of the focus than the orientation, values, and ways of operating. Even large companies, such as Robert Bosch and Wuerth, can share the attitudes, strategies, and values of their smaller, more typical counterparts and are generally viewed as belonging to the German Mittelstand.

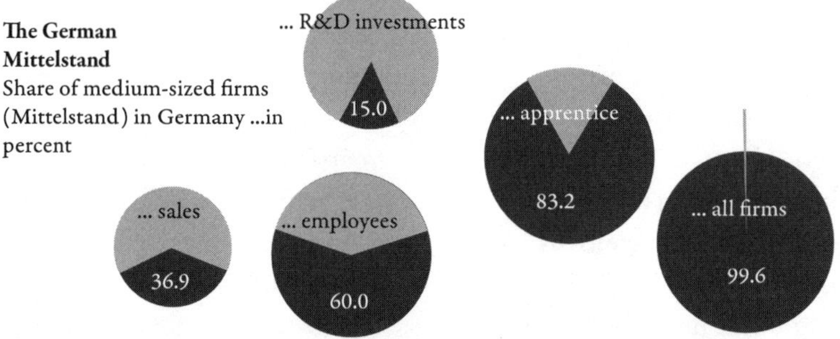

FIGURE 2.1 The Role of Small and Medium-Sized Enterprises in Germany
Source: Institut der Deutschen Wirtschaft, IDW, 2013.

In uncovering the key role played by the Mittelstand in driving the economic success of Germany, *Newsweek* points out that "this is the definition of *Mittelstand* success: to be a world leader in a niche market, the 'go-to' company even if the customers are half-way around the world, a 'hidden champion' (to use a German phrase) that benefits from globalization rather than being washed away by it. To be part of the *Mittelstand* is also to be capable of employing 50 to 500 people in a small town, meaning talented youth needn't head to the big city to find success. It's another way power—this time economic—is decentralized. The success of the Mittelstand, which generates the bulk of corporate revenues in Germany, is deeply intertwined with the country's support for manufacturing."[5]

The German Mittelstand is an economic heavyweight in several aspects. Not only do most firms belong to the Mittelstand, but most employees, 60 percent, are working for Mittelstand companies. Only one-fifth of German employment is in large companies, which is considerably less than in, say, the United States. And 83 percent of all apprentices came from the Mittelstand. Thus, the Mittelstand is a key source of educated human capital for the industry and service sectors in Germany. Most Mittelstand companies are too small to afford a specialized R & D division. Still, one-fourth of all the 350,000 R & D scientists and engineers employed in private industry are working within these small companies. In total, the German Mittelstand invested about 8.7 billion euros in 2013 in developing new products and production technologies, amounting to about 15 percent of all spending on R & D.

But the real difference lies in what the Mittelstand does, along with how it does it. According to *The Economist*, the Mittelstand is "often praised as a group for providing the backbone of the world's fourth-largest economy. Individually, they are world leaders in hiding their light under a bushel. They tend to be family-owned, tucked away in small towns and familiar only to the businesses that buy their specialized machinery and components."[6]

Perhaps this accounts for the widespread envy expressed in many countries toward the Mittelstand in Germany. The German Mittelstand generates not only a remarkable competitive advantage for production and manufacturing, but also a stability in employment and growth.

As is made clear in figure 2.2, like virtually every other developed country, Germany has hundreds of thousands of small companies, each employing a handful of workers. Similarly, Germany has a limited number of very large companies with thousands of employees, which command global name brand recognition. However, what Germany has and other countries do not is a vibrant and dynamic group of middle-sized companies. Scholars have long recognized the paucity of firms existing in the middle of the firm-size distribution, or what has been termed as "the missing middle."[7] In this respect Germany is different. Economic research has shown that in the United States, if firms grow, they tend not to stop growing until they attain a very large size.[8] Systematic empirical studies analyzing large data sets tracking the start-up, growth, and survival or failure of companies have shown that entrepreneurial start-ups in the United States tend to either survive

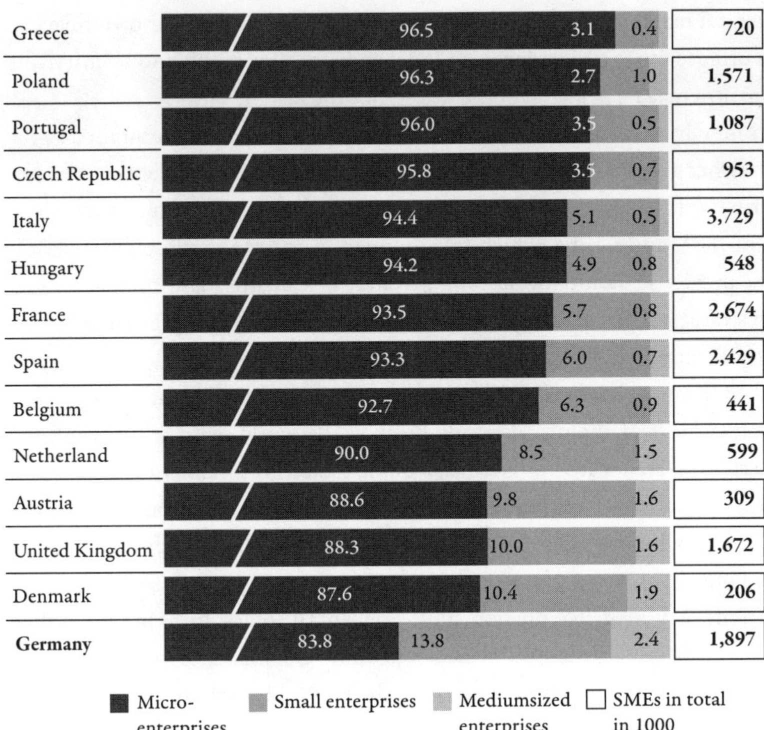

FIGURE 2.2 SMEs in Europe (% of all enterprises)
Source: Data from European Commission. Figure taken from Institut der Deutschen Wirtschaft, *iwd-Medien*, 28, 2013.

and grow or else fail.[9] Thus, in an "up or out" industrial structure, there is something of a hole in the middle of the firm-size distribution.

But the German Mittelstand is different. The German Mittelstand is characterized by several key qualities that are obscured when simply comparing numbers, or presence, with SMEs in other countries. The Mittelstand difference manifests itself in eight distinct, salient characteristics—firm governance, product strategy, human resources, organizational structure, planning time horizons and orientation, flexibility in production, ability to leverage local resources, and a global scanning for opportunities.

The first characteristic revolves around the ownership of the firm. First and foremost, only a handful of the Mittelstand companies are actually publicly held and listed on the stock market, or are governed by external private equity firms. Instead, most of the Mittelstand companies are family-owned. The family-owned and privately held Mittelstand companies resist growth through obtaining finance from external sources, especially where yielding control and decision-making is concerned, which could compromise independence and flexibility. This is evidenced by a debt ratio of German Mittelstand companies, which ranks among the lowest in the world. In addition, the debt ratios of the German Mittelstand are now at their lowest levels in decades.[10] Despite the low interest rates on the capital market, Mittelstand companies prefer to rely on their own financial power, which brings with it a high degree of independence, autonomy, and security. The Mittelstand mantra may be "survival of the fittest, not the fattest."[11]

There are compelling examples of Mittelstand companies that have succumbed to the temptation to either go public and be listed on a stock market or sell ownership to a private equity firm, such Villeroy & Boch, which was founded in 1748, Rosenthal, which was founded in 1879, and Grohe, which was founded in 1948. The subsequent performance of these previously family-owned and privately held Mittelstand companies suggests a shift in strategic focus, putting a premium on a fast but myopic growth in market share at the cost of sustainability.[12]

Family-owned firms are hardly a novelty in the leading developed countries. Still, Germany is different. Most of the oldest family firms in the world, with a long tradition spanning generations, are located in Germany. Some established, family-owned Mittelstand companies actually go back for centuries, such as breweries like Zötler, which was founded in 1447, or vineyards such as Weingut Fürst zu Hohenlohe Oehringen, which was established in 1242.

Manufacturing is a more recent phenomenon. Some of the oldest firms in the German manufacturing sector are still family owned, including a handful of firms that were founded long before the Industrial Revolution in the United Kingdom. For example, in 1340, the craftsman Johan Prym started the production of needles and buttons near Aix-la-Chapelle. Fast-forwarding to today, what ultimately became Wilhelm Prym GmbH & Co. KG, named after one of Johan's descendants, Wilhelm, in 1530, who was a goldsmith, is now a market leader in Europe and the United States in textile finishing. This Mittelstand company has operations located across the globe, with revenues of 350 million euros. The family continues to own the company and is now in its sixteenth generation of ownership. The longevity of this company is attributable to a fine balance invoking the mantra of the German Mittelstand—combining well-honed tradition with innovation. Wilhelm Prym GmbH & Co. has remained true to its principles and roots over the years, indeed over the centuries, but still has opportunistically expanded through fundamental innovations like the snap-fastener in 1903.

While family firms may know who they are, academics and scholars are less certain. In fact, dissonance and controversy reign in the scholarly literature about what actually constitutes a bona fide family firm. The definition varies to some degree across countries. For example, in the United States, a company is often classified as a family-owned firm when a family or individual owns more than 5 percent of the company's equity shares.[13]

An implication of this definition is that every company listed on a stock market with a private and individual investor owning at least 5 percent of the shares meets the criterion to be classified as a family-owned firm—even though there is no family! This definition clearly suffers by missing the important point, which is often called the *family-ness* of a family firm—the involvement of the family within the company beyond pure equity ownership. It is the presence of the family in the top management board and its role in the governance of the board of directors that make the real difference.[14]

In the German context, the Stiftung Familenunternehmen, or Foundation for Family Firms, distinguishes between two distinct categories to classify a company as constituting a family firm.[15] The first category is *owner-controlled firms* and consists of all firms that are controlled by a "manageable number of natural persons." Ownership and management do not necessarily coincide. In fact, 92 percent of all enterprises in Germany fall into this category.

The second category is labeled *owner-managed firms* and consists of all firms that are controlled by a "manageable number of natural persons" where at least one of the owners is actively leading and managing the firm. About 90 percent of all enterprises in Germany fall into this category.[16] Every third firm with revenues exceeding 50 million euros belongs to one of these two categories of family firms. Similarly, more than 150 family firms exhibit revenues exceeding the one-billion-euro threshold. The top 500 family firms in Germany employ over 4.5 million people worldwide and generate revenues exceeding 900 billion euros.[17]

Table 2.2 ranks the oldest family companies in Germany. Only a few, like the German Post, which was founded by the noble family of Thurn and Taxis, have become publicly traded companies on a stock exchange. Similarly, the parent firm of Merck KgaA, which was founded in Darmstadt over 450 years ago, was forced to split into two parts in 1916. One part, Merck KgaA, is still controlled by the founding family, which continues to serve as the major and largest shareholder. The other part, Merck & Co., is a publicly traded corporation on Wall Street.

A second key characteristic of the German Mittelstand is a strategy focusing on the quality, innovation, and technology of the product as sources of competitiveness, rather than relying mainly on price competition.[18] The strategy based on quality and innovation is consistent with a society and economy that has traditionally operated with a high value of its currency, rendering low-cost price competition relatively ineffective. After all, the post–World War II German economy was forged on combining a highly valued currency with very high labor costs. Thus, for some years, the Mittelstand companies had to operate and learn to survive and thrive in an environment where they competed against lower-cost producers located in low-cost countries. The key to surviving and thriving has been to develop products with the highest quality in the world. In order to maintain such high levels of quality, and to ward off competition from elsewhere, particularly from lower-cost producers enjoying the natural competitive advantages of a lower-valued currency and lower labor costs, the German Mittelstand has deployed a strategy focusing on innovation and technological improvements to enhance quality and maintain competitiveness in global markets. This has resulted in what Hermann Simon has painstakingly and meticulously documented—the *hidden champions* have emerged as the dominant producers and sellers in their product classes.[19]

TABLE 2.2

Family Firms in Germany

Company	Founded	Industry	Sales (in Mio €)	Employment
Achenbach Buschhütten	1452	Mechanical engineering mills	59.920	311
Isabellenhütte Heusler	1482	Metal processing	96.990	680
Deutsche Post	1490	Logistics	55,500.000	435,285
William Prym	1530	Push buttons	380.005	3,891
Stahlwerke Annahütte	1537	Threaded steel	224.000	500
Leoni	1569	Cable	3,810.000	61,591
Pfeifer Holding	1579	Wire rope and lifting systems	217.500	1,100
HahnemühleFineArt	1584	Art paper	25.430	180
Saxonia EuroCoin	1612	Coins	84.400	100
Heinz Holding	1622	Glass vessels	292.870	3.000
Merck KGaA	1668	Pharma and liquid crystals	10,741.000	39.230
WIV Wein International	1675	Vine direct distribution	48.290	5,400
Metrica Interior Gruppe	1681	Luxury interiors	82.650	300
Lukas Meindl	1683	Outdoor shoes	62.000	250
Dillinger Hütte Gruppe	1685	Steel / heavy plates	2,498.000	5,291
Lambertz	1688	Baked goods	552.400	3,450
Zapp	1701	Steel	338.600	1,000
Goldhofer	1705	Transport aircraft	141.600	650
Römheld Friedrichshütte	1707	Production technology	36.000	500

Source: David B. Audretsch and Erik E. Lehmann, "The Emergence of the Mittelstand Company: A German Perspective," working paper, University of Augsburg, 2015.

What almost all Mittelstand firms have in common is their strategic focus on market niches and their flexibility in the production process, enabling a handful of them to achieve the status of hidden champion. Otherwise, the Mittelstand is a rather heterogeneous group of firms, in particular with respect to size and governance, with the presence of families as a large shareholder for several generations.

The cornerstone strategy combining tradition with innovation by family firms contributes to the long-run perception among consumers of the product's quality, which obviously cannot be easily imitated by competitors. For example, pencils from Faber-Castell, which was founded in 1761, exhibit a long history of famous and prestigious consumers, such as Vincent van Gogh and Johann Wolfgang von Goethe. When questioned about what accounts for the obvious success emanating from a family working closely together for eight generations, Anton Wolfgang Graf von Faber-Castell, who is patriarch of the family-owned firm, invokes the mission statement dating back to his ancestors: "Tradition means preserving not the ashes, but the glow."[20]

A third important characteristic of the German Mittelstand is the nurturing and development of human resources, or what is more crudely referred to in other countries and contexts as the labor force. As discussed above, SMEs in Germany have realized that the apprentice system provides them with access to a resource that they have been able to leverage to develop and retain highly skilled and capable human resources. A study undertaken by the Institute for Leadership and Human Resource Management at the University of St. Gallen surveyed over 14,700 employees working at nearly one hundred SMEs in Germany and found that 97 percent felt a sense of community at their company. An additional 97 percent felt that the values of the company coincided with their own values. This sense of harmony between the workers and the Mittelstand reflects a determined strategy of German SMEs to get their employees to feel committed to their employer.[21]

From his experience, Herrenknecht clearly believes that being part of a family firm makes all the difference in his ability to leverage a highly skilled, motivated, and committed human resource base to deliver a quality and innovative product to customers throughout the world: "I believe that we pull together incredibly well, like a family."[22] As Herrenknecht explains, "We started 35 years ago, and many employees have now been at the company more than 30 years. They all pull together as a team. That is the core of a family business."[23] What Herrenknecht articulates is what scholars of family business have now identified through a large body of painstaking, systematic, detailed empirical analyses.[24] Such studies confirm that one of the strategies deployed by family business is to motivate employees beyond what they typically experience at a large, impersonal corporation, where work is all about the money. Rather, scholars of family business provide compelling documentation and analyses showing that employees in a family business are motivated not just by the wage but also by being part of a team.

For example, Reinhold Würth, who in 1945 founded a company manufacturing screws that has grown to operate facilities across the globe, attributes his own success as well as that of the company to having highly motivated and capable employees. Similarly, Wolfgang Grupp serves as both the owner and CEO of Trigema, a textile company in Germany.[25] Trigema manufactures T-shirts, polo shirts, and other textile products and sells in Germany as well as throughout the world. The high labor costs in the textile industry in Germany, with a mean hourly wage of 27.84 euros in 2013, poses a competitive challenge when compared to the hourly wage of three euros in China and an even lower wage of less than one euro in the Philippines.[26] Still, Trigema restricts its production to locations solely in Germany. When questioned about how Trigema is able to compete globally when burdened with such a cost disadvantage, the owner-manager of the company, Wolfgang Grupp, shares the key strategy deployed, which is the management of human resources. Most of the one thousand employees are working in or near Burladingen, a small village with fewer than thirteen thousand inhabitants located in the Swabian Jurain, an isolated region in southern Germany in the *Bundesland*, or state, of Baden-Württemberg. Not only does the Mittelstand company offer the guarantee of lifetime employment to every worker, but Grupp actually guarantees the same for their children as well!

Thus, part of the competitive advantage enjoyed by the German Mittelstand accrues from the superior motivation and work ethic of the employees, a kind of ubermotivation, inspired by the team atmosphere fostered by family-owned business. Just as the workers know that the family owners and managers will take that extra step for them, so too do they return the favor on the shop or factory floor. And it pays—the incidence of employee illness and the number of missed days at work are lower in family firms than public and nonfamily firms. For example, average rates of illness are about 3 percent and in many Mittelstand companies even lower. By contrast, the average rate of illness for large German companies varies between 4 and 5 percent. This means a small or medium-sized company has about ten fewer sick employees each day.

The formidable disadvantages confronting the Mittelstand from higher labor costs are therefore offset through greater motivation and productivity. The robust health of workers in the German Mittelstand translates into a savings of nearly half a million euros per year.

A recent study from the Institut für Weltwirtschaft (IfW), or Kiel Institute for the World Economy, demonstrates this type of cooperation and motivation prevalent in family-owned Mittelstand companies. In particular, the study documents how the global competitive advantage of family-owned firms in general, and the Mittelstand in particular, is based on the creativity and the innovative capabilities of the employees. The Mittelstand companies, in turn, respond by offering a wide scope of freedom and individual flexibility to the workers, such as allowing the worker to choose which hours and work space work best for him or her. The high level of confidence and trust placed in the workers of Mittelstand companies is expressed by the flexibility in allowing many employees to work at home, as well as to work during the morning or in the evening or even on weekends. For their part, Mittelstand employees provide the brainpower for generating a high rate of new products and product improvements.[27]

A key qualitative difference between the German Mittelstand and SMEs in other countries is the extensive boost in training, skills, human capital, and capabilities invested in young people through the German apprentice system. The apprentice system is part of the dual system of education in Germany and is discussed in detail in chapter 3. The dual system refers to the requirement that apprentices spend between one-half to just over two-thirds of their time at work in a company and the remainder of their time in formal education. Most of that formal education takes place at a *Berufsschule*, or vocational school. The apprentice system consists of well over three hundred *Ausbildungsberufe*, or recognized trades, where an apprenticeship can be completed. The apprentice system spans a broad spectrum of trades and professions, encompassing bricklaying, roofing, hair dressing, and plumbing.

This dual system of education generates several competitive advantages for both the employers and employees. First, this apprentice system imparts general technological knowledge on both a theoretical and a practical level, making those young people not only flexible in their employment but also an important source for accessing and absorbing state-of-the art technologies and ideas being developed elsewhere. Global competition is associated with shorter life cycles of products and processes.

The dual labor system, along with the system of apprenticeship, supports the Mittelstand companies in Germany against the challenges emanating from globalization. Instead of being a cog in a mass-production assembly line, where skills are constantly devalued, young people are challenged to assume responsibility in enhancing their own labor skills early in their lifetime and career. They learn early in life to be responsible for different tasks and how to cooperate with colleagues within a team context.

While most other countries have only scratched the surface of implementing a bona fide system of apprenticeship, the impact of long tradition and experience in Germany is broad and compelling. Around two-thirds of people younger than twenty-two have participated in the apprentice system. Of those, more than three-quarters actually complete their apprenticeship. This means that over one-half of people in Germany younger than twenty-two have completed an apprenticeship.

Many, but not all, Mittelstand companies participate in the apprenticeship program. Around 85 percent of all apprentices are working in Mittelstand companies. [28] The apprenticeship system offers the German Mittelstand a special source of competitiveness by providing a source of highly trained and skilled labor.

A fourth characteristic involves the organizational structure, which emphasizes decentralization and independent decision-making. As everyone who has ever worked in a large organization knows, ultimately the important and sometimes even not-so-important decisions get made up at the top. This is not the case in a family-run business. Or rather, the top is a lot closer to the bottom. In a family business the owner is typically the executive and manager. Combining these roles into one means that the business decisions involving risk, uncertainty, and liability are made in the context of the close ties that the family has with the employees and the community, which are especially close and have been nurtured over generations, since many of the German Mittelstand family businesses are located in smaller towns and communities.[29]

The flat decision-making structures of the German Mittelstand enable the companies to access know-how and ideas from their workers in a relatively efficient and seamless manner. The apprentice system delivers highly trained employees who not only are rich in technological and social competencies, but also provide a fertile garden of ideas. The Mittelstand has a tradition of leveraging the creativity and ideas of employees as a source of competitiveness in global markets. The work environment in the Mittelstand is typically anything but formal. Employees have direct access to management and are involved in decision- making. The decision-making and governance structures of the Mittelstand are noticeably flat rather than hierarchical. The feeling of alienation that characterizes employees in other work contexts is the exception, not the rule. This means that workers generally feel that not only are their ideas and input appreciated, they are also rewarded over time.

A 2010 study undertaken by the Cologne Institute for Economic Research found that only 46 percent of workers in large German companies felt that their ideas and creativity were appreciated and valued. In contrast, 61 percent in SMEs felt that they contributed to the entrepreneurial ideas of their companies.[30] Similarly, while only 59 percent of the workers in large German companies felt that they were involved in the decision-making process, nearly three-quarters of the workers in SMEs felt that they were engaged in the decision-making process. Perhaps this feeling of belonging and sense of place in a typical German Mittelstand company helps to explain the high rates of job satisfaction and low rates of job turnover prevalent throughout SMEs in Germany.

For example, decision-making and governance at Tobit AG are purposefully structured using a flat hierarchy to be conducive to flexibility. In the typical Mittelstand company, the CEO knows most of the employees personally, and in many cases since childhood. The flat hierarchies combined with deep and long-term relationships tend to facilitate communications about perceived problems, challenges, and opportunities, enabling the company to gather information and ideas fast and efficiently. Still, the important and most significant decisions are made at the top. The CEO makes the decisions as well as bears the risk.

A fifth characteristic of the Mittelstand is the long time horizons used for planning and decision-making. An extensive literature has shown that companies that are publicly held tend to have very short time horizons. Decision-makers typically obsess about the earnings for the next quarter. Quarterly profits, along with the other key financial indicators, can make the difference between a CEO keeping or losing her job in a publically held company.[31]

By contrast, most of the German SMEs are not publicly held companies. The focus is on longer-term goals, such as stability and survival, as well as providing value not just to the owners, but to a considerably broader set of constituents, including workers, company partners, and the community in which it operates. This lends itself to a longer-term time horizon, where the focus is less on quarterly performance than on long-term stability and development. No wonder that managers and CEOs in the German Mittelstand stay with their companies four times longer than their colleagues in large and public companies.[32] This long time horizon also pays off in terms of rich future dividends: "Most SMEs are working to secure the company's long-term existence and place great value on lasting relationships with customers, suppliers and other businesses. As an employee too, you are more than just 'one of the crowd.' Moreover, many SMEs take an active role in their regions by sponsoring education, culture and sport."[33]

A somewhat different aspect of the long-term orientation and focus of the German Mittelstand is that companies tend to be family friendly, especially when compared to SMEs in other countries and their larger counterparts within Germany. While other types of companies in different national contexts may be talking the talk, the German Mittelstand learned a long time ago how to walk the walk, which means taking employees' commitments outside of their jobs into account—especially challenging and demanding family situations: "The SMEs realized this long ago and are continually extending their family-friendly policies. These include flexible working hours—as well as the possibility of working from home, or even taking sabbatical leave."[34] These inner values, as Hermann Simon points out, are not only nice to have but are reflected in an impressive bottom line.

Another aspect of the long-term planning strategy of the German Mittelstand is the low incidence of employee turnover. Simon highlights the remarkably low annual turnover rate of about 2.7 percent. By contrast, the turnover rate for Daimler, which has the reputation of being a company with exceptional worker loyalty and low attrition, is still nearly twice as high, at 5.3 percent.[35] The mean annual employee turnover rate in Germany is even greater, 7.3 percent. In the United States, nearly one-third of workers leave their companies each year.[36]

The strong employee loyalty exhibited at Mittelstand companies, resulting in low rates of attrition and turnover, generates two types of cost savings and contributes to competitive advantage. The first is that only a small share of the investments in labor skills and accumulated experience of employees are lost through employee attrition and turnover. The second is that the costs incurred in screening, interviewing, vetting, and hiring new employees, along with their lower productivity during the learning phase of employment, are avoided, or at least minimized. When compared to the whopping mean employee turnover rate in the United States of 30.6 percent, Mittelstand companies are able to reap a considerable competitive advantage vis-à-vis global rivals and competitors. The low turnover rate of workers employed by the German Mittelstand translates into an average tenure spanning thirty-three years. By contrast, the high turnover rate in the United States translates into a mean tenure of less than four years.

More than thirty years employed by one Mittelstand company? As the owner and CEO of the Mittelstand company Trigema, Wolfgang Grupp, proudly explains: "Every year we celebrate several employees for their 40-year jubilee. They often start their career following their parents' footsteps and ties with a company by first serving as an apprenticeship and subsequently working their way up to greater levels of responsibility over the ensuing years."[37]

In highlighting the sixth key difference between the German Mittelstand and SMEs in other countries, *flexibility*, Tobias Groten, CEO and founder of Tobit AG, a software company started in the 1980s, forces employees to leave the company after five years. His philosophy adheres to the one-of-four rule. After five years, 75 percent of the employees have to leave the company, and only 25 percent are retained. These remaining 25 percent must be extremely flexible and unusual even in wanting to remain with the company. Still, this up-or-out policy implemented and enforced by Groten does not destroy or even erode the loyalty or motivation of employees—competitors or clients are pleased to be able to hire them and induce them to leave Tobit for their own companies. Groten considers his own human management policy the key to injecting flexibility: "New spirit comes from the freshmen, aged less than twenty-five years."[38]

Although Groten founded Tobit AG at the age of eighteen in 1986 and continues to serve as the CEO, he remains true to his entrepreneurial roots: "If you are established you are losing."[39] To maintain entrepreneurial flexibility and attitudes, Groten forces his employees to think and make decisions outside of the box in a firm culture devoid of stringent rules, which has proven conducive to disruptive innovations and new technologies. Groten prefers that his employees continually challenge their own ideas and those of their colleagues: "The question is not whether it is allowed or justified by myopic economic data. You must also be your own enemy and destroy ideas when they are stuck in a dead-end street."

Placing a premium on flexibility but also autonomy and independence, Groten becomes concerned if any single client accounts for a large share of Tobit AG's total revenue. Independence from any sole customer preserves flexibility in thinking, strategy, and decisions.

The relatively straightforward manner for efficiently communicating and scanning for ideas, reactions, and opportunities is conducive to a flexible reaction to exogenous shocks or changes in the business environment. Mittelstand employees can absorb changes and challenges without great concerns that such change will come at the cost of their own job or continued prospects for future employment.

One of the well-documented challenges in vertically organized and structured American corporations is that the incentives are not compatible with risk-taking for individual employees. The upside of a positive decision is limited, as the corporation reaps the returns, while a decision that is highly risky can have draconian consequences for the employee, such as termination of the employment contract. It has been often observed that one of the challenges of the large, vertically hierarchical American corporation is to induce employees to pursue riskier and highly uncertain decisions and behavior in order to spur innovation in a corporate context that ultimately punishes those very same employees when they do attempt to be innovative and entrepreneurial. An article in the *Harvard Business Review* explains "Why Big Companies Can't Innovate."[40] The reason is embedded in the structure and organization of the large, vertically hierarchical American corporation: "Big companies are really bad at innovation because they're designed to be bad at innovation."[41]

But not the Mittelstand companies. As the owner and CEO of the Mittelstand company Trigema, Wolfgang Grupp, asks rhetorically, "Why should I cut the wages from my loyal employees when one of my decisions was wrong?"[42]

Detlef Borghardt, the CEO at SAF-Holland, a Mittelstand supplier in the truck-and-trailer industry, explains that flexibility is not just a core strategy for the company, but grounded in its cost structure. Borghardt eschews the cycles of the typical American company oscillating between episodes of mass layoffs and hiring stampedes. Instead of a hire-and-fire strategy, Borghardt and SAF-Holland rely on flexibility in employment conditions. Over the last several years, when demand for the company's products was high, the company registered about forty-five thousand hours of overtime work. While this may cost more in the very short run, Borghardt is quick to emphasize the longer-run costs savings, because he avoids having to lay off workers during periods of slack demand. The overtime work provides SAF-Holland with a kind of buffer for demand fluctuations and other unforeseen shocks or unanticipated developments in the business environment. This buffer enables him to flexibly adjust the actual hours worked by his employees, sparing him both the costs of firing employees in a cyclical downturn and the high costs of searching for and hiring qualified employees during the upswing.[43]

A seventh important characteristic differentiating the German Mittelstand from its SME counterparts in other countries is its ability to draw on and enhance its competitiveness in global markets from local sources. The localized competitiveness of the Mittelstand draws on the strong and supportive involvement of the companies, including the owner-managers, in other firms and people spanning the entire total value chain of the company's main products. Typically this involvement and interaction involve relationships within the same town, city, or region. In particular, strong and deep relationships have been forged and nurtured with key suppliers and clients, in many cases over generations.

While their SME counterparts in other national contexts might be inclined to say, "It's none of my business," the German Mittelstand makes virtually every element involved in the supply chain its business. In particular, Mittelstand companies are involved in the process of product development with their key clients and suppliers and have invested in and fostered those relationships for decades all over the world. The trustful and respective relationships with the key stakeholders, suppliers, clients, house banks, and employees are strategic assets nurtured within the company. This strong and sustained relationships would not be possible with a frequent change in the management team. Rather, such deep relationships are firm specific and often include family members.

The eighth key characteristic distinguishing the German Mittelstand from SMEs in other countries is their aggressive and successful orientation toward opportunities beyond the national borders. How do we know that the German Mittelstand has an orientation toward discovering, creating, and acting upon opportunities outside of Germany? One indicator reflecting the robust external orientation is the strikingly high participation in exports. The export rate of the German Mittelstand is about 20 percent of output. While many of these export opportunities are within Europe, the Institut für Mittelstandsforschung, or Institute for Mittelstand Research, in Bonn, estimates that around 45 percent of those exports have a destination in Asia. This speaks to the competitiveness of the German Mittelstand, not just vis-à-vis larger counterparts within Germany, or even within the European Union, but also in the global context.

An example of this orientation toward opportunities outside of Germany is provided by Hark, a family-owned company, now in the fourth generation, which has become the world's leading orchid grower in laboratories. Hundreds of employees, mainly women in white skirts, are working with tweezers and scalpels in Lippstadt. A decade ago, Hark had only around thirty employees. However, in the subsequent decade, worldwide demand for orchids exploded. Hark was able to take advantage of this niche opportunity through a company innovation. As it discovered the skyrocketing of demand, Hark knew that a new type of production process would be needed to take advantage of new opportunities, mostly outside of Germany. Hark invented a special culture medium, making it possible to accelerate the growing process and enabling the company to take full advantage of opportunities for growing and selling orchids across the globe.

Hark established an additional laboratory in Kalamazoo, Michigan, in August 2013. With the slogan "Just add ice," Hark aggressively advertised their orchids throughout the United States—just add three ice cubes a week to the culture medium and the orchids will grow splendidly! Within just a few short years, their market share of the American market shot up to one-quarter of all sales.[44]

Hidden Champions

Small may be beautiful. But, at least in the case of Herrenknecht, it's productive as well. In 2013, Herrenknecht generated sales exceeding 1 billion euros. Herrenknecht is not the only family-owned Mittelstand firm that has generated an economic performance way beyond what might be expected from its size. In explaining why he latched onto a small subgroup of the German Mittelstand and celebrated them as hidden champions, the internationally acclaimed consultant Hermann Simon explains that he wanted to figure out why Germany has been consistently the world leader in exports: "I came across these world market leaders, mid-sized companies no one knew about. That's why I called them 'hidden champions.'"[45]

Simon defines a hidden champion as a firm that is either one of the top three companies in its product class in the world, or else is the leading producer on its continent, yet has sales not exceeding 5 billion euros. Only a small portion of the German Mittelstand consists of hidden champions.

Herrenknecht is far from being the only hidden champion in Germany. Rather, Mittelstand companies such as Micon, which produced the drilling equipment that contributed to saving the Chilean workers trapped in a mine, Poly-Clip System, which manufacturers the clip used to package meats, Tetra, which produces fish food, Abelton, which manufactures electronic music-mixing software and hardware, Arnold & Richer Cine Technik, which manufactures professional cameras, Mennekes, which produces equipment for charging electric vehicles, and Elektrisola Dr. Gerd Schilbach, which manufactures the premium enameled wire used in the Mars Rover are all examples of German hidden champions.

The impact and performance of these *uber-performing* firms, or the hidden champions, is even more striking. Over 150 of these companies have more than 1 billion dollars of sales. They created more than a million jobs in the last decade. According to Simon, while there are 2,500 hidden champions in the world, over half of them, 1,300, are located in Germany. Even though the United States has a population nearly four times greater than that of Germany, only 360 hidden champions are located in America.[46]

According to Simon, hidden champions include companies such as Hella, with its core businesses in vehicle lighting and electronics systems and components, but also companies like Gmund, which produces high-quality laid paper. What makes a hidden champion a champion, and why are so many German Mittelstand companies able to become and remain world market leaders in their product classes? Hidden champions in Germany are highly innovative. On average, hidden champions own five times as many patents as do larger and publicly owned companies. Hidden champions typically deploy the strategy of obscuring their innovative activities and limiting their transparency. Rather than patenting intellectual property, hidden champions have a propensity to keep new ideas and technologies a trade secret.

Hidden champions deploy the strategy of investing in close and long-lasting relationships with their key clients and developing customer specific solutions. As the owner and CEO of Weisser Spulenkörper, Manfred Starnecker, explains, "We develop specific solutions for our key clients." Weisser Spulenkörper is a hidden champion thanks to its high performance as a leading producer of technical plastic parts spanning six decades. Company success stems from a laser-like strategic focus on individual customer specifications. The innovation strategy of the company is similarly strongly focused on finding and delivering customer based solutions. As Starnecker explains, "Customer satisfaction and loyalty is the most important output of our innovation efforts."[47]

However, Starnecker also makes clear why the company prefers a strategy of trade secrecy over legal protection of intellectual property: "Patenting our solutions is not only time consuming and associated with costs but also reveals our efforts to others." Like Manfred Starnecker, other hidden champions typically prefer to shield their intellectual property along with their innovative activities not just from public scrutiny but also from their competitors, so that investments in research in development are almost always understated and remain under the radar. As Starnecker shares with considerable pride, "It is important that we are known and respected personally by our customers but remain unknown to our competitors."

This is why hidden champions often support close relationships with local universities and cooperate enthusiastically with them to generate new products and technologies. Such close cooperation also facilitates access to young talent, which provides one of the key strategic sources of competitive advantage—qualified and highly skilled employees. Since one of the disadvantages of being a hidden champion is that by striving to remain understated and hidden from the public and, more importantly, large global competitors, the champion also remains somewhat hidden from highly skilled employees and university graduates as a potential employer. By developing and nurturing close relationships with local universities, the hidden champion can compensate for its relative obscurity to potential highly skilled and high-human-capital employees. Thus, close geographic proximity to local universities is one of the key strategies deployed by hidden champions.

Another key strategy yielding a competitive advantage is leadership quality. Academic research has revealed that the CEOs of hidden champions have a tenure lasting about four times longer than do their counterparts at other companies. The stability and durability of leadership of the hidden champions is conducive to strong identification with the company, which in turn signals enthusiasm and team spirit and enhances discipline and trustworthiness for the employees. No wonder that the turnover of employees in hidden champion firms is 50 percent less than in large companies.

According to Hartmut Jenner, who serves as CEO of Kärcher, which is a world market leader of high-quality high-pressure cleaners and window vacuum cleaners, team spirit in a hidden champion mirrors that in a soccer club, where virtues like passion, burning ambition, and commitment take precedent. Annual employee turnover at Kärcher is less than 2 percent, a remarkable figure. Low employee turnover rates not only reduce the costs of having to hire and fire employees, but academic research has found that the willingness of a company to invest in the human capital of its employees depends strongly on the ability of the company to protect and appropriate the returns accruing from its investment in that human capital.[48] The success of hidden champions like Kärcher and Herrenknecht reflects a willingness of their employees to invest in lifelong learning activities and to remain with their companies throughout their working careers. In the context of the hidden champions, such high-cost investments in human capital pay rich dividends, both for the company and for the employee.

Hidden champions also exhibit considerably more resilience in the face of exogenous shocks. This reflects different modes and sources of obtaining finance. Hidden champions, as is the case for the typical Mittelstand company, tend to rely on finance from local and regional banks, which are relationship based. This enables the hidden champion to avoid diluting ownership, control, and influence, thus preserving the strategic advantage that underlies the competitive advantage. In contrast to their competitors located in the United States and the United Kingdom, hidden champions exhibit a high equity ratio along with large equity holders. That makes them independent not only from banks and their own interests in credit lending but also from the myopic stock market.

Hermann Simon also emphasizes that hidden champions differ in their strategic focus. For example, they tend to put a strong focus on narrow product class niches rather than on broad product categories, thus enabling them to be more targeted and efficient in investing their scarce resources. The core strategy of a focus on a narrow product class niche yields several strategic advantages. For one thing, focusing on a narrow and specialized product niche product typically accounts for only a small share of the total purchasing expenditures of their client and thus reduces downward pressure on prices. In addition, the products manufactured by hidden champions are often essential and indispensable to their customers, which tends to reduce the extent of any negotiating power and outside opportunities of their customers.

Another strategic advantage created by hidden champions comes from their efforts and commitment to continually and relentlessly improve their product and technologies until the top position in the market is attained. A hidden champion does not give up, at least not too early or prematurely. Rather, hidden champions exhibit remarkable persistence and tenacity in pursuing and implementing their core strategy of continual product quality improvement and innovation. The close relationships forged between key clients and hidden champions are conducive to continual quality improvements and incremental innovation. Thus, compared to other types of companies, hidden champions have two different and distinct sources spurring innovation and quality improvements—top clients and top competitors. According to Simon, such close and durable relationships with their key clients are the secret and power of the strategy driving the competitive advantage of hidden champions.

Just as the champions production processes are hidden, so too are the locations of their headquarters and production plants. To overcome the disadvantage of being hidden for consumers, clients, or employees, such companies have to put more effort and creativity into signaling their existence. For example, Otto Bock founded his company to manufacture prosthetics in 1919 as a response to the large number of injured veterans from World War I. Today, Otto Bock is a world market leader in producing highly innovative wheelchairs and prosthetics in Duderstadt, which is located in an isolated region in the middle of Germany, and in Salt Lake City, Utah. In 1988, four technicians from Otto Bock provided their services for free for all the athletes at the Paralympic Games in Seoul, South Korea. Their kind and generous service went largely unnoticed by the press and by the world. However, fast-forwarding to the most recent Paralympic Games, which took place in London in 2012, more than six thousand journalists and 2.5 million spectators followed the Games. This time, the thirteen repair shops and eighty technicians supplied by Otto Bock became something of a focal point of the Games. As Christin Gundel, chief marketing manager of Otto Bock, explains, "This engagement at the Paralympics leads to a great discussion in the social media and employment applications from all over the world." The social engagement of Otto Bock paid handsome dividends in terms of its human resource policy and its ability to attract the best and the brightest of the young generation. As Gundel reports, many well-trained and educated young people have a preference for employers with a social conscience and engagement who provide more than just a salary.[49]

The geography of the hidden champions also seems to contradict the conventional wisdom concerning locational advantages for innovation and competitiveness. Scholarly research has consistently shown that being located in a highly dense area tends to enhance the economic performance of firms.[50] These studies have made it abundantly clear that for a firm, especially for a small business, to perform well, it should be located within a densely populated agglomeration or cluster of similar and complementary firms. Just as Google is located in the agglomeration of California's Silicon Valley, Microsoft has its headquarters in Seattle. However, hidden champions typically eschew the larger cities and densely populated regions for the geographic isolation of smaller towns and even villages.

Wolfgang Epp, the director of the Chamber of Commerce in Reutlingen, which is located in the *Bundesland* of Baden-Württemberg, explains that a competitive advantage is accessed by locating in a particular region. According to Epp, it is the innovation capacity of the region that really matters. However, the innovation capacity of the region is shaped by the leading companies in that region. He also emphasizes the importance of having the entire value chain in production located in a single region, which enables companies to learn from each other and what each needs to be globally competitive and innovative.[51]

Epp points to the case of the development of the textile industry in the Swabian Jura region. Globalization has led to a crisis in the textile industry due to lower-cost competitors, principally in Asia and Eastern Europe, which rendered textile production in the Swabian Jura region unprofitable and seemingly unsustainable. However, in a strategic response to such global competitive pressures, the leading companies in the region shifted away from the production of textiles for the mass market and instead developed high-quality, specialized niches. Examples of these high-quality, specialized product niches include airbags and seats for cars and trains and wings for airplanes. In order to produce these specialized products, the textile companies had to work with several key hidden champions in the region, such as Mayer & Cie, which produces knitting machines, Groz-Beckert, which produces knitting needles, and Stoll, which also produces knitting machines. These hidden champions originated from the traditional textile industry and are now part of a cluster for the technical textile industry. Together with clients from the automotive sector, the life science industry, and medical technology and with the local university of applied science (*Fachhochschule*) in Reutlingen, a globally recognized focal point and cluster for technical textiles has emerged. The pride this region displays in building on its roots from the traditional textile industry but seizing the global opportunity afforded by its wings is evidenced by a bridge in the city of Albstadt. Rather than being constructed of steel and cement, the bridge is instead woven together by technical textiles. Spanning some one hundred meters, this bridge must be, if not the longest bridge in the world, the longest one consisting solely of technical textiles.[52]

Many of the 1,300 high-performing hidden champions of Germany are located in the relatively rural regions of the southwest of Germany, such as Heilbronn, Wertheim, Reutlingen, and Crailsheim. These small and obscure rural regions host several world market leaders. For example, Crailsheim in Baden-Württemberg, located close to Stuttgart, is called Packaging Valley Germany, named after a cluster of family-owned Mittelstand companies producing highly specialized machines in the packaging sector, with a particular focus on the chemical and pharmaceutical industries.

These small villages and towns where the hidden champions are sometimes located, are touristic hot spots, such as the southwest of Germany near Lake Constance, which serves as a magnet offering an attractive lifestyle for talented engineers and managers. A high quality of life with low costs of living, low crime rates, and low costs of housing can easily take priority over any disadvantage of being geographically isolated. In any case, thanks to the impressive German transportation infrastructure, any longing for the urban experience is only an enjoyable (high-speed) train ride away.

There are even hidden champions located in what can only be called obscure villages, such as Micon in Nienhagen, Mennekes in Kirchhundem, Tetra in Melle, and Poly-Clip System in Hattersheim. Thus, like the Mittelstand in general, Germany's hidden champions seemingly defy conventional wisdom about the relationship between geographic location and competitive performance.[53] Because they are uniquely equipped to draw on the resources of the *Standort*, or place, the German Mittelstand, and especially the hidden champions, emerge with a competitive advantage, not in spite of globalization, but rather because of the opportunities afforded by globalization.

Entrepreneurial Germany

In California's famed Silicon Valley, people typically associate small firms with entrepreneurial start-ups. Small is beautiful because it is entrepreneurial. Bold new ventures, such as Google, Facebook, Amazon, and Apple come to mind, where it takes the imagination, vision, and daring of entrepreneurs like Steven Jobs, Bill Gates, and Mark Zuckerberg to confidently launch their new venture, which ultimately creates an entire new industry and changes the world in a dramatic fashion. Extensive and exhaustive studies suggest that entrepreneurial start-ups play a crucial role in the evolutionary process by which new ideas that are ignored or rejected by the existing large and dominant corporations become commercialized and lead to breathtaking innovations, transforming entire industries and regions, and ultimately the world.[54]

To understand the role and impact of such bold start-ups, the scholarly field of entrepreneurship has emerged with the task of analyzing entrepreneurial activities within and across countries in order to generate a deep understanding of entrepreneurship and its impact on the world.[55] In particular, the scholarly field of entrepreneurship has developed a special focus on how and why business opportunities fuel the launch and success of new ventures.

A new firm is often the result of an entrepreneur who has identified an opportunity that is not being pursued or commercialized by an existing company. There are two key questions revolving around the role of such opportunities in scholarly thinking about entrepreneurship. The first is, where do the entrepreneurial opportunities come from? The second is, if these entrepreneurial opportunities are so compelling and valuable, why don't existing businesses pursue them? After all, business is about nothing if not about trying to profit from lucrative opportunities. Why would a viable, normal business pass on them?

A virtual army of scholars have dedicated their research to addressing both of these fundamental questions involving small business and entrepreneurship.[56] Opportunities are generally created by people with ideas. Where those ideas come from is as disparate as explaining how each person is different. But people have ideas. Some of those ideas are good, a very few of them are really good, and most are, well, not very good at all.

How can anyone know in advance which of the ideas is really good, or at least not bad? That is, how can anyone separate the wheat from the chaff? Because they are ideas and haven't been tried out, they remain, until implemented, simply that—ideas. No one can be certain what will actually be profitable and what will not. Thus, what has been characterized as constituting a *knowledge filter* is the gap between an idea that may or may not be viable and its implementation.[57]

For example, the idea that manufacturing and selling a personal computer might be profitable first came up in the 1970s at Xerox, where engineers and scientists had invented a new machine making personal computing possible. The trouble was, decision-makers at the company did not recognize the potential value of this idea or invention, and concluded that while it was an interesting device for sophisticated engineers to play around with, it had minimal potential commercial value. After all, their decision-making context was an era when people had become used to turning to mainframe computers as the solution to their computational needs.

When Steve Jobs got his hands on the new inventions, he saw opportunity where the decision-makers in the corporate hierarchy of Xerox saw only a waste of research and development resources. Jobs founded Apple Computer and ultimately launched not just a new business but ultimately an entire industry. The point is that the opportunity was actually generated through the research-and-development efforts by a successful, viable corporation, Xerox. However, the knowledge filter hindered Xerox from pursuing the new idea and commercializing it. Rather, it took an entrepreneur, in this case Steve Jobs, both to recognize and to act on that opportunity.

Another example of the knowledge filter in the context of a large research-and-development company creating an entrepreneurial opportunity is provided by IBM, which was trying to develop Scientific Data Systems (SDS)/SAPE software. Five IBM engineers, Dietmar Hopp, Klaus Tschira, Hans-Werner Hector, Hasso Plattner, and Claus Wellenreuther, all working for IBM in its location near Mannheim in Baden-Württemberg, were developing an enterprise-wide system based on this software, only to be told that it would no longer be necessary. Rather than abandon the project, they decided to leave IBM and start their own new company. In June 1972 they founded Systemanalyse und Programmentwicklung (System Analysis and Program Development), better known today as SAP. Thus, the opportunity was created in the organizational context of IBM, but was ultimately actualized and commercialized as an innovation in the organizational context of the new entrepreneurial start-up, SAP.

Entrepreneurship can provide a key role in the economy and in society by serving as a conduit for taking ideas created in one organizational context and getting them out into the market in the context of a new firm or organization. This was the case not just in the examples of Apple Computer and SAP, but also when Google was launched from ideas generated at Stanford University. But to highlight these wildly successful examples of entrepreneurial success obscures what is actually a strikingly low rate of survival of entrepreneurial start-ups. In fact, most ideas do not work out, or ultimately do not generate economic success, resulting in high rates of entrepreneurial failure. Most start-ups do not survive beyond a handful of months, let alone years.[58] This reflects the underlying basis on which small businesses are launched—no one is actually sure about the viability of the idea.

Thus, small business and entrepreneurship have become viewed as the process by which ideas and new products, processes, and services become actualized and find their way into the market. Because of the high risk and uncertainty involved, most of the start-ups don't survive very long. However, those ideas that are proven to be viable through actual market success help to fuel the survival and growth of the firm. Scholars have shown that, seen at a moment frozen in time, the typical industry looks like an inverted V, with lots of small companies at the bottom of the firm-size distribution, and only a few large ones at the top.

However, when seen through a more dynamic lens that tracks firms over time, the static view gives way to what is more like a conical revolving door. New ideas generate the start-up of lots of new firms, but only a small share of those are based on viable ideas and survive over time. Those entrepreneurial start-ups that do survive tend to grow into larger enterprises, ultimately displacing the larger firms with their antiquated products and services.[59]

In the American context, small business is really about new business, which evolves into business growth, if the entrepreneurial start-up is fueled by a viable idea. The start-up founded by Bill Gates along with his ragtag team of initial employees has given way to a global, megacorporation, Microsoft, just as Facebook, Google, and Amazon are innovative and dynamic, but certainly not small. At the same time are the hordes of start-ups, such as Napster, that try but ultimately fail before they can grow into a viable, competitive giant. As Andy Grove, one of the founders of Intel, wrote, *Only the Paranoid Survive*.[60]

But it is different in Germany. Thanks to the qualitative difference in Germany, especially where the family firms and hidden champions are concerned, stability is more characteristic of SMEs, and the frenzied turbulence and turnover that are characteristic of small business in countries such as the United States is more the exception than the rule. Rather, the German Mittelstand is more characterized by stability, incremental change, continuity, and improvement, in contrast to the more helter-skelter nature of SMEs in the United States. As the popular advertisement for Volkswagen in Germany pronounces, *Man weiss, was Man hat*—you know what you've got. So too it is with the German Mittelstand.

The German difference in small business, with its strong role for family business and focus on the long run, may seem to preclude the benefits from the type of entrepreneurial dynamism more characteristic of the United States and especially Silicon Valley. Without the freedom to fail, the entrepreneurial impulse was greatly inhibited.[61] Germany had limited the freedom of entrepreneurs to fail. Failed entrepreneurs in Germany simply did not get a second chance. Germany, like many of its European neighbors, had treated honest but insolvent entrepreneurs more or less like fraudulent criminals. By contrast, Britain will discharge a bankruptcy from debts after a relatively short twelve-month period. The bankruptcy laws in the United States are even more lenient. But in Germany, failed entrepreneurs could expect to take six years in order to get a fresh start, which is somewhat better than the nine years required in France. There were other dire consequences confronting bankrupt entrepreneurs as well. For example, in Germany a bankrupt entrepreneur generally could expect to be banned for life from being appointed to a senior executive position at the large, flagship companies.

No wonder that, over the years, many aspiring entrepreneurs simply left. More than fifty thousand German entrepreneurs and specialists are located in Silicon Valley, and an estimated several hundred start-ups with German founders are located in the San Francisco Bay Area, and in Silicon Alley in Manhattan and Brooklyn. Start-ups like Intraworld, Kollabora, Kitchensurfing, and WYWY are only a handful of the many examples of vibrant new entrepreneurial ventures founded by Germans in the United States. They are drawn not just by the access to venture and angel capital and other financial resources available to funding start-ups, but also by the mass of information technology and high-tech experts there, along with the networks, attitudes, and spirit.[62]

Yet another difference in the entrepreneurial landscape of Germany has been the prospects for new ventures and start-ups to grow, or become what is widely referred to as gazelles. Role models for bold and dynamic entrepreneurs have been abundant in America. Entrepreneurial visionaries such as Bill Gates, Larry Page and Sergey Brin, Steve Jobs, Jeff Bezos, and Mark Zuckerberg are recognized not just in the United States but throughout the world for the companies they founded and grew—Microsoft, Google, Apple, Amazon, and Facebook. A subsequent generation became inspired to start their own companies by these riveting role models who were not afraid to go their own way. It has been argued that they served as the driving catalyst underlying the emergence of what has been termed the entrepreneurial society.[63]

No such obvious entrepreneurs with global name-brand recognition existed in Germany to serve as role models and galvanize subsequent generations. The paucity of entrepreneurship in Germany has been reflected in the rankings of income and wealth. In the United States, such rankings are invariably headed by the famous founders of the bold and dynamic entrepreneurial successes. By contrast, the analogous top rankings of income and wealth in Germany have been consistently occupied by the aged heirs and successors of established Mittelstand family companies.

Thus, Germany did not seem capable of generating high-technology, knowledge-driven entrepreneurship because the model, values, and orientation of the Mittelstand focused on stability, continuity, and incrementalism, which were seemingly at odds with the model of bold and dynamic high-technology entrepreneurship emerging in the United States and elsewhere. Germany seemed so bogged down with its stagnant rate of economic growth, rising rates of unemployment, and meager start-up rates that the news media was rampant with headlines such as "Are We Still in the Champions League?" and referring to Germany as "The Sick Man of Europe."

In fact, there were compelling reasons to believe that entrepreneurship might not be incompatible with the German context. There have been historical episodes in Germany with a striking amount of bold and dynamic entrepreneurship. During the *Gründerzeit*, or the "Era of the Founders," dating back to the 1800s, a robust wave of entrepreneurs founded scores of new firms, some of which are still in existence and rank among Germany's most important companies. In just in a single year during this time, 1872, 432 companies went public on German stock exchanges. The number of joint-stock companies exploded from around two hundred prior to 1870 to more than one thousand just a few years later.[64]

However, the outbreak of World War I in 1914 put an end to the wave of entrepreneurial start-ups. Still, more than a handful of these start-ups have managed to survive well over a century and rank among the world's leading companies today, including Siemens (founded in 1847), Bayer and BASF (both around1860), Linde (1879), K + S (1889), Continental (1871), Daimler (1883/1890), Thyssen (1891), Fresenius (1912), Beiersdorf (1882), and Henkel (1876), to name just a few. These companies are still listed in the DAX 30, a blue-chip stock market index consisting of the thirty major German companies trading on the Frankfurt Stock Exchange, which is roughly the equivalent of the FT30 or the Dow Jones Industrial Average. One-third of the industrial companies still exist today. Including the two banks listed on the DAX 30, the Deutsche Bank (founded in 1870) and Commerzbank (founded in 1870) and the two listed insurance companies Allianz (1890) and Munich Re (1880), half of the major German companies have their origins dating back to the *Gründerzeit*.

Such longevity may be a double-edged sword. The *Economist* warns that "the giants are all ageing," suggesting that the dominance of old dinosaurs reflects a continent where attitudes are extremely risk averse.[65] Could the paucity of entrepreneurial activity be attributable to the dominance of the aged crowding out the prospects of would-be entrepreneurs, or is there simply a lack of creative entrepreneurs?

Shortly after the turn of the new century, the chancellor of Germany, Gerhard Schröder, no doubt reflecting the widespread frustration of nearly a decade and a half of German stagnation, ushered in bold new policies, reforms, and institutional changes. Only a few years earlier, in its 2000 meeting in Lisbon, the Council of Europe had identified entrepreneurship, along with investments in science, technology, and education, as the key to reigniting European growth. As the president of the European Commission at that time, the economist Romano Prodi exclaimed, "Our lacunae in the field of entrepreneurship need to be taken seriously because there is mounting evidence that the key to economic growth and productivity improvements lies in the entrepreneurial capacity of an economy."[66] Chancellor Schröder similarly recognized that the paucity of entrepreneurship was holding Germany back. Schröder's declaration of 2004 as "The Year of Innovation" may be as revealing as it was symbolic.[67] For a country bogged down with stagnant economic growth and alarming increases in the levels of unemployment, entrepreneurship held the key for reigniting Germany.

Both broad sweeping policy changes and institutional reforms were initiated by Chancellor Schröder to ignite German entrepreneurship. These included new programs providing funding and informational services facilitating the start-up of new firms. New sources for financing start-ups and small businesses, including loans and equity finance, were provided. These programs spanned all levels of government, from local governments to the Länder and the federal government in Berlin.

Financing was provided by the *Förderkredite* (microcredit) program. *Förderkredite* is administered through the Kreditveranstalt für Wiederentwicklung (KfW), which provided funding ranging from 10,000 euros to 25,000 euros to small and medium-sized enterprises. The *Gründerfond* provided up to 500,000 euros for starting new high-technology companies. This program was financed with 86 percent of the funding from government, and the remainder from third-party sources, such as venture capital. The EXIST program, which was initiated by the federal Ministry of Research and Education, had a focus on spawning spin-offs and start-ups from universities. It had an explicit mandate to promote university-based start-ups and foster a culture of entrepreneurship. Under the EXIST program, grants of up to 30,000 euros were provided to start-ups, but an additional 50,000 euros were available in Phase I and 150,000 euros in Phase II of the program to foster technology transfer and commercialization of research.[68]

What is particularly instructive about the EXIST program was that it involves regional partnerships including local governments, nonprofit organizations, and universities. Thus, an important and striking contrast with the now world-famous Small Business Innovation Research (SBIR) program in the United States[69] is that while the American program involves solely small businesses, the EXIST program unites key entities from the relevant region, including universities, government, nonprofit organizations, and entrepreneurs.

Figure 2.3 shows the location of the fifteen regions of Germany awarded support under the EXIST program, along with partnership regions. Each of these regions has a

FIGURE 2.3 The EXIST Program in Germany

particular technological focus and unique set of partners with the goal of igniting high-technology entrepreneurship in that region.

There is compelling evidence suggesting that Chancellor Schröder and Germany have succeeded in transforming the country from anemic "Sick Man of Europe" into, if not a hotbed of entrepreneurship, a country well on its way to becoming what has been termed by scholars an *entrepreneurial society*.[70]

In a recent article on entrepreneurship in Europe, the *Economist* raised doubts about Germany's shift toward entrepreneurship: "That an economy so copiously provided with the technically educated as Germany's has not produced a single globally important business-to-consumer internet company suggests a big problem with entrepreneurship."[71]

Konrad Hilbers, former CEO of Napster, argues that the problem is the lack of a risk-taking entrepreneurial culture in Germany.[72]

But wasn't it the same in Palo Alto, half a century ago, when the Fairchild eight left Shockley Semiconductor Laboratories to found Fairchild Semiconductors? In fact, they were denigrated the "traitorous eight" since an employment contract seemingly bound the employee to the company until she or he retired. Leaving the safety of a lifetime contract to found a new company was just an unthinkable risk. Entrepreneurial culture in the Silicon Valley was born when those eight engineers found the courage to leave Shockley and start their own company—the rest, including the succession of the "Fairchild childs " (Intel and AMD, among others) in Silicon Valley, is one of the most impressive stories of entrepreneurial America.[73]

Still, there is compelling evidence that Germany is evolving into an entrepreneurial society, or a country where entrepreneurship provides a driving force for economic growth and prosperity. For example, the three Samwer brothers, Marc, Oliver, and Alexander, founded several Internet companies. In particular, the brothers introduced a concept for a new business model in e-commerce that is based on speed, flexibility, and detecting market niches in the context of developing and transitional countries, such as Africa, South America, and Russia. Their vision was decidedly long term. Their new business model worked beyond anyone's wildest dreams. Nobody worldwide has systematically established so many important Internet companies as have the Samwer brothers.[74] Among other things, they created the e-commerce platform Alando, the market leader in Internet auctions in Germany, and Jamba, which became the market leader for wireless content such as music, pictures, games, and videos for mobile phones in Europe and the United States.

Another example of entrepreneurial success in Germany is highlighted by one of the Samwer brothers, Oliver, who is founder and CEO of the venture capital firm Rocket Internet. Samwer, in fact, distinguishes between the German and Silicon Valley breeds of entrepreneurship: "We are building companies within a factory and not in garages."[75] Rocket Internet is a large shareholder of several high-tech entrepreneurial start-ups in the business-to-consumer sector, including Trivago and Zalando SE.

Zalando SE, founded in 2008 in Berlin, is a multinational e-commerce company that specializes in selling shoes, clothing, and other fashion and lifestyle products online. Since its founding, Zalando has expanded to offer its retail services in fourteen European countries, along with several countries in Asia and South America. In 2014 Zalando went public through an IPO, which has resulted in a 2014 worth estimated to be in excess of 5 billion dollars.

In December 2014, the Samwer brothers announced that, together with the international consulting company Roland Berger, they were founding what they call a "superincubator," with the explicit goal of spawning and growing high-technology, high-growth entrepreneurial start-ups. As Charles-Duard Bouée, the CEO of Roland Berger, points out, this incubator will become the starting point of Terra Numerata, a digital ecosystem fostering entrepreneurship in Europe. It is termed a superincubator because it is still open to host and promote other incubators, as well as large and established companies, as an ecosystem that is attracting the top IT experts, potential entrepreneurs, and partners in building up a network like Rocket Internet.[76]

Entrepreneurship in Germany is alive and well.

Systematic empirical evidence analyzed in academic studies has confirmed that entrepreneurship has emerged in Germany as an engine of economic growth and jobs. A rich body of academic literature documents that those cities and Länder with the highest rates of new-firm start-ups also tend to exhibit the highest rates of economic growth and amount of employment creation.[77] Studies from earlier time periods provided compelling empirical evidence suggesting that economic growth rates and the creation of new jobs were actually lower in regions with a higher degree of start-up activity.[78] Apparently Germany has shifted from being a country where economic growth and job creation were promoted by large and stable companies during the 1970s and 1980s, to being driven by entrepreneurship and new-firm start-ups more recently.

While it is hard to understate the impact of the policy and institutional reforms initiated by Chancellor Gerhard Schröder in 2004, he was not alone in infusing entrepreneurship into Germany. In keeping with the decentralized nature of decision-making, institutions, and policy in Germany, there were considerable efforts made at the local level as well. Berlin, the metropolitan area spanning Munich-Nuremburg, Baden-Württemberg, and the Rhine-Neckar region provide compelling regional examples of an emerging entrepreneurial Germany.

The metropolitan area of Munich-Nuremburg boasts impressive large, high-technology based companies, such as Siemens, Airbus, BMW, and Audi, prestigious high-powered research universities like the Technical University of Munich, the Ludwig Maximilian University in Munich, and the Friedrich-Alexander University in Erlangen-Nuremberg, along with a score of high-profile research institutions, including a handful from the Max Planck Society and from the Fraunhofer Society. These nonprofit research institutions and universities have developed a laser-like focus on fostering the spillover of knowledge and ideas for innovation and commercialization, which ultimately fuels the growth and development of local economies.[79] A wave of entrepreneurial new ventures is launched every month in high-technology sectors such as biochemistry, electronics, engineering, and the life sciences. A number of high-technology entrepreneurial clusters have emerged in recent years, re-energizing these German regions and making them among the most dynamic ones in Europe and the world.

For example, in the Rhine-Neckar region several hundred firms have been created in the information communications technology (ICT) sector, with a particularly strong focus on open-source software. Similarly, Stuttgart, Heidelberg, and Karlsruhe all provide textbook examples of the role that top research universities and institutes, along with global companies such as SAP and IBM, can play in generating knowledge spillover entrepreneurship.[80] Without the fountain of research and new ideas spewing from these companies, universities, and research institutes, there would be no such entrepreneurship. At the same time, it is not clear that, without the entrepreneurship, the cutting-edge innovations and new product development would have taken place, at least in these regions.

The Baden-Württemberg region has also undertaken targeted strategies to spur entrepreneurship. To foster the innovative activities of these small companies, the government of Baden-Württemberg covers nearly half of the costs incurred in filing patent applications.[81] High-technology start-ups, such as the company founded by Saed Isfahani near Stuttgart, have blossomed. Saed Isfahani founded two high-technology start-ups—IWOT and ISOTEC—in Gerlingen, a small town close to Stuttgart. Each of these companies employs seven people. But small size has not deterred the companies from a number of key inventions, which have resulted in several notable patents in the resource and material industry.[82]

A somewhat different example is provided by Berlin, where entrepreneurship is driven and shaped by the creativity and opportunity seekers of the young generation, and which is emerging as one of the world's most mesmerizing entrepreneurial hot spots. The consulting company McKinsey estimates that each week in Berlin ten new high-technology and innovative ventures are founded. The entrepreneurial mecca of Berlin has drawn well over sixty thousand people in the digital industry to locate in Germany's capital city.[83] What is different about Berlin, however, is the paucity of corporate headquarters and research-and-development facilities. While some large, multinational companies have facilities located in and around Berlin, their headquarters and R & D divisions are actually located far away in cities such as Munich, Frankfurt, and Stuttgart.

Thus, the source of entrepreneurial opportunities is not company headquarters or research and development, as was the case for the founders of SAP. Rather, in the case of Berlin, the entrepreneurial opportunities and inspiration seem to emerge from the vibrant cultural scene. The former mayor of Berlin Klaus Wowereit's observation that Berlin was doomed to being *Arm aber sexy*, or "Poor but sexy," may have seemed like resignation acknowledging the inevitability of a dismal economic performance and status, but was actually a declaration of a dedicated policy initiative aiming to infuse the city with entrepreneurship.[84]

How far Germany has come since the doom and gloom prevalent throughout the 1990s, with renewed belief that entrepreneurship is compatible with the institutions, traditions, cultures, and societal orientation of Germany, is evidenced by a 2015 headline in the newspaper *Handelsblatt* proclaiming, "Der Mittelstand schlägt die Zuckerbergs und Musks," or the Mittelstand beats the Zuckerbergs and Musks.[85] The article reveals the startling findings of a study by the Global Entrepreneurship Monitor (GEM) based on a survey of 1,000 Germans and 1,100 Americans: "Entrepreneurs enjoy more recognition in Germany than in the United States."[86]

Conclusions

Every developed country has SMEs, and virtually every country has lots of them. That Germany has SMEs can hardly be a secret. The German difference is what it does with those SMEs, along with what those SMEs do for Germany. The German Mittelstand offers a distinct and unique role for SMEs.

Considering the quantitative definitions and categorization of what is meant by the Mittelstand, nothing particularly different or striking stands out. Based on the share of enterprises, employment, and sales accounted for by SMEs, Germany seems to be in line with other leading developed countries. However, it is the *qualitative* nature of the Mittelstand that has been Germany's secret strength. SMEs in Germany have a quality to them that sets them apart from their counterparts in other countries. It is the quiet and unnoticed exceptional strength of the Mittelstand that has, to a large extent, fueled the strong economic performance of Germany.

While scholars, policymakers, and business leaders have been mesmerized by the great successes of bold entrepreneurs such as Steve Jobs, Bill Gates, and Mark Zuckerberg, the more poignant and compelling secret of Germany is the economic prowess of thousands of small businesses that exhibit stability, a long-term focus, incremental change, and a commitment to quality enhancements. They are embedded in their communities and have deep ties with their employees and other constituents, and have provided the economic backbone and engine of Germany's remarkable economic surge and resilience.

Germany's commitment to and dependence on the Mittelstand were thought to preclude the development of dynamic high-technology entrepreneurs. However, contemporary Germany is proving that it can have it both ways, as a new generation has spawned headline-grabbing, bold, dynamic, and vibrant entrepreneurial start-ups. The CEO and director of Google, Eric Schmidt, has been so impressed by the recent emergence of entrepreneurial Germany that he recently prophesized that "Germany is well on the way to becoming a start-up Nation."[87]

This important secret of Germany is reminiscent of Sir Isaac Newton, who, when asked how he was able to come up with such pathbreaking new insights into physics, such as the laws of gravity, responded, "I merely stand on the shoulders of giants." The astonishing German success and economic resilience in an era of global turbulence are in no small part attributable to standing on the shoulders of midgets—the Mittelstand.

3 Poets and Thinkers

FOR A COUNTRY historically known as *Das Land der Dichter und Denker*, or the land of poets and thinkers,[1] Germany has achieved a mediocre performance by all of the main measures of educational attainment. For example, in the 2012 international PISA studies, undertaken by the OECD, Germany ranked just sixteenth in terms of mean student performance.[2] Not surprisingly, China ranked higher, but so too did Estonia, Poland, and Canada, with Vietnam closely following. In terms of performance in problem-solving, Germany ranked seventeenth, behind Korea and Japan, but also Italy and the Czech Republic.

At the university level, things look even more dismal for Germany. In the *Times Higher Education World University Rankings 2013–2014* compiled by Thomson Reuters, the California Institute of Technology (Caltech) is ranked the highest, closely followed by the University of Oxford, Harvard University, Stanford University, and the Massachusetts Institute of Technology (MIT). Not only is Germany glaringly absent among the top universities in the world, there are no German universities listed among the top twenty, or even among the top fifty.[3] The most highly ranked university is the Ludwig-Maximilians-University of Munich (LMU) at 57, right above the University of California at Davis. The Free University of Berlin (FU) is ranked at 86, closely followed by the Technical University of Munich (TUM) and the University of Heidelberg, Germany's oldest university established in 1386.

However, the seemingly lackadaisical educational performance of Germany by these widely accepted international standards and criteria poses something of a paradox. While the educational performance may seem dismal and even second-rate, Germany is the envy of the world in terms of producing perhaps the most important ingredient for what drives economic performance in the contemporary globalized economy—human capital. For example, the World Economic Forum ranks Germany among the very top countries for human capital, along with Switzerland, Singapore, Finland, the Netherlands, and Sweden.[4]

The secret is, in fact, not that Germany has high levels of human capital. Rather, it is what Germany does to generate such enviable levels of human capital, even when it seems burdened by mediocre primary and secondary education and universities. Perhaps there is something to be learned from the comparison with its world champion soccer team. How did the German *Nationalmannschaft*, or national soccer team, manage to amaze the world with its masterful World Cup victory in 2014 when not a single player ranks among the highest paid and presumably best players in the world? The world's richest player, Cristiano Ronaldo, earned $73 million, with a salary of $49 million in 2014, followed by Lionel Messi, with total earnings of $65 million and a salary of $42 million.[5] These were voted as the two best soccer players in the world in 2014. There are no German players among soccer's elite. The highest paid German player is Bastian Schweinsteiger, who earned a paltry $16 million, with a salary of $13 million.

Just as the soccer superstars are found in countries such as Portugal, Argentina, Spain, and Brazil but not in Germany, so too are the educational superstars for K-12 education in South Korea and Finland but not in Germany, while the university superstars are unequivocally found in the United States and United Kingdom but not in Germany. As with soccer, the secret may be in the teamwork, in the way that each individual player or organization interacts and interfaces with the others by playing its role to become part of a bigger team that ultimately proves to be unbeatable and the envy of the world. This chapter is devoted to examining the German secret of excelling in human capital, research, and science, even when, on the surface, it appears that it does anything but excel.

The Wirtschaftswunder

In their meticulous and careful analysis, the former president of the Kiel Institute for the World Economy, Herbert Giersch, and two of his key colleagues at that time, Karl-Heinz Paqué and Holger Schmieding, painstakingly analyze what fueled the Wirtschaftswunder.[6] The MIT scholar Robert Solow was awarded a Nobel Prize for identifying the keys to economic growth at that time: plants and factories, or physical capital, and people to work in those plants and factories, or labor. But the German advantage fueling the Wirtschaftswunder lay elsewhere—in its people, and especially in its workers. In particular, the workers manning Germany's newly reconstructed and rebuilt factories in industries such as automobiles, steel, and machinery were superbly trained through the highly vaunted apprentice and dual labor systems.

That the highly skilled workers of Germany even had factories and plants to work in following the devastation in the homeland wrought by Hitler's and Goebbels's *Totaler Krieg*, or total war, was something of a *Wunder*. The new postwar Federal Republic of Germany had little to work with, but here history and circumstances intervened. Thanks in no small part to the generosity of the United States in providing ample funds for investment through the European Economic Recovery Plan, or what is more commonly referred to as the Marshall Plan, the newly founded Federal Republic of Germany was able to rapidly rebuild its capital stock.[7] The bombed-out ruins of factories that equipped a nation at war with tanks, naval ships, and other military equipment were quickly replaced by sleek and efficient new plants and factories producing consumer goods such as automobiles and household goods and producer goods such as steel and machine tools.[8]

The engineers formerly deployed in fighting the war and working in armament factories were freed up to produce industrial and consumer goods. These highly qualified engineers and managers, which Hitler had euphemistically named "Speer's Kindergarten,"[9] provided a skilled labor force to fuel the rapid recovery of postwar Germany. It was not just their human capital as managers and engineers, but also their discipline and experience, that contributed to the uniquely skilled labor force.

A few of them turned to entrepreneurship and started new companies, such as Joseph Neckermann, while others became inventors, such as Ernst Heinkel in aviation, or directors and managers in the heavy manufacturing industries, such as Hans-Günther Sohl at Thyssen, Otto Beitz at Krupp, and Heinrich Nothoff at Volkswagen. Still, most found employment as highly skilled engineers in industry. While other countries, such as the United States and the United Kingdom, also had their engineers, the German engineers offered a big competitive advantage—despite their high skill levels, they were inexpensive, reflecting the low postwar wages prevalent in Germany.

Perhaps more than any other company, Volkswagen is associated with the spirit of the time of Germany and its Wirtschaftswunder. Volkswagen, which literally means the "people's car," was a brainchild of the Nazis designed to give the masses what they wanted—an inexpensive and accessible automobile that they could afford to purchase, operate, and drive. The dream for producing such a people's car was actualized by Hitler's famous protégé, Albert Speer, who focused on the twin strategies of minimizing the resources allocated in producing the car and deploying assembly line mass production. These twin strategies were essential because, with the country on the verge of yet another world war, resources could hardly be diverted from the build-up for the seemingly inevitable conflict. The development of mass production in churning out thousands of vehicles ensured not only the lowest possible cost per unit but also that production followed a "Made in Germany" strategy that reduced the country's dependence on production by any foreign entity. Ferdinand Porsche designed a system of mass production for the Nazis that ultimately enabled wartime mobilization in Germany, just as his counterpart, Henry Ford, accomplished for the United States.[10]

The Nazis, of course, did not survive the war. But Volkswagen did. And so too did the original twin strategies of resource saving and mass production, albeit for the new postwar model that helped to fuel the Wirtschaftswunder—the VW Beetle. Anyone old enough to remember the VW Beetle recalls a highly reliable car that was inexpensive but of high quality and reliability.

The wildly popular VW Beetle broke one production record after another. Heinrich Nothoff, who served as CEO of Volkswagen during that time and was a typical *Wirtschaftskapitän*, or captain of industry, articulated the all-encompassing company goal—to become the world market leader with the people's car.

Figure 3.1 shows the explosion of the production of the Beetle during the era of the Wirtschaftswunder. The Beetle, officially named the Volkswagen Type 1 and informally called the "Bug," was a two-door, four-passenger, rear-engine car, which had a remarkable production run until 2003. With over 21 million Beetles manufactured, it remains the longest-running and highest-volume manufactured car in the world from a single design platform.[11] That one of the authors learned to drive with his father's VW Beetle is no *Wunder*, considering when he first acquired his driver's permit.

It took highly trained engineers and skilled workers to turn the hunks of metal into the Beetle at Volkswagen. The geopolitical tensions of that era made their own surprising contributions. With the outbreak of the Korean War in 1950 and the onslaught of the Cold War, fears about the rise and dominance of the communist countries shaped Germany in a way that few could have imagined only a few years earlier. Germany had rapidly evolved from *Feind* to an important and trusted ally working side by side with the Western allies as a buffer against a hostile Eastern bloc.[12]

In the London Agreement on German External Debts of 1952, or the London Debt Agreement, the Western creditor nations agreed to relinquish about one-half of the reparations from World War II. Just as important was the flood of loans to and investments in Germany from the United States. Not only would a rapid recovery of Germany from

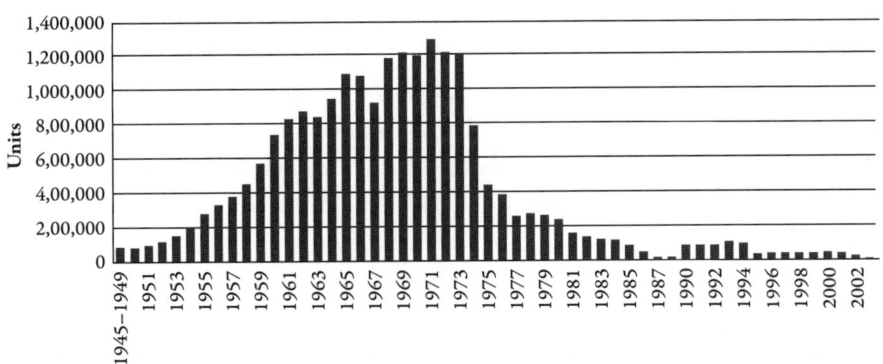

FIGURE 3.1 Annual production of the Volkswagen Beetle
Source: Data from Volkswagen.

the devastation of the war benefit the Western trading partners and provide a lift for their own economies, but it would also help to shore up the determination and resilience against the communist threat from the East.

The Korean War in the first part of the 1950s triggered a dramatic increase in the demand for steel and machinery by the United States. There was only one Western country with excess capacity in production at that time, Germany. Thus, the exports from Germany in steel, machines, and chemical products began to flow in increasing amounts to the United States. Companies like Volkswagen, Thyssen, Krupp, Höchst, BASF, and Mannesmann emerged as the backbone of the German Wirtschaftswunder. The heartland pumping out record amounts of manufactured goods, the Ruhr Valley, rapidly surged ahead as one of the wealthiest and most dynamic economic regions in the world. The fear precipitated by the rapid spread and dominance of communism throughout Eastern Europe, and especially in the Soviet Union, had solidified Germany as an invaluable and trusted ally and partner, with a long-lasting boost for not just its economic recovery from the war but for the Wirtschaftswunder.

The Dual Education System

As not just Germany, but in fact the entire world, began to recover from the devastation wrought by two world wars, the greatest demand, and therefore the focus of production, was basic goods and commodities for consumers and producers. For consumers this meant automobiles, washing machines, housing, and clothes. For producers this meant iron, steel, and machinery.

Churning out the demanded producer and consumer goods provided jobs, and increasingly good jobs, for workers, not just in Germany or in the United States, but throughout the developed world. Most economists and other scholars characterized the workers employed in factories and plants churning out mass-produced washing machines, sewing machines, and automobiles from meticulously constructed assembly lines as being unskilled. In other countries, and in particular the United States, this meant not having a university or college degree and possibly not even having finished high school. But the paucity of formal education was thought not to matter because the main demands on industrial workers thrown onto the assembly lines of mass-produced goods was to be reliable and consistent in performing a very small but focused set of manual tasks that were then repeated with clocklike regularity over the course of a work shift. This wasn't rocket science, hence the classification of "unskilled workers."

What was not different in Germany was that the typical worker engaged in manufacturing had never attended a university or college. But this is where the similarities ended. Although German factory workers typically had never attended, let alone graduated from, a university, they did have a very different advantage—formal and informal training. This training came through an educational system that is strikingly different from that found in the United States. American factory workers simply ended their education, either abruptly by dropping out or through the decision not to extend their education beyond high school.

By contrast, German workers were being trained to develop valuable skills from an early age. While the gymnasium prepares students for matriculation at a university, the *Realschule* prepares students for skilled work. Students from the *Realschule*, like their counterparts from the *Gesamtschule* and *Hauptschule*, typically do not matriculate at a university but rather become skilled workers. While the typical American industrial or service worker may receive training to acquire specific skills suitable for the workplace in a training program offered by an employer, or perhaps by a community or technical college, by contrast, German workers accumulate valuable labor skills even before they are teenagers.

The pragmatic and job-oriented training and education of young people gets a real boost from the *Lehrstellen*, or apprentice system. Unlike the Anglo-Saxon countries, such as the United Kingdom or the United States, Germany has what is termed as a dual education system, where some young people are prepared to matriculate at a university, while others are prepared to be highly skilled workers.

There are something like 342 recognized *Ausbildungsberufe*, or trades, that offer in-company training and classroom instruction in both technical and social fields. Examples of an *Ausbildungsberuf* are a plumber, pharmacist, and airline mechanic, but trades are also prevalent in banking and other service-related industries. The typical *Ausbildungsberuf* requires the apprentice to split her or his working time between the employer and an educational training institution, such as a vocational school, or *Berufsschule*. Nearly every city in Germany has at least one *Berufsschule*. As of 2013, over 1.4 million students were enrolled in 1,559 *Berufsschulen*.[13] The training as an apprentice will typically last between two and one-half and three and one-half years, at which point the apprentice will work full time. Hands-on training and practical experience is part of every apprenticeship, where highly targeted and specific skills are learned, such as those required in information technologies.

This makes graduates from the dual system flexible for different tasks and positions for a broad range of firm and industry contexts. In a rapidly changing global economy, the dual education system provides firms with a high degree of flexibility, as highly skilled and trained workers can be assigned to a broad spectrum of new, and in many cases, evolving job categories. Business administration-related apprentice training programs are actually supervised and certified by the local chamber of commerce, to ensure that the skills learned by the apprentice match the needs and standards of the local business community.

Often the local *Berufsschule* and local industry build close relationships, resulting in mutually reinforcing benefits. For example, Hochschule 21 in Lower Saxony has over seven hundred partnering companies located in the region. After graduating a master, the best students are eligible to enroll at universities for a bachelor's degree program.[14]

Thus, while substantial parts of each American generation battle frustration and alienation with an educational system that may meet the needs of university-oriented students but not those who will ultimately be engaged in manual and service jobs, their counterparts in Germany are receiving exactly the kind of training and investment in skills needed to compete, succeed, and thrive.

As a result of the dual system of education, considerably fewer young people in Germany matriculate, let alone graduate, from a university, while many more opt for the apprentice system to invest in becoming a worker with skills that will give a competitive advantage in the workplace. In 2013 only 28 percent of Germans aged between twenty-five and thirty-four had attained a college or university education, while the mean equivalent for the entire OECD countries was 39 percent.[15] At the same time, around two-thirds of young Germans began an apprenticeship, of which about three-quarters were able to complete their training and education as an apprentice.[16] While the rest of Europe and even the United States struggle with alarming rates of youth unemployment, which was around 50 percent in Spain and Greece in 2014, Germany's youth unemployment rate remained below 8 percent. However, because there is no analogous set of institutions in the United States and United Kingdom, most scholars and policymakers have been slow to recognize the value created by the German dual labor force system in general, and the apprentice system in particular. When scholars, thought leaders, policymakers, and decision-makers in business compare education in Germany with that in other countries, and in particular with the United States and United Kingdom, they see substantially lower rates of young people attending and graduating from the university. What they tend not to see is that these are the very same young people who are gaining highly valuable labor skills that generate considerable value not just for themselves but also for their employers, for their industries and regions, and ultimately for the entire country. However, because of low university matriculation and graduation rates, Germany was never classified as being a strong country in terms of human capital, education, or knowledge. Rather, it was typically classified as having a moderate level of human capital and operating as a moderate knowledge economy. What has been continually overlooked was the sleeping giant of highly skilled workers who had not attended or graduated from universities, especially when their labor skills are contrasted with their counterparts in other countries manning assembly lines, factory floors, and a myriad of other manufacturing and service jobs.

During the era of the Wirtschaftswunder, labor didn't seem to matter. As the Nobel Prize–winning economic growth model posited by MIT economics professor Robert Solow made abundantly clear, what mattered was factories, plants, and machines, or what was referred to as physical capital.[17] Labor was simply something that was thrown into the production process to man the mighty assembly lines fueling mass production of manufacturing, such as automobiles, steel, and tires.

In the Anglo-Saxon countries of the United States and the United Kingdom, much was made about the alienation and despair of workers, both those on the assembly lines of the great factories, and clerical white-collar workers, meticulously keeping track of them and their performance. The sociologist William H. Whyte, for example, scorned the deskilling of the once proudly independent American worker. In his best-selling book *The Organization Man*, Whyte lamented that what had replaced the proud American mavericks of earlier generations were men who, above all else, delivered obedience and conformity to their employers.[18] According to Whyte, "Loyalty among employees was more important than individual brilliance. Team players were valued more highly than mavericks. The individual was always subordinated to the greater good of the company."[19]

Only with hindsight did it became clear that, in fact, what kind of labor was matched up with capital did make a difference in the level of economic performance. This discovery came when another Nobel Prize–winning economist Wassily Leontief meticulously analyzed patterns of international trade and determined that, contrary to the assumptions made by most scholars, policymakers, thought leaders, and decision-makers in business, the United States had a comparative advantage in goods and products that were based largely on labor and not so much on physical capital.[20] Leontief's finding contradicted the prevailing thinking, that the United States, as the industrial leader in the free world, would have a comparative advantage in physical capital and not labor. After all, coming out of World War II, "The United States found itself an economic lord set far above the destroyed powers, its once and future competitors among both Allies and Axis powers. . . . While European and Japanese powers were being pulverized, new American factories were being built and old ones were back at work."[21]

As Europe and Japan lay in ashes, perhaps it is not surprising that estimates of the world's entire stock of physical capital placed something like two-thirds in the United States. As the distinguished British historian Robert Payne gushed, "There never was a country more fabulous than America. She sits bestride the world like a Colossus; no other power at any time in the world's history has possessed so varied or so great an influence on other nations. Half of the wealth of the world, more than half of the productivity, nearly two-thirds of the world's machines are concentrated in American hands; the rest of the world lies in the shadow of American industry."[22]

One would have thought—no, would have assumed—that, given the rich abundance of factories, plants, and machines in the United States vis-à-vis the rest of the (decimated) world, the comparative advantage in goods and products with high physical capital content would surely be in the United States. This certainly reflected the prevalent thinking in economics. According to the most compelling theory of international trade in the scholarly discipline of economics, the Heckscher-Ohlin[23] model, the proportion of factors of production determines the structure of trade, which in turn reflects the underlying comparative advantage. An abundance of physical capital relative to labor will be reflected by the export of capital-intensive goods. Conversely, a paucity of physical capital and a relative abundance of labor will be reflected by the export of labor-intensive goods. Since the United States had an abundance of physical capital relative to any other and all other countries, it stood to reason that it would export capital-intensive goods and important labor-intensive goods.

But Leontief found exactly the opposite. Despite the relative abundance of physical capital enjoyed by the United States, his meticulous research documented that the United States was actually exporting labor-intensive goods and importing-capital intensive products.[24]

Scholars immediately set out to resolve what quickly became known as the *Leontief Paradox*. As scholars scrambled to resolve the Leontief Paradox, they began to question the underlying assumption that labor consisted of unskilled workers engaged in repetitious, mechanistic work. Rather, they began to introduce additional factors of production into their models and analyses reflecting the important roles played by human capital, skilled labor and knowledge.[25] Apparently not all workers were the same. Some had more human capital than others. Some were more highly skilled than others. The resolution to the Leontief Paradox was that the United States was actually exporting goods that were human capital and knowledge intensive. Studies analyzing data and trade patterns over the post–World War II era clearly showed that the United States exported goods that were indeed labor intensive, as Leontief had found, but that labor was rich with human capital. Those industries with the comparative advantage tended to be classified as high technology, such as computers and pharmaceuticals.[26] Similar studies for Germany identified a clear comparative advantage in industries with a high component of skilled labor. Germany clearly had a comparative advantage in moderate-technology industries that relied heavily on skilled labor, such as automobiles and machine tools.[27]

The End of the Miracle

When exactly the Wirtschaftswunder stopped being such a *Wunder* has been subject to considerable speculation and debate. However, in their highly influential treatise on the subject, *The Fading Miracle*, Herbert Giersch, Karl-Heinz Paqué, and Holder Schmieding left little doubt that the miracle had long since faded by the fall of the Berlin Wall.[28] Still, the *Zeitalter*, or era, of globalization, which was ushered in by the events of November 9, 1989, no doubt hastened the deterioration of Germany's long vaunted postwar economic performance.

Economic growth stalled and unemployment began to rise shortly after the country was unified in October 1990—a trend that would worsen for well over a decade. The tried-and-true formula that had served postwar Germany so well in generating both economic stability and prosperity no longer seemed to work. For example, between the mid-1980s, right before the Berlin Wall fell, and a decade later, subsequent to German reunification, employment within Germany in the ten largest companies fell in absolute terms. During this same period, employment in these companies outside of Germany rose, quite drastically in some cases. The outsourcing and offshoring articulated by Thomas Friedman in his influential book *The World Is Flat* apparently was not restricted to the United States.[29] The loss of competitiveness in the traditional companies and industries in Germany also resulted in waves of corporate downsizing.

For the first time since its ascendance out of the rubble of World War II, Germany began to question the efficacy of its prized and highly valued economic and social asset—the dual system of education along with the its vaunted system of training apprentices and workers. If the dual system of education and the skilled labor force were no longer sufficient to generate competitive companies and industries in the rapidly emerging globalized economy, perhaps they had become antiquated and superfluous, if not an actual burden.

Speculation and debate about why exactly the Wirtschaftswunder had run its course were numerous and animated. Some argued that the financial resources shifted toward helping the new *Bundesländer* in the eastern part of the recently reunited country were proving to be too much of a burden for the western part to handle.[30] As billions of Deutschmarks were transferred from taxpayers in the west to invest in modernizing an alarmingly outdated infrastructure, along with social transfers, real estate, and housing, something of an investment bubble erupted in parts of the new *Bundesländer* in the east. Other arguments emphasized what seemed to be the role and response of West German industry in acquiring parts of the industry and integrating former competitors into their own value chains. In addition, there were new demands, problems, and challenges. Combining two countries is not simple. Nor is having an additional 18 million new citizens to integrate. Thus, Germany during the postunification period was inward looking, trying to address these new and unprecedented challenges, and struggling.

Lessons from America

Germany, however, was not the first country vulnerable to competition from abroad. In fact, the decade of the 1980s was fraught with economic anxiety in the United States. Plant closings, downsizings, and layoffs became widespread, particularly in the Midwest, earning it an unfortunate characterization as the Rust Belt. The once mighty factories of the American heartland that had churned out endless production lines of automobiles, steel, tires, and ovens had been humbled by a flood of imports pouring out of Europe and, especially, from Japan. The traditional manufacturing strengths of the United States, where it had been widely assumed to be the comparative advantage, were exposed as having a glaring competitive disadvantage, all within the span of a few short years, leading Lester Thurow, who at that time served as dean of the prestigious Sloan School of Management at the Massachusetts Institute of Technology, to worry that the country was "losing the economic race."[31] Writing in the mid-1980s, Thurow lamented that "today it's very hard to find an industrial corporation in America that isn't in real serious trouble basically because of trade problems. The systematic erosion of our competitiveness comes from having lower rates of growth of manufacturing productivity year after year, as compared with the rest of the world."[32]

Scholars along with leaders in business and public policy were at a loss as to how to regain America's competitive strengths. One response, such as *The Rise and Decline of Great Powers*, by the Yale University scholar Paul Kennedy, reflected a deep pessimism and a resignation to the perceived inevitable economic, political, and social decay pervasive throughout the United States.[33]

A very different perspective came at the end of the decade from the important and influential study *Made in America: Regaining the Productive Edge*, by a "dream team" of twenty-three top interdisciplinary scholars at the prominent and prestigious MIT Commission on Industrial Productivity, assembled and directed by Michael L. Dertouzos, Richard K. Lester, and Robert M. Solow.[34] The authors rejected the pessimism inherent in the view that American economic decline and loss of competitiveness was inevitable. Rather, they proposed a bold and careful strategy for American economic renewal. The authors detailed a meticulous blueprint for boosting productivity and competitiveness in the very same industries, such as automobiles and steel, which had given way to lower-cost imports pouring out of the more efficient and competitive factories from international rivals in Japan and Europe.

In fact, restoring American economic supremacy is exactly what transpired in the following decade, the 1990s.[35] Economic growth and job creation took off, as unemployment continued to fall, so that by the end of the decade, a prevalent conclusion was that not only had unemployment been wiped out once and for all, but that the business cycle also had been overcome, its devastating downturns and recessions now a thing of the past. The stock market started climbing and never stopped, at least not until the next century was in sight. The awe-inspiring economic American boom became the envy of the world.

The view from the other side of the Atlantic, in Germany, was crystal clear: while the MIT Commission on Industrial Productivity had been prescient in rejecting the inevitability of American economic decline, it was blindsided by the actual engine of renewal and growth fueling the resurgence of economic leadership and supremacy in the United States. The surge in American economic growth and competitiveness did not come from any revival in the traditional manufacturing industries, such as automobiles, tires, and steel. In fact, the economic crisis in those industries continued to deepen as the decade rolled on. Rather, the resurgence of US economic performance came from an unexpected and entirely unforeseen direction—new high-technology industries, such as personal computers, software, information technology, and biotechnology, along with knowledge-intensive services in finance, health, and education.

The view from Germany bogged down by its dismal economic performance of the 1990s may have been full of envy, but there was no delusion when it looked across the Atlantic at what the Nobel laureate in economics Joseph S. Stiglitz proclaimed to be "the most prosperous decade in history" in his widely read and influential book *The Roaring 1990s*.[36] All of these newly emerging and thriving industries had one thing in common. They were based less on the stalwart of the post–World War II era, physical capital, than on what has emerged as the mantra for economic success and prosperity in the era of globalization—knowledge and ideas. They were about brains, not brawn.

Germany seemed to be narrowing the gap in the standard of living with the United States throughout the post–World War II era, so that on the eve of the fall of the Berlin Wall at the end of the 1980s, it seemed fairly certain that a process of convergence was taking place. But just a few years later, America was racing ahead, enjoying what Stiglitz termed as the best economic performance in the country's history, while Germany was left behind, sputtering with sluggish economic growth and rising levels of unemployment. The widely assumed process of convergence between the two countries had seemingly reversed itself.

What was the difference? Thought leaders and policy analysts did not have to look hard and far. Scholars had already identified the key difference—knowledge. Just as Robert Solow had uncovered the key ingredient to economic prosperity in an earlier era—factories and plants, or what the economists call physical capital[37]—Paul Romer, a professor of economics at the University of California at Berkeley, formalized in economic models what policy and business leaders were already beginning to realize—knowledge and ideas had become the driving force for economic growth, jobs, and competitiveness.[38] Just as physical capital and labor are the key inputs and resources used to produce manufactured goods and products, knowledge and ideas are the key ingredient in generating innovations.[39] Globalization had rendered many of the traditional manufactured products no longer competitive in the high-cost and expensive locations of North America and Europe. But a new source of competitiveness was emerging—innovation.

Once-mighty industrial giants such as General Motors and U.S. Steel, which rose to global dominance through massive investments in plants and factories, were being displaced by the new high-tech start-ups, like Microsoft and Apple Computers, with their gleaming and trendy new campus-like facilities. This new breed puzzled old-school experts at first. Where were the factories? Where were the smokestacks? But this new breed of economic success thrived not in spite of a paucity of physical capital, but rather because of it. Similarly, places like Silicon Valley emerged with a mesmerizing economic performance, even as the old industrial cities Detroit, Cleveland, and Pittsburgh sputtered and stalled.[40]

Looking across the Atlantic, Germany recognized a strategy for turning the forces of globalization into economic opportunities, one that had worked for at least one country—innovation. The traditional strategy of relying largely upon skilled labor to fuel international competitiveness, employment, and economic growth had seemingly reached its limitations in the new global era.

At the dawn of the final decade of the last century, it was the ability to innovate that bestowed competitive advantage, and this meant brains mattered more and brawn less. But where did this knowledge and idea exactly come from? Here the scholars were less sure.

Three main types of sources were identified as creating the all-important knowledge fueling innovation, which in turn drives competitive advantage. These important new sources of competitive advantage are leveraged by firms like Microsoft but also places like Silicon Valley to gain a competitive edge and ultimately a sustained economic performance.[41] That is, the very same underlying forces shaping competitive advantage held for firms and industries as well as for regions, states, and entire countries.

The first source of knowledge is research and development, or R & D. Companies undertake R & D with the purposeful intention of generating innovations.[42] For example, the semiconductor was the result of research undertaken in the research laboratories of AT&T. The widespread reputation of Silicon Valley as being the most innovative place on earth is attributable in no small part to the large investments in R & D made by the multitude of high-technology companies populating "the Valley."[43]

The second source of knowledge is from research undertaken at universities and scientific institutions. University research has been used to fuel a broad range of innovations, such as the drink for athletes Gatorade, which came from research undertaken in the laboratories of the University of Florida, to the MP3 play3er, which came from research undertaken at a Fraunhofer Institute. Numerous studies have shown that those places with strong research universities, such as Silicon Valley and the Research Triangle region of North Carolina, also tend to exhibit superior economic performance.[44]

The third source of knowledge comes from workers. If they have a high degree of human capital, they are more capable of generating and contributing to innovative activity. Most studies measure and even characterize human capital in terms of formal education and highest degree attained or number of years in school.[45]

In terms of what mattered—R & D, university research, and human capital—there was one indisputable leader in the world, the United States. Not only did the United States account for a high share of the total investment of R & D during the 1990s, but it was by far the leading country in terms of R & D investment, either in absolute terms or as a share of gross domestic product.

If the United States dominated R & D, its leadership in terms of university research may have been even stronger. While it may be contested whether Harvard University is better than its perennial rival, Yale University, not to mention MIT, the University of Chicago, or Stanford University, there was no doubt that the best universities were in the United States. Other than Oxford University and Cambridge University, there were scarcely leading universities to be found anywhere outside of America.

In terms of the third source of knowledge that fuels innovative activity, human capital, the United States was again the indisputable leader. Thanks to its rich, vital, but also varied and diverse population of colleges and universities, the United States was the world leader in terms of having workers who had attended and graduated from colleges and universities. If valuable ideas come from people, the United States was the country with people educated and prepared to generate that new knowledge.

Thus, for all three of the main sources of knowledge that matter for innovative activity—R & D, university research, and human capital—the United States was by far and away the undisputed leader in the world during the decade following the fall of the Berlin Wall. However, there were still nagging suspicions that even a mighty arsenal of these knowledge inputs might still not be enough to generate the crucial innovative activity that was so desperately needed to drive competitiveness in the era of globalization.

The concern was that just having ideas and knowledge is not a guarantee that they will automatically result in innovations. There is a great gulf between a cognitive process, or an idea, and actually putting that idea into action and obtaining a positive result. As the great philosopher, writer, and scientist Johann Wolfgang von Goethe pointed out more than two centuries ago, "Knowing is not enough, we must apply; willing is not enough, we must do."[46]

A key mechanism driving the theoretical models of endogenous growth in the scholarly discipline of economics is the assumption that investments in knowledge automatically spill over from the organization where they are undertaken and result in commercialized innovative activity.[47] What works in theory doesn't always work so smoothly in practice. In fact, there were glaring examples highlighting key inventions that did not automatically spill over into commercialization and innovative activity. For example, the generous funding to American universities for research by federal agencies such as the National Institutes of Health (NIH) and the National Administration for Space Agency (NASA) created numerous new ideas and inventions that were unable to find their way into the market. The problem was apparently a maze of bureaucratic approvals, restrictions, and requirements posing formidable challenges to actually commercializing new ideas emerging from university research.

Senator Birch Bayh was so concerned about the paucity of commercialized university research emanating from federal funding by the US governmental agencies that he admonished his colleagues in the US Senate that "a wealth of scientific talent at American colleges and universities—talent responsible for the development of numerous innovative scientific breakthroughs each year—is going to waste as a result of bureaucratic red tape and illogical government regulation."[48]

Senator Bayh's warning challenged the efficacy of government and societal investments in new knowledge if knowledge remained simply that, and was not commercialized for innovative activity, at least not within the country funding the investments in knowledge, the United States: "What sense does it make to spend billions of dollars each year on government-supported research and then prevent new developments from benefiting the American people because of dumb bureaucratic red tape?"[49] Senator Bayh argued that, if the country was not able to appropriate the returns, in terms of economic growth, employment and competitiveness, from its costly research investments, then perhaps it would be advisable to abstain from, or at least reduce expenditures on, federally funded academic research.

Scholars subsequently characterized as *the knowledge filter* the very real-world problem of barriers to commercializing new knowledge and generating innovative activity from that knowledge.[50] The knowledge filter consists of factors and conditions preventing or impeding the spillover of knowledge for commercialization and innovation.

While scholars articulated and assigned a name to the concept articulated and described by an army of leaders in public policy and business, Senator Bayh set about to create a legislative and policy mandate to penetrate that knowledge filter. Together with his colleague in the US Senate, Robert Dole, Senator Bayh championed a new mandate in the form of legislation and policy to spur innovative activity and reignite American economic growth, employment creation, and competitiveness. Consequently, Congress enacted the Bayh-Dole Act in 1980.[51] The Bayh-Dole Act represented an explicit attempt to facilitate knowledge spillovers from universities for commercialization and ultimately economic growth.[52] In particular, the Bayh-Dole Act reassigned the intellectual property rights of inventions emanating from federally funded research from the funding federal agency to the university actually undertaking that research.

A large body of scholarly literature has emerged assessing the efficacy of the Bayh-Dole Act in penetrating the knowledge filter.[53] Most of the empirical evidence, both scholarly and otherwise, has ranged from the strongly positive to the wildly effusive. For example, *The Economist* gushes, "Possibly the most inspired piece of legislation to be enacted in America over the past half-century was the Bayh-Dole Act of 1980. Together with amendments in 1984 and augmentation in 1986, this unlocked all the inventions and discoveries that had been made in laboratories through the United States with the help of taxpayers' money. More than anything, this single policy measure helped to reverse America's precipitous slide into industrial irrelevance. Before Bayh-Dole, the fruits of research supported by government agencies had gone strictly to the federal government. Nobody could exploit such research without tedious negotiations with a federal agency concerned. Worse, companies found it nearly impossible to acquire exclusive rights to a government owned patent. And without that, few firms were willing to invest millions more of their own money to turn a basic research idea into a marketable product."[54]

Similarly *Business Week* concludes that "since 1980 the Bayh-Dole Act has effectively leveraged the tremendous value of academic research to create American jobs, economic growth, and public benefit. The Act has resulted in a powerful system of knowledge transfer unrivaled in the world. One would think that the combination of public benefit and the productive, job-creating effects of the Bayh-Dole Act would be a winner in every sense."[55]

A different attempt to penetrate the knowledge filter was enactment by Congress of the Small Business Innovation Research (SBIR) program. Congress enacted the SBIR program in 1982 with an explicit goal of reinvigorating jobs and growth through enhancing the innovative performance of the United States.[56] In particular, the explicit mandate created by Congress was to promote technological innovation, enhance the commercialization of new ideas emanating from scientific research, increase the role of small business in meeting the needs of federal research and development, and expand the involvement of minority and disadvantaged persons in innovative activity.

The SBIR program consists of funding from eleven federal agencies to small businesses through a grants program. As of 2012, SBIR awards amounted to around $2.5 billion annually to small firms for innovative activity. The magnitude of the SBIR grants range from $100,000 ($150,000 at the National Institutes of Health) for a Phase I award, to $750,000 for a typical Phase II award.

The efficacy of the SBIR program in penetrating the knowledge filter has been analyzed in considerable detail by the Board on Science, Technology and Economic Policy of the National Research Council of the National Academy of Sciences. There is considerable empirical evidence suggesting that the SBIR has facilitated the commercialization of knowledge and ideas generated at universities and private companies.[57] These studies generally conclude that the SBIR has generated entrepreneurship and innovations that might otherwise not have occurred.

Studies finding that the SBIR facilitates penetrating the knowledge filter are remarkably robust. A positive impact of the SBIR on entrepreneurship, innovation, and overall economic performance is found across a broad spectrum of disparate methodologies, such as case studies, interviews with officials administering the program at the funding federal agencies, broad-based surveys of recipient firms receiving SBIR support, and state-of-the-art econometric studies.

Studies identifying the impact of the SBIR in enabling firms and entrepreneurs to penetrate the knowledge filter have generated six important findings. First, most of the inventions and new ideas would never have been commercialized without SBIR funding.[58]

Second, there are more start-ups, and in particular technology-based start-ups, as a result of the SBIR program. A significant number of high-technology start-ups simply would not exist in the absence of SBIR funding.

The third important finding is that the SBIR program enhances the growth performance of recipient firms. Fourth, the SBIR program tends to enhance the likelihood of survival for recipient firms. In particular, the SBIR provides a mechanism enabling entrepreneurial start-ups to survive what has been characterized as the valley of death.

Fifth, the commercialization of research undertaken in university laboratories has been enhanced as a result of the SBIR. The last important finding in assessing the impact of the SBIR is that the program has spurred the entrepreneurial activity of researchers and scientists at universities. The empirical evidence highlights a significant number of university scientists and engineers who had started companies but in the absence of the SBIR program might never have engaged in entrepreneurial activity. Equally important, the demonstration or contagion effect of SBIR-funded scientists and engineers who have become entrepreneurs has induced other colleagues to also start a business.[59]

The knowledge filter does not exist solely in the realm of knowledge created by universities. Rather, poignant examples exist highlighting the existence of a formidable knowledge filter choking off or at least impeding the spillover of knowledge and ideas for commercialization and innovation. For example, many of the key components of the personal computer, such as the keyboard and screen, were actually invented in the research-and-development facility of Xerox, Xerox Park. When the scientists and engineers behind these crucial inventions suggested to the decision-making hierarchy at Xerox that they had created a potential innovation with extraordinary market value, they were met with rigid skepticism. Company executives rejected the idea of going into a new and unknown product line when the company was already the world's dominant producer of copy machines.

Scholars would subsequently interpret the uncertainty and asymmetries inherent in new ideas in knowledge as contributing to the inevitability of the knowledge filter, not just for research undertaken at universities but also for research undertaken in virtually every organizational context. Because of the uncertainty inherent in new ideas and knowledge, no one can predict what the market valuation of any new idea or invention will actually be. The asymmetry reflects the high variation in expected market valuation of new ideas across different people. In fact, Steve Jobs got wind of the newly invented personal computer at Xerox Park. Where the executives at Xerox saw a wasted investment, Jobs saw the rich promise of a lucrative new market.[60] It actually took Jobs's entrepreneurial activity in founding the new company, Apple, to provide the conduit for the knowledge and ideas funded by and created within the organizational context of Xerox to spill over for commercialization and fuel the innovative activity that would launch what would ultimately prove to be one of the innovative giants of this generation, Apple Computer. Scholars provided not just compelling examples such as Steve Jobs founding Apple Computer, but also systematic empirical studies confirming the key role that entrepreneurship plays as a conduit of knowledge spillovers from the organization investing in and creating new knowledge ideas to a newly founded company actually commercializing those ideas through innovative activity.[61]

Thus, the United States had emerged with global leadership not just in the key aspects involved in creating new knowledge and ideas—R & D, university research, and human capital—it also led the world in one of the key conduits for the spillover of that knowledge from the cognitive realm of ideas to actualization through entrepreneurship. While high-profile entrepreneurial companies such as Apple, Nike, Ben and Jerry's, Dell Computers, Microsoft, and Starbucks captured the attention of Americans, perhaps just as impressive were the thousands of unknown entrepreneurs choosing not to pursue careers in large corporations but rather to set off on their own.[62]

Combining the two essential ingredients—knowledge and entrepreneurship—fueled an explosion of economic growth, job creation, and prosperity that the country had never known before.

The results, measured in terms of economic performance—growth, job creation, and productivity gains—showed it. Economic growth, new jobs, and productivity all stood at record levels by the middle of the 1990s. Unemployment had virtually vanished in the country. The Dow Jones Industrial Average soared, along with the real estate market, leading more than a few scholars and economists to proclaim that the business cycle had finally been defeated. Joseph S. Stiglitz celebrated "the most prosperous decade" in the history of the world![63]

This innovative performance, and even more importantly, this economic performance clearly reflected American dominance of knowledge factors and inputs and the strong, driving force of entrepreneurship to transform those new ideas into viable, innovative products. The United States was the undisputed global champion in terms of patented inventions. The US comparative advantage in knowledge-intensive industries, or in products requiring a large input from factors such as R&D and human capital, was clearly exhibited in trade patterns. Meticulous studies documented that the United States was a strong exporter of goods and products in high-technology industries and other industries that are knowledge based and highly innovative, such as computers, semiconductors, pharmaceuticals, and software.[64]

Rethinking Universities and Research

Things were considerably different in Germany. The country not only lagged in the holy trinity of knowledge inputs and factors—R & D, university research, and human capital—but perhaps even more alarming, it was falling further and further behind.

R & D as a share of gross domestic product (GDP) was below 2.4 percent by 2004. Germany clearly lagged behind world leaders such as Sweden, which had an R & D intensity of 4.0 percent, Japan, with an R & D intensity of 3.2 percent, Switzerland, with an R & D intensity of 2.8 percent, and the United States, with an R & D intensity of 2.5 percent.[65] With its emphasis on, and historical comparative advantage in, the traditional manufacturing industries such as machine tools, metalworking, and automobiles, high-technology and newly emerging industries were not a high priority and did not play a large role in Germany. This, in turn was reflected in a lower R & D intensity in Germany than in many key trading partners and competitors, such as the United States, Sweden and Japan, which clearly had lost the comparative advantage in those industries and, in turn, relied on R&D-intensive industries for their competitiveness.

In terms of the gold standard of human capital, the share enrolled in tertiary, or higher, education, Germany ranked among the lowest countries in Europe and in OECD countries. By 2001, fewer than one-third of German students were enrolled in tertiary education.[66] By comparison, nearly one-half of the comparable age groups were enrolled in tertiary education in Britain, 49 percent in Korea, 69 percent in Sweden, and 42 percent in the United States. This suggested that the level of human capital lagged considerably below that of most of its counterparts, both in Europe and in the OECD, where the average was 48 percent.[67] Again, historical strengths bestowing a comparative advantage in Germany in the traditional moderate-technology industries, which had served Germany so well for so long, had directed a significantly higher share of young people into acquiring industrial skills through the apprentice system rather than from attending universities. Thus, in terms of human capital, Germany simply didn't measure up.

The third leg of the stool supporting knowledge and innovation consists of universities and related research institutions. This should have been an area of strength from which Germany could launch a new era of knowledge-based innovative activity. But it wasn't. In fact, the once proud and mighty world leader in research and ideas, the German university, now was encumbered by at least three glaring deficiencies.

The first deficiency involved the mission and orientation of the university. A century ago, when it stood as the undisputed leader of university research, Germany, in fact, set the standard for universities throughout the world. As the scholar R. Seven Turner concluded in his doctoral thesis at Princeton University, "The Prussian Universities and the Research Imperative, 1806–1848," "Scholars of most European nations contributed to this heroic age of organized learning, but German scholars played the pre-eminent role."[68]

The German university had attained such lofty prominence by the second half of the nineteenth century thanks in no small way to Wilhelm von Humboldt.[69] Historically, the landscape of not just Europe, but also the United States, consisted of universities under the dominance and control of the church and the state. The alarming fate of Copernicus when he challenged papal authority, arguing that earth revolved around the sun, was certainly more rule than the exception.

The historical and institutional linkage between the church and the university was challenged and disrupted by Wilhelm von Humboldt, Alexander's older brother, in Berlin during the early 1800s. Humboldt was a giant in philosophy and linguistics who, among other things, served as the Prussian minister of education and later founded the University of Berlin (now Humboldt University Berlin) In particular, Humboldt triggered a new tradition for universities centering on freedom of thought, learning, intellectual exchange, and research and scholarship as their salient features. According to Humboldt, "'The purpose of the universities is to cultivate learning in the deepest and broadest sense of the word,' not for some practical or utilitarian end, but for its own sake as preparatory material of spiritual and moral education (*Bildung*)."[70] The historian Daniel Fallon suggests, "Perhaps the most remarkable fact about the widely admired German university of the nineteenth century is that it had no clear precedent. The university idea was struck, virtually *de novo*."[71]

As the Humboldt model for the university diffused through first Europe and subsequently to the other side of the Atlantic, universities became free from parochial constraints, leading instead to the nonsecular university committed to independence of thinking, learning, and research. Rather than simply serve as vessals for transmitting what was approved and advocated by the church and state to subsequent generations, scholars were introduced to a radically new priority: "Whoever wishes to enter upon a scholarly career, upon him is the demand to be placed that he not merely have learned the knowledge at hand, but rather that he also be capable of producing knowledge out of his own independent activity."[72]

Humboldt left a very different mandate and mission for universities than what existed when he arrived. What has become known as the Humboldt model of the university was not just free from the dictates of the church and the state, but also pursued the discovery of new knowledge, or what was called *Wissenschaftsideologie*. According to Turner, "*Wissenschaftsideologie* glorified discovery and creativity within the universities. . . . It assumed that one obtains academic knowledge through the rigorous applications of well-defined methods of investigation which moreover means that the tools of discovery can be made available to large numbers of students."[73]

The founder of the American Psychological Association, who would subsequently go on to serve as president of Clark University, G. S. Hall, observed in 1891, "The German University is today the freest spot on earth. . . . Never was such burning and curiosity. . . . Shallow, bad ideas have died and truth has always attained power. . . . Nowhere has the passion to push on to the frontier of human knowledge been so general. Never have so many men stood so close to nature and history or striven with such reverence to think God's thoughts after Him exactly."[74]

The world leadership of the German university with its Humboldt model diffused throughout the continent and across the Atlantic over the succeeding century. That Germany should find itself at an economic disadvantage not in spite of, but because of the state of its universities toward the close of the twentieth century seemed startling. As the former president of Harvard University and former ambassador to the Federal Republic of Germany, James B. Conant, pointed out with insightful prescience in 1964, the German university is "the best in the world—for the nineteenth century."[75]

What had happened to so drastically reduce the one-time leader in university research and education to becoming an object of pity? One answer, of course, was that German universities had been decimated by Hitler, the National Socialists, and World War II.[76] Germany had been the leader in generating Nobel Prize winners since 1901, when Wilhelm Conrad Röntgen was awarded the very first Nobel Prize in Physics. However, this totally changed after 1935 thanks in no small part to the legacy of Hitler and the National Socialists.[77]

But a deeper answer is provided by Daniel Fallon, who views the German university as "a heroic ideal in conflict with the modern world."[78] In fact, the mission and orientation of universities in the economy and society had evolved considerably elsewhere in the world, especially in the United States and United Kingdom.

The German "heroic ideal" of knowledge for its own sake, inherent in the Humboldt model of the university, had indeed diffused throughout Europe and across the Atlantic. In the early post–World War II years, when the economy may have conformed best to the growth model articulated by Robert Solow, where plants and factories, or physical capital, served as the engine of economic growth, jobs, and competitiveness, there was little economic use for what the university had to offer, which was essentially new ideas. After all, factories required machines combined with unskilled or perhaps moderately skilled workers, but the lofty ideas percolating at universities seemed to be extraneous to industry and the world of commerce. Universities may have made an important contribution in passing along the great traditions of Western culture and civilization from generation to generation, but they were generally regarded as an economic drain rather than as a crucial resource in generating economic performance.

But as the source of competitiveness shifted from brawn to brains, or from physical capital to knowledge, the role of universities changed. As the 1970s and 1980s ushered in the demise of the postwar economic model where the driving force of economic growth and prosperity was physical capital, scholars and policymakers began to turn toward a new source of economic growth, employment creation and competitiveness—knowledge and ideas. Where the university had been largely viewed as extraneous to economic performance during the initial decades following World War II, policymakers, business leaders, and university officials started to realize that the university was needed to provide a crucial and valuable resource and asset driving economic growth. After all, universities are all about generating new ideas.

A new mandate, mission, and orientation for universities in America was emerging. This new mandate was to include research and teaching, not just in the traditional academic disciplines, where value was determined and influenced by the discipline itself—"knowledge for the sake of knowledge"—but also in fields where knowledge "can contribute to solving the problems and challenges prevalent in society."[79] Those problems range from the social to the economic and to business. The main point was that the mission of American universities became highly responsive to the demand for knowledge and ideas, not just from the traditional academic disciplines themselves, but from particular interests within society.

In fact, this outward orientation of American universities, where values were influenced by external parties, was not entirely new. There were striking examples of American colleges and universities that had been mandated with goals external to the inward-looking traditional academic disciplines. For example, in an effort to win World War II, the US Government turned to key American colleges and universities for help in generating the ideas and technologies to develop the next generation of weapons and equipment. This partnership between the federal government and the universities was so fruitful that it made a significant contribution to the allies' ultimate victory in the war.

Vannevar Bush was one of the young engineers who played a key role in working with the universities to develop the nuclear bomb. He was so impressed by what we today would characterize as the knowledge spillovers from the university that, following the allied victory, he championed a refocus of the mission of university research. Bush laid out a compelling case for a new and expanded role for universities in contributing to societal needs in his highly influential book *Science: The Endless Frontier*.[80]

Vannevar Bush's bold new mandate for American universities in 1945 was, in fact, not entirely without precedent. Almost a century earlier, an even more fundamental mandate had been crafted for American colleges and universities to respond not solely to the values of the inward-looking ivory tower, but also to include outward-looking societal values. President Abraham Lincoln signed into law the Morrill Act, widely referred to as the Land Grant Act, in 1862. The Morrill Act provided a land grant from previously federally owned land to each state on the condition that it would be dedicated in perpetuity to fund agriculture and mechanical colleges that would have dedicated benefits accruing to that state. In order to fulfill the mission mandated by the Morrill Act, the designated land-grant universities had to develop an effective set of institutional mechanisms facilitating the spillover of knowledge in general, and science and technology in particular, that would contribute to the economic performance of the state. It is certainly far from a coincidence that the United States has held the comparative advantage in many agricultural products, despite high labor costs, for the 150 years subsequent to passage of the Morrill Act. Through the link between state-of-the-art research, teaching, and dedicated support services from the land grant universities to the agricultural sector of the states, American farms and agriculture have remained far and away the most productive in the world.[81]

As knowledge and ideas increasingly replaced physical capital as the driving force underlying economic performance, the role of universities in the economy also started to change. Universities in the United States were increasingly viewed not just as institutions promoting social and cultural values but as a key catalyst for economic growth and prosperity.

In shifting the mission and orientation of the university from the traditional Humboldt model, where the values and goals were dictated by the inward-looking traditional academic disciplines themselves, the universities may have realized that, thanks to the compelling precedent and experiences garnered by the land grant universities, they did not have to reinvent the wheel. What could be learned from the experiences of the land grant universities is that doing basic research and coming up with new ideas and knowledge does not automatically translate into having a positive impact in the targeted community. Rather, new interdisciplinary and applied fields had to be developed that did not adhere to any disciplinarily determined values but rather to the needs, demands, and interests of an external community.

But even this new set of applied and outward-looking interdisciplinary programs and fields, which took research, ideas, and insights generated from the traditional basic disciplines and applied them to generate solutions to particular and targeted problems, challenges, and contexts, proved not to be sufficient in facilitating the spillover of knowledge from the university to the outside community. In addition, land grant universities realized that a broad range of mechanisms, institutions, and offices mandated with enabling and enhancing the transfer of knowledge, ideas, practices, and technology from the university to the targeted community, such as agricultural extension services, were essential to ensure the transfer of technology and spillover of knowledge from university research to actual applications for constituent groups.

As American universities began to extend their fundamental mission away from a fixation on research and teaching in the traditional academic disciplines to add on new applied and cross-disciplinary fields with an outward orientation, such as biochemistry, nanotechnology, business schools, informatics, schools of public policy and life sciences, they also began to develop institutions, mechanisms, and offices promoting the transfer of technology and knowledge spillovers from university research to society. Examples of what has been characterized as conduits of knowledge spillovers include offices of technology transfer, science parks, incubators, innovation centers, and offices of engagement.[82]

Thus, the orientation, mission, and mandate of the American university have evolved from the Humboldt model to what has been characterized as an entrepreneurial university. Fundamental disciplinary research still matters in the entrepreneurial university, and in fact is still undeniably the heart and soul of what has been characterized as the university in the entrepreneurial society. But a campus visit to the typical American university suggests an evolution characteristic more of an archaeological dig. The way the university has changed over time can be traced by a concentric ring reflecting the development and shift from the Humboldt model to the entrepreneurial university. At the core of the campus are typically not only the most beautiful and impressive ivy-covered buildings and carefully manicured landscape, but also the home of the traditional and recognizable academic disciplines. A second ring reveals the more modern but also utilitarian architecture of the newer applied and interdisciplinary fields and programs, such as the business school, informatics school, and school of public policy. For example, at Harvard University, the famous and highly esteemed school of business is actually not in Cambridge but located on the other side of the river, in Boston. On the fringe of the campus is the third ring, consisting of very recently constructed buildings housing the science parks, incubators, offices of technology transfer, and innovation centers. The architecture of American university campuses generally reflects this important and fundamental shift away from the Humboldt model and toward the new, contemporary entrepreneurial university.[83]

But not in Germany. At least, not through the remainder of the previous century. The universities in Germany were simply left behind, bearing the weight of the ponderous centuries-old model of the university crafted by Humboldt.

A second liability burdening universities in Germany was constraints on funding. In the early years following World War II, even the best public universities in the United States were still mainly funded by state governments. Tuition was kept low to maintain accessibility to all students regardless of family incomes and resources. But as the cost of universities exploded in the 1970s, state legislatures could not keep up. The prohibitively high cost of participating in the frontiers of research exploded. Not only did tuition rates jump to painfully high levels, but as the state legislators balked at financing universities clawing to maintain or move ahead in the brutal markets of academic competition, American universities turned to new sources of finance, such as sponsored research, but also philanthropic support from generous alumni, foundations, and benefactors.[84] The levels of endowment in most major research universities are now in the billions of dollars. Harvard University, for example, now has an endowment of $36.4 billion, which is greater than the GDP of one-half of all the countries in the world.[85]

Harvard's endowment, which exceeds the GDP of ninety countries, falls between the GDP of Jordan and Latvia.[86]

But not in Germany. Throughout the last century, finding new sources of finance to fund increasingly expensive research and education was almost impossible in a culture with a tradition of tuition-free education and a paucity of philanthropic participation. It simply wasn't done. This, of course, placed German universities and scientists at a considerable resource disadvantage vis-à-vis their rivals and counterparts on the other side of the Atlantic. No German university has anything remotely approaching the resources available to the top private universities, such as Harvard University, or even the endowments of public research universities, which have now risen to substantial levels in the billions of dollars.

Consequently, Germany suffered from what is called the *brain drain*. Attracted not just by higher salaries but also more enticing working, teaching, and research conditions, top scientists and other academics fled the more meager levels of compensation and uninspiring teaching and research conditions for lucrative offers in North America and the United Kingdom, but also on the continent in Austria and Switzerland.[87]

The third liability involved a relative homogeneity of German universities. Most students attended the universities located within geographic proximity of their home. Since funding came largely from the Länder, there was a paucity of competition among the universities, resulting in a rather bland and homogeneous profile of the typical German university. By contrast, the university landscape in the United States was rife with innovation and diversity, resulting in a rich heterogeneity of colleges and universities with a broad and diverse profile of strengths, ranging from excellent four-year colleges, such as Amherst and Williams, to single-gender colleges, such as Smith, to private research universities, such as Emory University and Washington University, and finally to public universities, such as the University of Wisconsin and the University of California. Each had their strengths and weaknesses, their advocates and critics, but taken together formed a diverse boutique of rich research and educational opportunities.

Germany was falling behind. Not just in terms of one of the pillars upon which the knowledge economy and society depends, but on all three pillars—R & D, universities, and human capital. Public policy and business leaders had a name for this crisis, which was echoed throughout the media—*Die Innovationskrise*, or innovation crisis.[88] As *The Economist* observed in its typically understated fashion, "German Innovation: No Bubbling Brook."[89]

Germany: Land of Innovation

And then Germany woke up. As the economic misery and helplessness of drifting continued throughout the final decade of the previous century, Chancellor Helmut Kohl, who had begun his remarkable tenure as the leader of Germany in 1982, navigated West

Germany through the tensions of the Cold War, and then unflinchingly led the country through the process of reunification in 1991, announced a bold new policy direction to squarely address the *Innovationskrise* in January 30, 1996, his *Initiatives for Investment and Employment*.[90] There was no doubt that the new policy priority targeted innovation and entrepreneurship. The first and main part of the program focused on the "creation of new and innovative firms."[91]

However, it would not be until several years later, under Chancellor Gerhard Schröder, that the country actually was able to embark on this bold new direction, shifting toward a knowledge-based, innovative economy as a main priority. The striking success of American policies fostering linkages and partnerships between universities and industry, such as the Bayh-Dole Act, along with the inspirational success of new and entrepreneurial firms, led to a rethinking and reformulation of the role of research, human capital, and the universities.

One aspect of the new policy approach in Germany was to interpret science and research, not as an isolated activity at the periphery of the economy, but rather as a cornerstone of innovation and ultimately economic performance. Thus, "research is not an end in itself," as the German Ministry for Education and Research (Bundesministerium für Wirtschaft) pointed out in 2012.[92] Rather, research undertaken at universities and nonprofit institutes should fuel economic growth and new jobs. A new mandate for the role of science and research was ushered in by the German Ministry of Economics combined with the Ministry for Education and Research (Bundesministerium für Bildung und Forschung), which declared that "all parts of the innovation process, starting with basic research up to the diffusion of new products and procedures, should be linked up." New economic policy strategies involving networks and regional clusters emerged as a priority for economic policy. In order to spur not just cooperation with private industry but also the acceleration of technology transfer and knowledge spillovers, offices of technology transfer began to proliferate across German universities and research institutions.

In 2002 the Employee Invention Act was amended, which effectively abolished the traditional ownership of intellectual property created from university research.[93] In particular, the reform introduced a new policy where the university is assigned the ownership of the intellectual property from research undertaken at the university, but the inventor, who is typically a professor or scientist, has a claim to one-third of the revenues expected to accrue from any commercialization of that intellectual property.

At the same time the patenting process of university inventions was centralized into regional patent agencies (RPAs) and taken away from the technology transfer offices (TTOs) of the university. This new policy was designed to facilitate economies of scale in university patenting and at the same time to free resources for the TTO to concentrate on supporting the researchers in the process of commercializing their inventions rather than becoming bogged down by the legal and bureaucratic jungle of patenting intellectual property.

Chancellor Gerhard Schröder declared 2004 to be the *Jahr der Innovation*, or Year of Innovative Activity. Many of our economist colleagues in Germany at that time wrote off Chancellor Schröder's slogan as simply another example of vacuous political rhetoric designed to dupe a naive public. In hindsight, the *Jahr der Innovation* signaled that, under Chancellor Schröder's vision and leadership, the country was embarking on a set of fundamental and far reaching economic and social reforms, not the least of which placed the highest priority on transforming Germany into a knowledge and innovation driven *entrepreneurial society*.[94]

Transforming Germany from being the sick man of Europe to a knowledge-driven and innovative entrepreneurial society did not come easily Professor Dr. Klaus Zimmerman, who served for years as president of the prestigious and influential German Institute for Economic Research Berlin (Deutsches Institut für Wirtschaftsforschung Berlin) and serves now as president of the Institute for Study of Labor in Bonn, pointed out that "at the end of 2005 Germany oscillated between a fundamental breakthrough embracing economic and social reform and simply giving up on those reforms. The first stirrings of modernizing an antiquated economy and social welfare state were only beginning to be recognized. Grave reservations and concerns impeding sweeping reform posed a considerable political and social challenge."[95]

In hindsight, the *Jahr der Innovation* in 2004 was anything but vacuous rhetoric. It marked the opening volley for significant and fundamental changes in Germany, with innovation as the centerpiece of the new German economic strategy. The *Innovationspakt*, or Innovation Agreement, made through the budgeting process between the Chancellor's Office and the Bundestag, or parliament, guaranteed that the portion of the federal budget allocated to knowledge and human capital in general, and research in particular, be given priority. The budgets of the Federal Republic reflected this priority over the ensuing budgetary fiscal years. As employees and members of the Max Planck Society during those years, we witnessed the president of the Max Planck Society at that time, Professor Dr. Peter Gruss, announcing the surprisingly substantial increases in the annual budgets. While Chancellor Schröder's reforms called for austerity and tightening in many other parts of the budget, such as social services, the chancellor's vision identifying investments in research and human capital as the keys to reigniting German economic competitiveness and growth was reflected in the sudden and considerable annual increases in budgets of not just the Max Planck Society but most of the institutions receiving funding from the *Bund*, or federal government, for research, such as the German Science Foundation and the research institutes comprising the prestigious Leibnitz Society.

Expenditures on research and development in Germany started to increase gradually but noticeably, from a low of 2.4 percent of GDP in 2007 to over 2.8 percent by 2012. While many European countries, such as France, Portugal, Spain, Italy, and Sweden, were unable to increase their share of GDP allocated to R & D, Germany was clearly shifting its priority toward research and innovation.

The Schröder administration also addressed all three of the main constraints hindering the competitiveness of German universities and their contribution to the innovative capabilities of Germany. The *Exzellenzinitiativ*, or Excellence Initiative, was introduced by the German Ministry of Education, together with the German Science Foundation, in the middle of the first decade of this century, to allocate more funding of cutting-edge research, enhance human capital in Germany, and spur the international competitiveness of German research and universities. The additional funding was not spread equally across the entire university landscape, but rather was targeted among the promising areas of excellence, which was interpreted by many commentators as an attempt to create what was referred to as "elite" universities, which presumably could compete with the cutting-edge research and world's leading universities in any particular field.

One of the key impacts of the *Exzellenzinitiativ* was to spur differentiation and specialization, through what was called *Profilbildung*, or the development of a specific research profile, leading German universities to become less homogeneous and increasingly heterogeneous with unique strengths and strategies.

University education, along with overall elementary and secondary school education, was also fundamentally reformed, not just to align it with the new European mandate of the Bologna Educational Process launched in 1999, but to modernize education and enhance human capital. The gold standard of human capital, the entrance rate or share of an age cohort enrolled in tertiary education, increased throughout the first decade of this century, from 32 percent in 2001 to 46 percent by 2011. While measured levels of human capital lay below those in France and Switzerland in 2001, Germany had jumped ahead of those countries a decade later.

Table 3.1 shows the variety of types of institutions of higher education in Germany. In order to facilitate the spillover of knowledge from the upgraded research and education at the universities, a wave of new institutions and mechanisms, ranging from offices of technology transfer to incubators and innovation centers, were initiated at universities and research institutes. The Technical University of Munich (TUM), which is ranked perennially among the very strongest in Germany, began referring to itself as the Entrepreneurial University.

Fachhochschulen, or technical colleges, have a strong focus on the needs of the industry and providing students with the skills that will make them appealing in the labor market. Students enrolled in the *Fachhochschulen* typically have a clear focus on the job market and the employability. While universities are mostly located in large cities and metropolitan regions, as figure 3.2 shows, *Fachhochschulen* are also established in more isolated and less dense regions in the periphery to provide key skilled workers for local industry. It is not surprising that *Fachhochschulen* not only became a main source of skilled labor for local industry, but have also emerged as a valued partner for joint research and development projects. In some regions with a low presence of public universities, as in East Germany, *Fachhochschulen* serve as an important conduit for creating and transferring

TABLE 3.1

Higher Education in Germany, 2014

	Public universities (number of students enrolled)	Private universities (number of students enrolled)	Students (public)	Students (private)	Staff (public)	Staff (private)
Universities	86	20	1,656,258	18,087	522,773	3,941
College of Education	6	0	24,899		3,664	0
Theological universities	13	3	2,217	339	684	86
Art colleges	48	3	34,115	1,069	13,624	323
Universities of applied sciences (*Fachhochschulen*)	119	88	729,004	117,513	103,440	12,537
Administration colleges	28	1	32,574	806	5,420	18
Total	300	115	2,479,067	137,814	649,605	16,905

Source: "Deutschland in Zahlen 2014," Institute der Deutschen Wirtschaft Köln, 113.

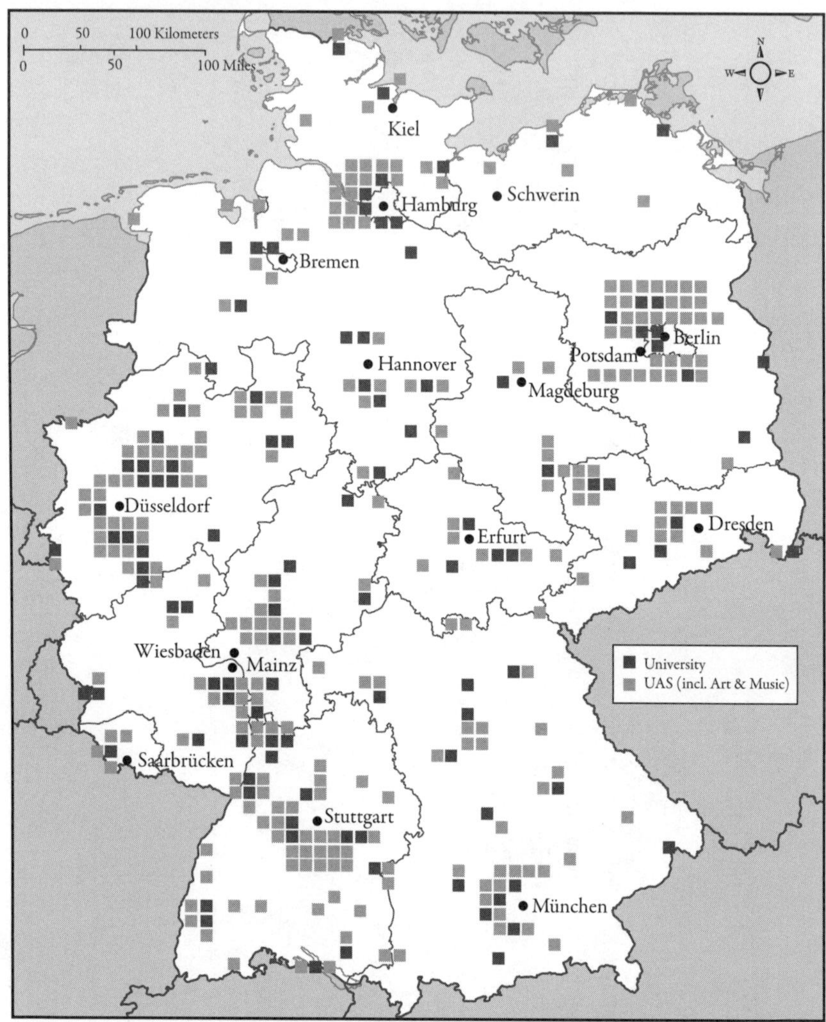

FIGURE 3.2 Location of universities and universities of applied sciences
Source: Erik E. Lehmann and Alexander Starnecker, "Introducing the Universities of Applied Sciences," in David B. Audretsch, Erik E. Lehmann, Albert N. Link, and Alexander Starnecker (eds.), Technology Transfer in a Global Economy (Heidelberg: Springer, 2012), 103.

knowledge and innovations, as evidenced by the high level of external funding for research and above-average patent activities.[96]

Germany has another great asset in its arsenal of knowledge and human capital-creating institutions that is almost without precedent in other countries. The research landscape is ripe with nonuniversity research institutions and institutes, ranging from the highly celebrated ninety some research institutes comprising the Max Planck Society, to the Fraunhofer Institutes and the numerous institutes contained in the umbrella organization of the Leibnitz Society. Steinbeis affiliations have a focus on applied R & D, consulting, and training off-the-job.

TABLE 3.2

Research Institutes in Germany

Institute	Branches	Founded	Staff	Budget (in euros)
Fraunhofer	67	1949	23,000	2 billion
Max Planck Society	83 institutes (5 abroad)	1948	16,998	1.6 billion
Steinbeis	about 1000	1983	1,708 3,544 freelancer	145 million
Helmholtz	18 Centers, 7 Institutes	1958	36,000	3.76 billion
DLR e.V. (German Aerospace Center)	32	1907	8,000	798 million, Aerospace > 1 billion
Leibniz Society	86	1700	17,500	1.53 billion

Source: David B. Audretsch and Erik E. Lehmann "Academic Sources of Knowledge Spillovers in Germany", working paper, Augsburg University, 2014.

Table 3.2 shows some of the most important nonuniversity research institutions in Germany, ranging from the Fraunhofer Society, with its mandate on applied research, to the Max Planck Society, whose mandate is more toward basic and fundamental research and science. One indicator of the prominence and significance of the Max Planck Society, but far from the only one, is the eighteen Nobel Prize winners affiliated with it in the period since 1948.

The new innovation policy approach aggressively encouraged these institutions, which had previously worked in isolation, and in some cases competitively with hostilities and rivalries, to join together in an effort to enhance the knowledge spillovers and linkages from the more basic and fundamental research, to the applied research, and ultimately toward commercialization and innovation. For example, the *Exzellenzinitiativ* generally called for a consortium of complementary programs spanning multiple institutions in a region, and not just a single university department or program.

Conclusions

The United States and Great Britain can boast that they undoubtedly have the very best universities in the world. Countries such as Finland and South Korea are admired for the rigorous and highly effective primary and secondary education.

The secret to Germany is that, while it may not have the best of any particular level of education and research in the world, it does have an impressive and improving strength at all levels of research and education. At the base is what still may be the best system in the world for training and qualifying skilled labor, which contributes considerably to the competitive advantage in many manufacturing and service industries. When combined with the very high levels of education in the German school system and what is emerging as a highly competitive research environment at the universities and numerous world-class research institutions, the country has recovered from being the sick man of Europe to a thriving knowledge- and innovation-driven economy and society.[97] After all, Germany is still the country of poets and thinkers.

4 Roots and Wings

HEIMAT. IT WOULD be hard to find something that elicits more emotion and feeling in the hearts of Germans than this word that means "home." The identity of Germans revolves around and is shaped, or *ausgeprägt*, by *Heimat*. Who he or she is and becomes, personal values, and what ultimately directs and drives aspirations and decisions can be traced back and linked to *Heimat*. Each December, more than 1,400 *Weihnachtsmärkte*, or Christmas markets, are organized in Germany. Similarly, there are around 9,900 *Volksfeste*, or local folk or people's festivals, each referred to as a *Heimatfest*, or celebration of the *Heimat*. The entire world, of course, is familiar with the grandest *Heimatfest*, which is *Oktoberfest* in Munich, dating back to 1810, but now attracts more than 6 million annual visitors. As a reflection of their significance to Germany and Germans, several *Heimatfeste* are part of the national cultural heritage.[1]

If it is the soaring eagle that captures the independence and freedom of Americans, it is the deep and anchored roots of the mighty oak tree, or the *Eichen*, that best reflects the significance of rootedness to Germans. When the great scholars, poets, writers, and philosophers Johann Wolfgang von Goethe and Friedrich von Schiller met in Weimar some two centuries ago, they dedicated their lives to celebrating and articulating the significance of those roots.

In America it's different. It is no secret that the United States was formed by people who chose to leave for the New World. The rootlessness and willingness to move to take advantage of the next opportunity is at the core of the American identity. After all, this is a country that viewed the dictate "Go west, young man" as opportunity, not defeat. The Statue of Liberty, the country's leading image, welcomes new generations who have left their homes, to start anew by joining those who had previously done the same.

After the Civil War, for the first time in American history, the national and federal government preceded the state and local. Even the grammar changed. Prior to the Civil War, when the emphasis was on the autonomy of each state, the correct grammar was "The United States are . . . " Subsequent to the war, the plural gave way to the singular, reflecting the final and irreversible emergence of national unity over the autonomy and independence of the local, "The United States is . . . "

But it's different in Germany. The history of Germany as a unified state is not like that in France, Great Britain, or the United States, and this is reflected in the feeling of *Heimat*, which is more local compared to the proud nationalism reigning in other countries. At the end of the fifteenth century, Europe was fragmented into about 450 different autonomous states, most of them located within the territory of the Sacrum Imperium Romanum Nationis Germaniae, or the Holy Roman Empire.[2] The empire never achieved the extent of political unification formed in France, evolving instead into a decentralized, limited elective monarchy composed of hundreds of subunits, principalities, duchies, counties, and free imperial cities, among other domains. Along with the heterogeneous and fragmented political landscape also came a fragmented and decentralized, or autonomous, identity.[3]

What the Statue of Liberty is to Americans, Hermanns Denkmal, or the Memorial to Hermann, is to Germans. Hermann, or Armenius, united the various bands of Germanic tribes to ward off and ultimately defeat the Romans at the Battle of the Teutoburger Forest in AD 9. It was Armenius who defended the *Heimat*.

When asked what he thinks about Germany, the NBA star Dirk Nowitzki reflects about his *Heimat* as the small town where he grew up: "I think of my parents' house nestled in the hills of Katzenberg. It is a beautiful, idyllic place."[4] Nowitzki recalls as a student in the eleventh grade having to sit in the back of classroom because he was far and away the biggest kid in the class, and the teacher holding up the book he was required to read, "easily five or six hundred pages of Goethe."[5]

It was Goethe who is commonly attributed with observing nearly two centuries ago that "the greatest thing a father can give his son is roots. The second greatest thing is wings to escape those roots."[6] Of course Goethe had it right. Contemporary Germany has also gotten it right. Dirk Nowitzki is not alone, both in being shaped, or *ausgeprägt*, by his roots, but also in having the wings to pursue opportunities that lie way beyond that *Heimat*. This chapter suggests that one of the secrets of Germany is the mixture, integration, and nurturing of roots along with wings to escape or at least see beyond those roots that has contributed to its strong economic performance and resilience.

The Mandate

Germans are, of course, not alone in having an emotional connection to their home. Parisians love Paris, Texans love Texas, and you don't have to read the bumper sticker to know how New Yorkers feel.

So what's different about Germans? Actually, nothing. What is different, however, is not the people, but rather the place, or rather, the legislated decentralized and local decision-making mandated by the *Grundgesetz* (*lex fundamentalis*) with the character of a constitution first enacted following World War II and more recently after the reunification in 1990.

After the horrors of Adolf Hitler followed by the devastation from the war, both the occupying Allied forces and political leaders were wary of centralizing political and economic power. Under National Socialism, Hitler had fueled his grab for power by centralizing both economic and political power. Rapid cartelization of the major companies and industries made conformity to the National Socialists difficult to resist.[7] Similarly, political power was quickly shifted under National Socialism away from the states and regions to the capital, Berlin. Thus, one of the most crucial cornerstones when the Federal Republic of Germany was established on May 23, 1949, was to ensure that history would never repeat itself by anchoring decentralized authority and decision-making firmly in the roots of the Länder and at a more localized level. In declaring, "Today a new Germany arises," Konrad Adenauer, who was president of the West German Parliamentary Council and was subsequently elected as the first chancellor, was assuring both citizens of his newly formed country and the rest of the world, *nie wieder*—never again.

The *Grundgesetz* mandates that each *Bundesland*, or state, retains considerable authority and autonomy in making decisions, as well as in having the fiscal authority to tax and fund those decisions. Thus, the *Bundesland* of Bavaria is actually referred to as the *Freistaat von Bayern*, or the Free State of Bavaria. What it is free of is restraints, controls, but also the identity and image of an external force, or the central government. The same holds for the *Bundesländer* of Saxony and Thuringia following reunification in 1990.

STANDORTPOLITIK

It is not just the *Grundgesetz* that protects the autonomy and independence of German regions and localities. Equally compelling is the legal and constitutional mandate for local governments to engage in policies to shape, influence, and enhance the economic performance of the relevant place, whether a *Bezirk* (district), *Stadt* (city), or *Land* (state)—*Standortpolitik*. There is no equivalent word for *Standortpolitik* in English. *Standort* means place. *Politik* means policy. But strung together, *Standortpolitik* is a, not just German word, but unique concept that can be translated to mean *the strategic management of place*.[8]

Standortpolitik refers to the legal but also political and social mandate for governments at each place, or *Standort,* in Germany, to engage in strategies to enhance competitiveness and ultimately economic performance. Barely taught in university courses on economics or political science today, the concept of *Standortpolitik* has been largely ignored by scholars.

There are notable exceptions. The Nobel Prize–winning economics professor at MIT, Paul A. Samuelson,[9] referred to the German scholar Heinrich von Thünen, who lived between 1783 and 1850, as the "founding father of regional or geographical economics."[10] In his pioneering work, first published in 1826,[11] von Thünen developed a theory explaining trade and regional agglomeration of industries, services, and different types of agriculture around cities. Fast-forwarding to today, however, *Standortpolitik* as an approach to and mandate for economic policy has hardly been more than a blip on the radar screen of economists and other scholars. It was not until recently that *Standortpolitik* has been translated to mean the strategic management of place.[12]

The mandated decentralized emphasis on generating a strong economic performance at the local level is facilitated by *Ordnungspolitik,* which, according to the German minister of finance, Wolfgang Schäuble, "is an institution that lays the groundwork for reliable long-term policymaking and that by itself can counteract undesirable fiscal and economic developments."[13] *Ordnungspolitik* provides the legal mandate for the government to undertake *Standortpolitik* and engage in policies to enhance competitiveness and economic performance.

However, it should be emphasized that the governments at the local, city, state, and national levels do not possess a monopoly in engaging in *Standortpolitik.* Rather, the private sector (*Industrie*) and the workers in unions (*Gewerkschaft*) are very actively engaged in *Standortpolitik* through the process of *Konsens,* or crafting a consensus in the goals, strategies, instruments, and implementation of *Standortpolitik.*

The mandate for *Standortpolitik* and *Ordnungspolitik* in Germany dates back several centuries. The king Frederick William I of Prussia was the first monarch in continental Europe who established freedom of trade and religious liberty in an effort to actively foster industrial location and spur economic development in his kingdom. In particular, the Prussian king implemented a policy to attract what we today would term as human capital and talent from other regions of Europe, which contributed to making Prussia one of the most prosperous and dynamic regions of Europe. The Prussian king also founded universities in his kingdom and promoted not just the field of engineering but also management and administration. Prussia was the first state introducing compulsory school attendance, reflecting the king's recognition of the importance of education and human capital, even back then. The institutional, social, and political roots for what today are the bedrock underpinnings of the German economy, *Standortpolitik* and *Ordnungspolitik,* helped to transform Prussia into a leading industrial region before the outbreak of World War I, and Berlin into one of the world's industrial, but also cultural, hot spots.[14]

Standortpolitik and *Ordnungspolitik* are the cornerstones for the post–World War II German economy.[15] These cornerstones cement the German approach to a market economy with strong social support, which is differentiated from the American and British versions, and is commonly referred to as the *soziale Marktwirtschaft*, or the social market economy. The German approach of the *soziale Marktwirtschaft* encompasses a set of institutions and policies to provide both freedom of choice and individual initiative but also social responsibility. In contrast to a pure laissez-faire market economy free of government intervention, or the opposite, socialism or communism, the German *soziale Marktwirtschaft* combines private enterprise and decision-making with government regulation and intervention on the national, regional, and local levels to establish fair competition and maintain a balance between economic growth, employment, good working conditions, social welfare, and public services.[16]

Thus, *Standortpolitik* and *Ordnungspolitik* combine to provide the institutional framework for a delicate balancing of national and local interests and decision-making in shaping the direction of the economy and society. Professor Dr. Hans-Werner Sinn, president of the highly influential IFO Institute in Munich, was recently asked what other countries, such as the United States, could learn from Germany. His answer consisted of a single word—*Ordnungspolitik*.[17]

Decentralization

It would be a mistake to misinterpret the strong overall economic performance of the entire country, Germany, within the legalized mandate for and framework of *Standortpolitik*, as insulating every *Standort*, or city and state, from economic distress. In fact, as the recent economic performance of specific cities, regions and states in Germany suggests, there are no guarantees (see table 4.1).

As figure 4.1 shows, places such as the Länder of Bavaria and Baden-Württemberg have exhibited very strong economic performances, reflecting highly successful local strategies. While unemployment exceeds 20 percent in Spain, 25 percent in Greece, and 10 percent across the entire European Union, it is only 3.8 percent in Baden-Württemberg and 3.5 percent in Bavaria.[18] This exceptional economic performance clearly reflects the success of the strategic management of those particular places, or a decentralized and local *Standortpolitik*, and not the entire country, as evidenced by other places in Germany, such as Bremen, with an unemployment rate of 11.2 percent, and Berlin, with an unemployment rate of 12.2 percent.

Just as Thomas Friedman declared in his best-selling book focusing on the impact of globalization, *The World Is Flat*, Germany, too, is flat. While Friedman has been misinterpreted as suggesting that the economic performance throughout the world will converge, in fact, the University of Toronto business professor Richard Florida set the record straight by arguing that the opportunities afforded by globalization actually result in a "spiky"

TABLE 4.1

ECONOMIC PERFORMANCE ACROSS BUNDESLÄNDER

State	GDP/capita in € (2003) 2013	Public R & D spending in millions of € (2003) 2013	Patents/100.000 Inhabitants (2003) 2013	GDP in millions of € (2003) 2013	GDP growth (%)	Exports in millions of € (2003) 2013
Baden-Württemberg	(29,466) 37,472	(12,322) 20,336	(121) 138	(314,649) 407,245	(−0.37) 0.94	(107,682) 173,262
Bavaria	(29,360) 38,429	(11,348) 15,305	(109) 118	(363,997) 487,987	(0.05) 0.99	(106,702) 167,494
Berlin	(23,941) 30,642	(3,107) 3,781	(27) 27	(81,195) 109,186	(−2.33) 1.15	(9,137) 12,823
Brandenburg	(17,579) 23,751	(550) 975	(13) 13	(45,285) 59,125	(−0.32) 0.68	(5,098) 13,112
Bremen	(36,180) 43,085	(641) 755	(26) 24	(23,977) 28,578	(0.57) 0.45	(10,737) 14,675
Hamburg	(47,338) 53,611	(1,435) 2,198	(57) 43	(82,020) 97,731	(−3.05) 0.79	(19,667) 49,157
Hesse	(32,951) 38,490	(5,107) 7,098	(62) 36	(200,689) 235,685	(−0.28) 0.93	(34,278) 57,376
Mecklenburg–Western Pomerania	(17,132) 22,817	(395) 770	(12) 11	(29,772) 37,061	(−0.70) −1.07	(2,926) 7,189

Lower Saxony	(22,601) 30,149	(5,240) 6,747	(35) 38	(180,518) 238,981	(−0.32) −0.02	(51,285) 77,631
North Rhine Westphalia	(26,287) 33,621	(8,460) 12,190	(43) 40	(475,132) 599,752	(−0.90) −0.14	(120,698) 179,357
Rhineland Palatinate	(23,296) 30,420	(1,678) 2,465	(53) 26	(94,505) 121,579	(−0.23) 0.23	(28,591) 46,650
Saarland	(24,130) 31,834	(277) 470	(33) 25	(25,652) 32,056	(−0.29) −1.32	(9,493) 13,309
Saxony	(18,536) 24,226	(1,841) 2,829	(19) 24	(80,337) 99,894	(0.92) 0.25	(15,144) 31,465
Saxony Anhalt	(17,423) 23,196	(531) 752	(16) 10	(44,173) 53,004	(−0.49) −1.19	(5,381) 14,873
Schleswig-Holstein	(23,050) 27,684	(732) 1,141	(22) 17	(64,972) 78,702	(0.25) −0.05	(11,668) 19,055
Thuringia	(17,053) 23,168	(798) 1,130	(31) 25	(40,627) 51,034	(1.14) 0,49	(6,323) 12,153
Germany	(26,024) 33,355	(54,462) 79,028	59 (269)	(2,147,500) 2,737,600	(−0.38) 0.43	(664,392) 1,093,811

(continued)

TABLE 4.1 CONTINUED

State	GDP/capita in €(2003) 2013	Public R & D spending in millions of € (2003) 2013	Patents/100.000 Inhabitants(2003) 2013	GDP in millions of €(2003) 2013	GDP growth(%)	Exports in millions of € (2003) 2013
France	(25,600) 31,300	(34,569) 46,549	(129) 126	(1,587,902) 2,059,852	(0.9) 0.2	(411,442) 560,226
Spain	(18,600) 22,300	(8,213) 13,392	(23) 33	(783,082) 1,022,988	(3.1) −1.2	(206,084) 349,120
Italy	(23,300) 25,600	(14,769) 19,834	(77) 70	(1,341,850) 1,560,024	(0) −1.9	(327,610) 474,679
United States	(35,000) 39,900	(256,132)	(117) 90	(10,175,654) 12,625,631	(2.8) 2.2	(919,643) 1,703,336

Source: "Deutschland in Zahlen," Institut der deutschen Wirtschaft, Cologne, 2014.

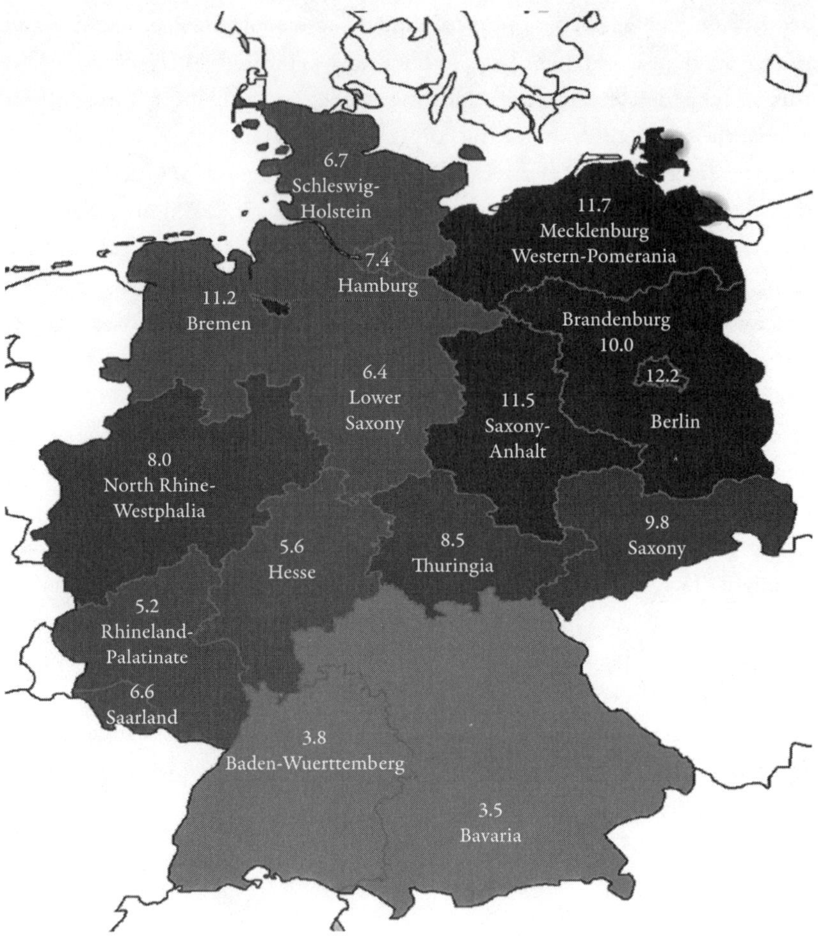

FIGURE 4.1 Unemployment Rate (%) in German Länder, 2013
Source: David B. Audretsch, *Everything in Its Place: Entrepreneurship and the Strategic Management of Cities, Regions and States* (New York: Oxford University Press, 2015).

geography of economic performance, which describes a vast heterogeneity of economic performance, rather than a uniform one.[19] Accordingly, Germany too can best be characterized by a heterogeneous, spiky, spatial economic performance, reflecting variations in the success of different approaches to *Standortpolitik* by the various cities and Länder.

Why is this decentralization in decision-making so central to the recent German economic success, even while the rest of Europe has been paralyzed with economic stagnation and misery? What is no secret is that the engine of economic prosperity in the leading developed countries shifted away from plants and factories, or physical capital, to ideas and creativity, or knowledge, during the last years of the previous century.

For the decade following last century's midway point, Detroit was the richest city, not just in the United States, but in the world.[20] What did Detroit have that was the envy of other places? Plants and factories, or physical capital—to manufacture automobiles and ship them all around the world.[21] The large corporation was the source of well-paying jobs and security and the basis for the wealth and growth of cities like Detroit. Thus, policies that promoted the competitiveness of the corporation were tantamount to promoting the competitiveness of the place, in this case, Detroit. "What`s good for General Motors is good for America," the former chairman of GM Charles "Engine" Wilson declared.[22]

Just as Detroit was the wealthiest city in the United States, its counterpart in Germany was the Ruhrgebiet, or Ruhr Valley. The Ruhrgebiet benefited from massive investments in factories and plants that churned out a record output of manufactured goods and products. Like General Motors, Ford, and Chrysler which fueled impressive growth for decades in the Motor City, the great steel companies of Thyssen, Krupp, and Mannesman transformed the Ruhr Valley into one of the fastest-growing regions in the world. The German Wirtschaftswunder was accomplished on the manufacturing brawn of the Ruhr Valley.

Long before the end of the last century, however, something had changed. It was no longer the mighty factories of Detroit or the Ruhr Valley that served as the locomotive of economic growth, jobs, and competitiveness. Rather, what caught everyone's attention was Silicon Valley, where plants and factories, or physical capital, are noticeably absent. Even before the turn of the century, it had become clear that what mattered for economic performance—jobs, growth, and competitiveness—was, in fact, not physical capital but rather ideas and creativity, or what economists characterize as *knowledge*. It was brains and not brawn that mattered.

Local Advantage

The shift in what drives economic growth away from the traditional economic factor of physical capital to knowledge, or ideas and creativity, had important implications for the role of regions and cities in particular, as well as spatially decentralized decision-making more generally. At first policymakers and thought leaders interpreted the emergence of knowledge in a rapidly globalizing economy to signify the demise of cities, localities, regions, and states as meaningful economic entities. As the title page of *The Economist* proclaimed back in 1995, globalization seemingly resulted in *the death of distance*.[23] The Internet was triggering a spatial revolution in terms of the geography of production. According to *The Economist*, "The death of distance as a determinant of the cost of communications will probably be the single most important economic force shaping society in the first half of the next century."[24]

The Internet, cellular telephone, and other new modes of communication had seemingly rendered place unimportant. After all, with a flat earth, people could be connected and busily accessing and exchanging information 24/7. It didn't matter where they were physically located, as long as they could plug in and log on.

But scholars and thought leaders in business and policy quickly discovered that not only did place still matter, but in the era of globalization and the Internet, and at a point in time when ideas and creativity were the driving force underlying economic success, it seemed to matter more than ever. In a direct response to Thomas Friedman's flat earth, the UCLA economics professor Ed Leamer argued that geographic proximity provides special advantages to both firms and individuals.[25]

The importance of geographic proximity may have surprised the intellectual community, but it wouldn't have surprised Glen Frey. Just as he was forming the rock band the Eagles, Frey befriended Jackson Browne. Jackson arranged for Glen to move upstairs from him in a rather beat-up, old house in Echo Park, located in the foothills near downtown Los Angeles. Frey recalls that he would be awakened each morning to the sounds of Jackson repeating the same verse of song he was trying to write thirty or forty times, adjusting notes and chords, and trying out different lyrics and melodies. Suddenly the music would cease, followed by ten minutes of silence and then the whistle of a teakettle. And then Jackson would start the whole cycle again for the next verse. Glen Frey recalls that he had always wanted to learn how to write songs but never knew—that is, until he moved in upstairs from Jackson Browne. As he listened to Browne "apply elbow grease every day," a light bulb went on: "I learned through Jackson's ceiling and my floor exactly how to write songs."[26] Perhaps had he not lived upstairs there would have been no Eagles, or at least not the group where the members wrote their own songs.

That is what economists call a knowledge spillover. The knowledge, insight, and creativity involved in songwriting spilled over from Jackson Browne to Glen Frey, only in this particular case perhaps it should be called a knowledge spill-up. It is the geographic proximity to the source of the knowledge that provides the platform for accessing knowledge spillovers. This holds not just for songwriting but for pretty much everything where ideas, knowledge, and creativity are concerned.

Scholars slowly but systematically uncovered that, contrary to conventional wisdom, location and geography mattered more than ever in a technological, globalized economy.[27] Location holds the key to accessing and ultimately implementing invaluable ideas. Steve Jobs got the idea that he could successfully launch a personal computer business because he lived within close geographic proximity, in Palo Alto, to the company that had invented all of the main components of a personal component, Xerox. Just as Glen Frey had to live in the same house to understand how Jackson Browne wrote songs, Steve Jobs had to live in the same place as the computer engineers working at Xerox, to fathom what the personal computer was all about and what its potential value might be.

Scholars subsequently generated a body of literature providing compelling empirical evidence that innovative activity tends to cluster within close proximity to the source of the knowledge generating those innovations.[28] An important implication was that investments in plants and factories, as well as labor, may be geographically unbounded and eager to move to the most favorable location, but where ideas and creativity are concerned, they are pretty much bounded within close proximity to the knowledge source where they were generated. This means that places, whether a community, city, region, or state, might not really have much control over the location of manufacturing plants and factories, or rather the decisions that their owners and managers make about where to locate them. As Thomas Friedman famously observed,[29] globalization opened up the floodgates for manufacturing companies to outsource and offshore their activities to the least expensive and most favorable location. The first decade of this century witnessed thousands of manufacturing jobs in all of the developed countries outsourced and offshored to less costly production in least-developed countries such as India and China.[30]

When it came to the production of standardized manufactured goods, relying principally on combining low-skilled workers on assembly lines engaged in repetitive tasks that minimized thinking place did not matter anymore. According to the former dean of the Sloan School of Business at MIT, Lester Thurow, "A seismic shift in technology has either seduced or forced, depending upon your views, national business firms into becoming global business firms. With the new computer-telecommunications technologies, a profit-maximizing company must make its products wherever in the world they are the cheapest to make and it must sell its products wherever in the world the greatest profits are to be earned. If the firm does not find the cheapest places to produce its products and the most profitable places to sell its products, others will. The firm that doesn't go global will be driven out of business by those that do. . . . From the point of view of business, improvements in communications have made global sales and outsourcing possible, highly profitable, and necessary, all at the same time."[31]

Or rather, as Thomas Friedman famously pointed out, it was a race to the bottom. The low-wage and low-cost location won, at least until an even lower-wage and lower-cost location nudged it out.[32]

However, when it comes to thinking up new ideas in an original and creative fashion, or producing carefully crafted products with high levels of performance and reliability, place matters more than ever. This means that those places—communities, cities, and states—that are best situated to recognize their strengths and build on those strengths tend to enjoy the best economic performance because knowledge, creativity, and ideas tend to be spatially localized.[33] Just as scholars have come to recognize that local decisions, conditions, and policies are the key to generating competitive advantage and strong economic performance,[34] so too do policymakers and thought leaders increasingly look to localized decision-making at the city or state level as the key to jobs, growth, and competitiveness.

For example, the European Union created a new policy emphasizing the creation of local and regional strategies to enhance competitiveness and economic performance at the local level—the Smart Specialization Strategy (RIS^3). In particular, the European Union requires each region to propose a Smart Specialization Strategy in order to become eligible for funding under the European Cohesion Funds.[35] The proposal must identify a region's relative strengths and weaknesses and ways to build upon those strengths.[36] If the European Union's Council of Europe in its 2000 Lisbon Agenda prioritized knowledge and entrepreneurship as the driving forces that needed to be harnessed in order to reignite economic growth, jobs, and competitiveness, it is the Smart Specialization Policy that recognizes that the focus of this policy needs to be at the local, and not national or European, level.

The stringent political and economic decentralization, or federalism, that was imposed by the Allies during their occupation of Germany might have seemed to some like a form of retribution for Germany's waging and losing yet another war. While such decentralization of decision-making may have bestowed gains in terms of political stability and mitigating tendencies toward economic extremism, few understood at that time that localized decision-making, institutions, and policy contributed positively to economic performance. After all, if localization was so important, why did the French concentrate so much economic and political power in Paris? And why did the English do the same in London? The same could be said for country after country, including the Americans with their formidable concentration of political and economic power and decision-making in the capital, Washington, DC. Thus, while the Germans seemed content shifting so much authority and decision-making to the Länder and cities, and even erecting their newly formed capital in what could be called a minor city at best, Bonn, none of this seemed particularly consequential when compared to the harsh reparations imposed on Germany by the Allies in the Treaty of Versailles.[37]

But this quirk of history ended up bestowing Germany with a surprising source of competitive advantage based on the decentralized nature of institutions, policymaking, decision-making, and authority at the local level in an era when generating new knowledge, facilitating that knowledge to spill over for use by firms and people in that region, and then commercializing that knowledge are the engine of economic performance. Because of the legal, social, and historical mandates for each place to proactively engage in policies to ensure a strong economic performance, cities, states and regions in Germany have developed the institutions, financial authority, understanding, and expertise in devising and implementing *Standortpolitik*.

The *Bundesland* of Bavaria provides a compelling example of how *Standortpolitik* can be leveraged to transform a region and generate a strong and sustained economic performance. Prior to the 1960s, Bavaria was an economically backward agrarian state with unemployment rates well above the German average, dependent on monetary transfers from all other German Länder, in what is legally rooted in the *Grundgesetz* as the *Ausgleich*. Bavaria had always been rural and agricultural and had been largely unaffected by the Industrial Revolution that had transformed other Länder, such as North Rhine Westphalia, Baden-Württemberg, and Saarland into vibrant manufacturing-driven regions. This paucity of industry turned out to be an advantage for Bavaria after World War II. Rather than focusing its investments on rebuilding and recreating old and existing industries, its *Standortpolitik* led Bavaria instead to invest in seeding new and cutting-edge knowledge-based and high-technology industries.

Thus, the *Standortpolitik* of Bavaria focused on the policies and institutions that were important not for the old industrial manufacturing industries, such as steel and iron, but rather for creating knowledge and ideas that would fuel the new high-technology industries. The strategy focused on creating and funding a series of key research institutes, which ultimately proved invaluable in Bavaria's surging economic performance.

The *Standortpolitik* in Bavaria seeded several important industry and innovation clusters through strategic investments in the research infrastructure at twenty-six universities and other higher-learning institutions, three major research establishments, twelve Max Planck Institutes, and thirteen Fraunhofer Society establishments. Today the *Standortpolitik* of Bavaria has a pronounced focus on biotechnology, material sciences, nanotechnology, and automatization.[38]

In 1957 Germany's first nuclear reactor (named "FRM I") was put into operation by the Technical University Munich (TUM). Decades later, this investment paid off handsomely, with the emergence of a high-technology cluster involving material sciences and radio-pharmaceuticals. Similarly, an important cluster in the defense industry, along with aerospace and aeronautics, is now located in the Munich region, which totals over one hundred companies engaged in the production of radio and radar systems, tanks, and jet fighters. One of the many heritages of Bavaria's *Standortpolitik* is the decision made by the European Aeronautic Defence and Space Company (EADS) to develop and manufacture numerous high-technology products in the Munich and Augsburg regions, including Airbus, Eurocopter, and the European GPS system "Galileo."

The example provided by Bavaria highlights the key role that *Standortpolitik* can play in sustaining the economic performance of a city, region, or state, and highlights four distinct pillars—factors and resources, the spatial structure and organization of economic activity, the human dimension, and policy and institutions.[39] The first pillar refers to the endowment of key inputs into economic activity, such as physical capital, human capital, skilled workers, university research, R & D, and the creative class. The second pillar focuses not on the amount of those key resources but on their spatial structure and organization. This analyzes the extent to which economic activity is organized in a cluster of complementary firms, specialized in one type of industry or in diverse industries, managed by a large company with market power or diffused in entrepreneurial start-ups. By contrast, the third dimension focuses on people. In particular, the extent to which people interact and are linked through networks facilitates spillovers. In addition, leadership along with the image and identity of the place contributes to economic performance. The final pillar involves the role of policy and institutions, which can enhance the effectiveness of the other three pillars.[40]

Many, if not most, countries have tended to centralize these pillars at the federal or national level. For example, there is an explicit mandate to ensure a strong level of economic performance in the United States, but this mandate is explicitly at the federal or national level, and not at the state or local level. According to the Employment Act of 1946,[41] "The Congress hereby declares that it is the continuing policy and responsibility of the Federal Government to use all practicable means consistent with its needs and obligations and other essential considerations of national policy, with the assistance and cooperation of industry, agriculture, labor, and state and local governments, . . . for the purpose of creating and maintaining, in a manner calculated to foster and promote free competitive enterprise and the general welfare, conditions under which there will be afforded useful employment opportunities, including self-employment, for those able, willing, and seeking to work, and to promote maximum employment, production, and purchasing power."[42]

While the Employment Act of 1946 does assign to the government the responsibility of ensuring strong economic performance, it also assigns that responsibility to the federal and not the state or local level, because it is "the continuing policy and responsibility of the Federal Government . . . to coordinate and utilize all its plans, functions, and resources for the purpose of creating and maintaining . . . conditions under which there will be afforded useful employment opportunities. . . . The Congress has placed on the President the duty of formulating programs designed to accomplish the purpose of the Act."[43]

Thus, while other countries, such as the United States, centralized key decision-making, public policy, and ultimately the responsibility for a strong economic performance in the federal government, by contrast, they have been decentralized to the state and local levels in Germany through *Standortpolitik*. As other countries and supranational organizations such as the European Union find themselves scrambling to decentralize innovation and entrepreneurship policies to the local level, Germany finds itself with the legal, historical, social, and institutional mandate requiring each *Standort* to take responsibility for its own economic performance in what some scholars and thought leaders refer to as the knowledge economy and others as the entrepreneurial society.[44]

In striving to attain and sustain a strong economic performance, the German Länder have assumed responsibility for ensuring the alignment of the four pillars shaping economic performance. In terms of key resources and assets, German Länder and cities have made substantial investments in education, training, and knowledge. For example, funding for the world-class institutes comprising the Max Planck Society is generally shared between the *Bund*, or federal government, and the Länder. The Max Planck Institute of Economics, where we both worked during the first decade of this century, was located in Jena, and financing was shared equally between the federal government and the state of Thüringen. In fact, there are three Max Planck Institutes located in Jena, which have contributed substantially to its economic vitality. As *The Economist* gushes, "The city of Jena provides a tantalizing glimpse of the way Germany could be going. If you seek Paradise, go to Jena."[45] (The train station in Jena is in the part of the city named Paradies, or Paradise!)

Similarly, financing for the Center for European Economic Research (ZEW) in Mannheim is financed in part by Baden-Württemberg, which provides cities and the entire region with key economic and business insights and trends. In fact, the German landscape is littered with similar institutions, ranging from basic research and applied research, such as the Leibnitz Institutes and the Fraunhofer Institutes, to institutions providing a linkage and networking function, and institutions, such as the Social Science Research Center Berlin (Wissenschaftszentrum Berlin fuer Sozialforschung, WZB) and the Kiel

Institute for the World Economy, which provide some of both. Membership in the prestigious Leibnitz Gesellschaft, or Society, ensures that such research institutes maintain a delicate balance between local and national interests. These are just a few examples of the rich mosaic of institutions, organizations, and agencies that are at least partially sponsored at the local level, typically with considerable federal financial support, in order to enhance the economic performance of the particular *Standort*.

Global Opportunities

Germany has rich roots not only deeply embedded in culture and tradition but also in legal institutions at the local and state levels, or at the *Standort*. It also has the wings to escape those roots. These are the wings of learning, knowing, and experiencing other cultures, contexts, and nations.

It starts with language. When David arrived in Germany in 1984, he did not speak German. He quickly discovered that, back then, Germans who spoke English were the exception, so that he quickly realized that learning German was essential. Academic conferences, lectures, seminars, and colleagues all were conducted in the native language—German. Just as French was prevalent in France, Italian in Italy, Greek in Greece, German was the language in Germany.

Foreign visitors in France find that this is still the case today. The same holds for Italy. But something has changed in Germany. Most people understand and speak English. It is virtually de facto that the educated youth are fluent in the global language. Visiting Germany today is reminiscent of visiting the Netherlands, Denmark, or Belgium three decades ago—you can get by with English just fine.

The EF English Proficiency Index (EF EPI), which is the world's most comprehensive ranking of countries for adult English skills, reflects this trend.[46] As figure 4.2 shows, in a sample of sixty-three countries where English is not the official or community language, Germany is ranked tenth, in the highest group of countries, attesting to a high level of proficiency. In the group classified as having attained medium skills in language, grammar, and spelling are Spain (20), Portugal (21), Italy (27), and France (30). Most strikingly, Germany has surged ahead of these Western European partners. By contrast, some of the newer members of the European Union in the east, where the Russian language had been the mandatory foreign language for decades, actually exhibit a greater proficiency in English than do some of the West European countries—Poland (6), Estonia (8), Slovenia (11), Romania (16), and Hungary (17) are all ranked in the top group.

Most importantly, the study concludes that German adults speak English at a highly proficient level, which has improved considerably over the past seven years. This was not always the case. As the study reveals, the difference in skill levels between age cohorts in Germany is actually larger than anywhere else in Europe. Poor English skills among

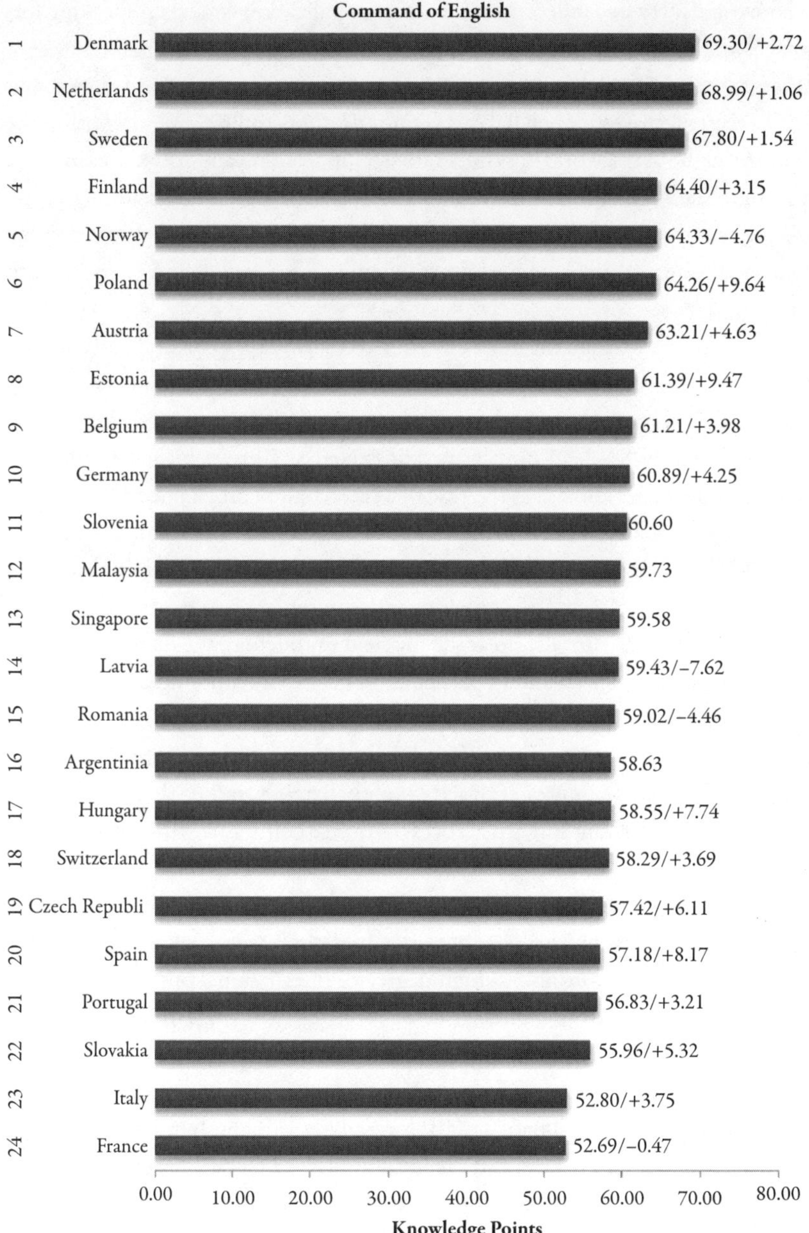

FIGURE 4.2 German Proficiency in English

Source: www.ef.com/epi.

Germans above age forty-five reflect an earlier, pre-globalization era, when speaking foreign languages was not such a priority.

More than is the case for some of its European neighbors, Germany has realized that to recognize, create, access, and then harvest economic opportunities not just within the country, but throughout the world, it is imperative to understand and speak the language of globalization. The high and impressive levels of proficiency in English among young adults indicate that the average adult proficiency will improve in Germany in the coming years. If only the cohort of the young adults is taken into account, Germany ranks fifth in the world.

It is Germany's youth who are the most determined to leave roots behind and embrace their wings. A decade ago, students preferred to study only at their local university. Opportunities to study abroad at a foreign university typically led to a firm shaking of the head. It is different today. Students now seemed possessed by *Wanderlust* and *Fernweh*, or the desire to be somewhere abroad, as the title of a recent study proclaimed.[47]

This impression is backed by the evidence. In 2001 only about 50,000 students studied abroad. One decade later, in 2011, the number of students studying abroad had exploded by nearly threefold, to 140,000. While the increased interest of students in having an overseas experience has left virtually no academic field untouched, the increase has been the greatest in the social sciences, and in particular in business, economics, management, and the study of the law.

Germany's youth is answering the call of globalization. In their determined preparation to harness the opportunities afforded by globalization, rather than succumb as victims, they prioritize learning and experiences in diverse cultural, institutional, and national contexts.

In keeping with the distinct identities and strategies of the different German *Bundesländer*, the external orientation to global opportunities also varies across German cities, states, and regions. Frankfurt exhibits a high degree of international openness and integration, which is reflected in the highest level of proficiency in English in the country. The strong global orientation of Frankfurt has no doubt contributed to its competitive advantage and strong economic performance as one of the world's top financial centers. Not only is the European Central Bank (ECB) located in Germany, but so too are scores of other banks, insurance companies, and the headquarters of global corporations. Similarly, Länder such as Baden-Württemberg, Bavaria, and Hesse all rank among leading export regions, while the newer Länder from the former East Germany lag behind.[48]

At least part of Germany's economic success and resilience in thriving on globalization, even while many of its neighbors have been defeated, are attributable to the shift in attitudes and self-perception in Germany, from being a large country in Western Europe to being a small country in a large, globalized world. An irony may be that, while the fall of the Berlin Wall on November 9, 1989, and the subsequent reunification of the country on October 3, 1990, created a larger country, Germany went from being a large country in a divided continent to a small country in a big world. In fact,

Germany, newly reunified and larger by 18 million people, struggled with the rapidly globalizing economy during the 1990s. Growth was stagnant, and unemployment rose to double digits by the turn of the century.

The economic struggle impeding Germany in adjusting to a rapidly globalizing economy is evidenced by the sharp decline in manufacturing employment of 1,307,000, while it increased in foreign subsidiaries by 189,000 between 1991 and 1995.[49] The outsourcing and offshoring of jobs was even more drastic in particular industries and sectors. For example, in chemicals domestic employment decreased by 80,000, but at the same time employment outside of Germany increased by 14,000. Similarly, electrical engineering jobs within Germany went down by 198,000, and in automobiles 161,000 jobs were lost in Germany, while 30,000 jobs were added in foreign countries.[50]

The German public was dismayed by what was interpreted as a betrayal of the social contract inherent in the German model of cooperation and consensus among the main partners of industry, unions, and the public sector, which was articulated by the lament in the headlines of one of the most important newspapers in the country, *Die Zeit*, "When Profits Lead to Ruin—More Profits and More Unemployment: Where Is the Social Responsibility of the Firms?"[51] Between 1991 and 1998 employment in Germany actually fell by over 1 million jobs, from 39 million to less than 38 million, which corresponded to a decline in the employment rate from 67 percent to less than 64 percent. At the same time, the unemployment rate skyrocketed from just over 5 percent in 1991 to nearly 10 percent by 1998, leading *The Economist* to lament, "As economic growth stalls yet again, the country is being branded the sick man (or even the Japan) of Europe. This is inevitably casting a cloud over Europe's single currency, the euro."[52]

As economic misery in the form of stagnant growth, rising unemployment, and diminished prospects spread across the country, Germany responded around the turn of the century by looking outward. Political leaders, policymakers, and thought leaders realized that, although the fall of the Berlin Wall had led to the reunification of the country and the departure of allied occupation and influence, with the apparent assumption of independence and autonomy, the rapidly globalizing economy had exactly the opposite impact of increased interdependence and reliance, not just with European neighbors but with the entire world. Germany had become a small country in a large world.

Learning, being comfortable with, and ultimately mastering the language of globalization, English, became *selbstverständlich*, or simply taken for granted, among the educated and professional class. By 2004, 97 percent of Germans had a basic knowledge of English, and one-quarter had attained fluency.[53]

But language was just the start. More important was the rapid diffusion of an attitude and orientation toward looking outside of the country for influences and especially opportunities. Prior to the fall of the Berlin Wall in November 1989, the economies of Western Europe and developed countries were at least somewhat independent and autonomous. Anyone who remembers the franc in France, guilder in the Netherlands, drachma in Greece, lire in Italy, schilling in Austria and deutschmark in Germany would recall a time when not just currencies, but also economies and institutions still had considerable autonomy and uniqueness.[54] Before the era of globalization, countries had remarkably different systems of education, health, social security, and even ways of marrying people, as David's own marriage in Berlin at Rathaus Schöneberg in 1986 testifies.

But globalization changed all that. We heard a speech in Stuttgart by the former minister president of Baden-Württemberg, Lothar Späth, where he boldly challenged Baden-Württemberg to become radically more open by facilitating the admission of international students to universities and offering courses taught in the English language. He noted that generations of students all around the world had gotten to know the United States by studying in America, and that Germany had to make studying at its universities more accessible. In fact, as the focus of companies, universities, and governments shifted toward a global orientation, the focus for opportunities also shifted from the domestic to the global.

During our years working in the Max Planck Society, we experienced an organization that was determined to do everything possible to be accessible to foreigners. As in many German firms and organizations, English became a de facto working language. Meetings were typically held in English. Doctoral dissertations started being written in English. While the French struggled with trying to maintain an exclusivity for their language, the attitude in Germany was to understand that the opportunities were now global and no longer just local or domestic. Just as the first federal chancellor, or *Bundeschancellor*, Konrad Adenauer had argued that economic success was a prerequisite to being able to afford the social safety net during the Wirtschaftswunder of the postwar era, so too did Germany at the turn of this century recognize that economic success was a prerequisite for the vitality and confidence that would ultimately drive and sustain German culture, traditions, and language. By embracing globalization and harnessing at least some of the opportunities afforded by globalization, Germany emerged as one of the most vital and dynamic economies in Europe.

How exactly was this accomplished? An advantage of the consensus model of Germany is that once a direction or opportunity is recognized, institutions, organizations, and agencies – a rich and potent system – are on the same page and work together to realize their goals. The Max Planck Society was no exception to a change in perception, recognizing that the locus of opportunities was shifting from the national to the global.

As the world suffered from the global recession starting early in this century and plunged into despair following the financial crisis triggered by the collapse of Lehman Brothers in 2007, a raucous debate emerged in the United States concerning how best to stimulate the economy. One side, led by economists and thought leaders such as Paul Krugman, advocated drastic increases in government spending as a classic Keynesian response to what was perceived to be deficient demand.[55]

The other side, associated with conservative think tanks such as the Heritage Foundation, argued that reducing taxes was the appropriate response to the sharp fall in demand.[56] The one thing everyone seemed to agree on is that the world recession had led to deficient demand, which could be restated as a paucity of opportunities. Demand and opportunities had to be restored through intervention, one way or another.

Germany took a different approach to the global economic crisis. Even though Germany lives in the same world as the United States, globalized Germany did not perceive the economic crisis as a commensurate crisis of demand. Rather, it perceived the recession as a catalyst for looking for opportunities in other places, and not just within Germany or even within Europe. The reaction to the economic crisis in the United States and other countries was the same as in previous crises: the perception and reaction considered the country autonomous and therefore responsible for creating its own demand.

What is striking about the German reaction is that it was reminiscent of how small countries have always responded to economic downturns—they understand that they are small countries in a big world and cannot autonomously control or even shape aggregate demand, but rather must take it as exogenous, or given in a large world. Countries like Denmark, Sweden, and the Netherlands have survived and even thrived for decades not by complaining that their own domestic economies do not generate sufficient opportunities but rather by searching for, creating, and ultimately serving opportunities existing outside the country. Germany had become a small country in a big world.

Everyone knows that today Germany is the export leader in the world. But this has not always been the case. As recently as 1995, the export share of GDP of Germany, at 22 percent, was below that of Italy, at 29 percent, and just above that of Spain, at 21 percent. The export share of France was only slightly lower at 20 percent.

But in response to the fall of demand, or shortage of opportunities, resulting from the global recession and financial crisis, Germans, in firms, governments, and nonprofit organizations and as individuals, started looking overseas for opportunities. And they found them. In particular, they found opportunities to expand economic activity in China. Between 1999 and 2010 exports to China from Germany exploded by nearly 700 percent. While the value of exports, of course, increased within the eurozone, that increase was considerably less, 85 percent. Despite the highly valued euro, exports doubled in that same time period to countries not in the eurozone.

It would be a mistake to infer that the explosion of German exports "just sort of happened" without a great effort to identify, create, and harvest economic opportunities. One interpretation of the export statistics is that they reflect overall internationalization activities in their myriad forms, such as partnerships, foreign operations, networks, and consortia. Exports generally don't "just sort of happen."

On January 8, 1992, President George H. W. Bush alarmed the world by first vomiting at a banquet hosted by the prime minister of Japan and subsequently fainting. President Bush had traveled to Japan to convince the Japanese to purchase American-manufactured automobiles, in an effort to spur US exports. The Japanese responded that they would be more inclined to purchase automobiles, regardless of their origin of manufacture, if the steering wheel were placed on the correct side. As in the United Kingdom, the Japanese drive on the left side of the road, but apparently the companies in Detroit didn't take this into consideration and were attempting to sell the Japanese automobiles with steering wheels on the wrong side!

The point is that it takes more than manufacturing something and hoping that the rest of the world will notice and enthusiastically change its buying patterns and run to purchase it. Rather, it can often take careful and meticulous relationship building, listening to potential partners, suppliers, and customers, learning about their product and service needs and what exactly constitutes the opportunity and how it can best be provided. While the Americans whined about a deficiency of aggregate demand for their products, or simply a lack of opportunities, the Germans actually did something about it. They went to China. But not just China. They went and looked all around the world, got to know potential customers, partners, and suppliers, learned the language of those partners, and in doing so emerged not just as the global export champions, but perhaps even more importantly, the champions at harnessing global opportunities. Many German firms increased their international activities drastically within the last decade and operate on a high level.

Figure 4.3 illustrates the share of total sales accounted for by foreign sales in the leading German companies listed on the stock market. While some companies like Deutsche Post, Deutsche Telekom, and Lufthansa had a predominantly domestic focus a decade ago, today they are decidedly international. With only a few exceptions, Germany's top companies are now global players with an international orientation.

While America seemed oblivious to the needs and demands of consumers outside the country, and therefore ignored and ultimately missed numerous potential economic opportunities, Germany has been better equipped to meet such demands. A host of institutions, programs, and incentives shifted the attention of individuals, firms, and nonprofit organizations to looking for opportunities not just in Germany but elsewhere in the world.

For example, the Max Planck Society was founded in Germany to advance basic research and science. The scientific and academic prowess of the Max Planck Society has been leveraged to identify, create, and help harvest opportunities for innovation and business throughout the world. This is illustrated by the development of one of the world-leading clusters in neurosciences, Martinsried, which sprung up from the Max Planck Institute of Neuroscience in Munich as the scientific and research catalyst. The Max Planck Institute of Neuroscience has succeeded in attracting several Nobel Prize scientists and has emerged as an invaluable source of knowledge not just in basic research for academics but also as a source of ideas and technologies that have spurred innovation and growth. Similarly, the nearby Innovation and Founding Center Biotechnology (IZB) has attracted leading scientists and engineers from around the world to the Max Planck Institute, which to date has launched over sixty start-ups in the neurosciences.[57]

Recently the Max Planck Society has added a number of institutes outside of Germany. We were members of the Max Planck Society when the decision was made by the president of the Max Planck Society, Professor Dr. Peter Gruss, with the approval of the directors of the various individual institutes, to open up the new Max Planck Institute Florida for Neuroscience. The rationale and logic for locating a Max Planck Institute at this location was to provide a mechanism to absorb the knowledge created and to be

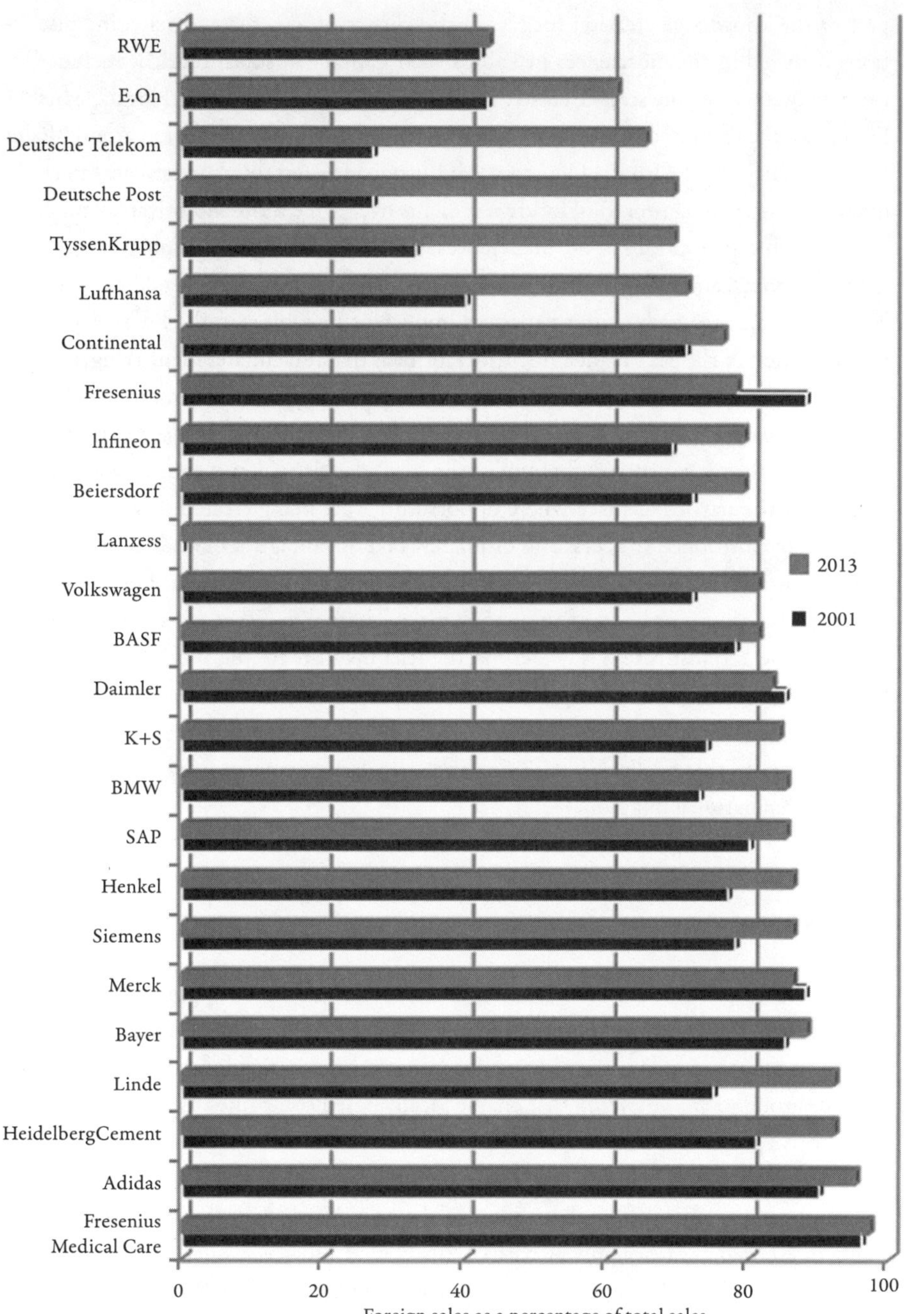

FIGURE 4.3 Share of Sales of Leading German Companies in Foreign Countries
Lanxess was founded in 2004 as a spin-off from Bayer AG.
Source: Wirtschaftswoche, June 30, 2014, 39.

part of the knowledge creation process in the cluster of research and scientific institutions involved in the biosciences in Palm Beach County in south Florida. Included in this newly emerging life science cluster is the Scripps Research Institute Florida, which is located on the campus of Florida Atlantic University in Jupiter. The region around Palm Beach County along with the Governor Jeb Bush made substantial investments in creating the life sciences cluster. BioFlorida represents over three thousand private companies and research organizations in the life sciences, spanning biotechnology, pharmaceuticals, medical devices, and bioagriculture, with an employment in 2013 of over 84,000 people. This life science research cluster generates important new ideas in the life sciences. An interpretation of the Max Planck Institute Florida is that it facilitates identifying new opportunities located outside of Germany as well as providing a mechanism to take advantage of those opportunities. Peter Gruss made it clear, and the directors of the individual scientific institutes concurred, that unless the Max Planck Society went international by locating at the particular place where opportunities are being created, it would not be strategically positioned to access and ultimately take advantage of new ideas.

A rich mosaic of nonprofit and governmental agencies, institutes, and organizations provide mechanisms or linkages to opportunities external to Germany. The German Economic Research Institute (DIW Berlin), the Kiel Institute for the World Economy, the CESIfo Institute in Munich, the numerous Fraunhofer Institutes, and the Center for European Economic Research (ZEW) in Mannheim are all examples of organizations and institutions that facilitate identifying and articulating opportunities that are not just local or even national but global.

Conclusions

Having the wings to identify, create, and harvest not just domestic opportunities but also those throughout the world has paid off for Germany. So, too, has having the roots to link those global opportunities to carefully designed local institutions and organizations crafted through *Standortpolitik* that enable locally based companies to generate globally competitive goods and services.

How profitable and beneficial Germany's combination of roots and wings is clear from the empirical evidence. Throughout most of the post–World War II era, the standard of living in Germany was roughly at parity with France. However, since the beginning of this century, the standards of living in Germany and France, as well as that in many of its other European neighbors, began to drastically diverge. In 2004 GDP per capita was about the same in Germany and France. By 2014, per capita GDP had grown to $38,291 in Germany, yet only to $34,141 in France, suggesting that the standard of living had increased in a decade 12 percent more in Germany than in France. The diverging trajectories in economic performance and standard of living may be largely attributable to the roots and wings of Germany.

5 (Infra)Structure

VISITORS RETURNING FROM Germany invariably gush about the high speeds they drove their rental Mercedes or BMW on the autobahn. Others recant their impressively comfortable journeys travelling on the ICE, the high-speed, long-distance trains, not to mention the rich thicket of local and regional trains, subways, trams, and buses, all making mobility not just easy but a joy. Perhaps the more thoughtful are particularly enthused about the dazzling and diverse array of museums, theaters, opera houses, symphony halls, and galleries, reflecting a vital and dynamic cultural scene.

What all of these have in common is they represent various dimensions of the same thing—infrastructure. One of the two main textbook definitions of infrastructure is "the fundamental facilities and systems serving a country, city, or area, as transportation and communication systems, power plants, and schools."[1] That Germany boasts of some of the most impressive infrastructure in the world is hardly a secret. What may be less understood is that such infrastructure investments are at least partially attributable to the recent stunning economic performance and resilience of Germany.

There is, however, another definition of infrastructure. The first and primary definition offered is "the basic, underlying framework or features of a system or organization,"[2] or what might commonly be referred to as structure. As the *New York Times* columnist David Brooks, in his thoughtful essay "The Good Order," points out, "Communities need order to thrive and cooperate since where there is chaos and disorder there is distrust and withdrawal. The main job of local leaders is to provide the basic infrastructure of security: roads, police, honest judges and orderly schools."[3]

The purpose of this chapter is to suggest that the very infrastructure in Germany that impresses visitors so deeply is more than a shiny façade. Rather, it reflects a deeply rooted but also legally mandated role of organization and structure, which has proven not just to bestow a certain quality of life but also to deliver an enviable standard of living. In particular, this chapter identifies how Germany is able to provide structure, organization, and order in a chaotic and frenzied modern world, and how such structure contributes to a strong economic performance. While structure may be a rather abstract, albeit important, concept, more to the point, economic success in Germany can be attributed to specific and targeted investments in infrastructure.

Structure

Americans value freedom more than anything else. After all, it is a country founded on the battle cry of "Give me liberty or give me death." As the official motto of the state of New Hampshire proclaims, "Live Free or Die." Even a placard campaigning for next November's election advises, "I Love Freedom: Vote Republican." The distinguished historian James M. McPherson explains in his bestselling treatise on the Civil War era, *Battle Cry of Freedom*, that after winning their freedom as mandated by Abraham Lincoln's Emancipation Proclamation, many of the former slaves had opportunities to remain on the plantation for wage work.[4] But many chose not stay. Rather, as McPherson points out, they took to the open road to experience and to celebrate, what had been denied them for generations—freedom. Look at the major forms of art and culture that are uniquely American—most notably jazz. It is about the expression and celebration of freedom, if nothing else.[5] What do most Americans want to pass along to the next generation? Freedom—especially the freedom from being subjected to coercion from political and economic powers. Perhaps a little more cynically, or at least thoughtfully, the Rhodes scholar and later actor Kris Kristofferson penned the lyric that made the singer Janis Joplin a household name, "Freedom's just another word for nothing left to lose."

But Germany is different. Of course Germans value freedom. Most Germans now consider the defeat of Hitler and National Socialism in 1945 by the Allies, the new constitution of the Federal Republic of Germany (the *Grundgesetz*), and a solid anchoring of the country first in Western Europe and then, following the fall of the Berlin Wall, in the expanded European Union as securing their freedom. But Germans also value something else highly—beauty. German culture and sensibilities are a descendant of classical Greek values—which appreciate and hold beauty to rank among the greatest values. If Americans want to pass along freedom to the next generation, the driving prevailing value of Germans is to pass along beauty to future generations.

But beauty is not just in the eye of the beholder. In Germany, beauty is embedded in a sense of structure. Consider the most compelling music ever composed in Germany, the national treasure of the great classical composures. Where would the beauty of Beethoven, Handel, Bach, or Wagner be without structure? When Germans look to civic life, their neighborhoods, districts, cities, states, and to the entire country, they see a political and social landscape that is formed and defined by structures. Certainly the primacy of architecture and planning in German cities reflects the primacy of structure.

However, the role of structure extends far beyond buildings and architecture. It reflects a certain way of thinking, or organizing thoughts, arguments, and orientation. The imperative for structure is reflected by a language that is dictated far more by structure than, say, the Romance languages. The German language, for example, is notorious in its rigid rules requiring where exactly in a sentence the verb must appear. As the American author Mark Twain observed some 150 years ago in his treatise "The Awful German Language," "There are ten parts of speech, and they are all troublesome. An average sentence, in a German newspaper, is a sublime and impressive curiosity; it occupies a quarter of a column; it contains all the ten parts of speech—not in regular order, but mixed; it is built mainly of compound words constructed by the writer on the spot, and not to be found in any dictionary—six or seven words compacted into one, without joint or seam—that is, without hyphens; it treats of fourteen or fifteen different subjects, each enclosed in a parenthesis of its own, with here and there extra parentheses which enclose three or four of the minor parentheses, making pens within pens: finally, all the parentheses and parentheses are massed together between a couple of king-parentheses, one of which is placed in the first line of the majestic sentence and the other in the middle of the last line of it—*after which comes the VERB*, and you find out for the first time what the man has been talking about."[6]

As Mark Twain surely would have confirmed, he who masters the rules of German grammar and sentence structure masters the language. By contrast, the free format of the Romance languages, but also English, can leave a foreign speaker bewildered and lacking orientation. If German is the language of classical music, with its heavily imposing structures, the Romance languages are better characterized by jazz, with its spontaneity, inspiration, and free format.

The cultural imperative of *Struktur*, or structure, is reinforced by a legal mandate for creating, nourishing, and sustaining fundamental structures in German society and the economy. This legal and constitutional mandate compels governments at the national, state, and local levels to create, nourish, and sustain structure and order as a means to generating a strong and prosperous economy. *Ordnungspolitik*, which was introduced and explained in chapter 4, can be literally translated as policy to maintain order. It involves the establishment of rules and provides the legal framework ensuring an orderly and effective functioning of the economy. *Ordnungspolitik* provides the basis for legal actions by the government with the goal of sustaining, modifying, and enhancing the economic order.[7]

The framework created by *Ordnungspolitik* relies on market mechanisms but at the same time includes a mandate to prevent economic power from being concentrated in just a few hands or firms. It also makes provisions for the configuration of property rights, for rules ensuring economic competition, such as prioritizing economic competition by prohibiting cartels and collusion, and for the configuration of contracts (*Vertrags- und Haftungsrecht*).[8]

Wolfgang Schäuble, minister of finance, explains *Ordnungspolitik*: "I would also like to point out that it is not just new thinking that we need. Rather, it is often equally important to recall older ideas and approaches that may have fallen out of the limelight in the meantime. For example, we in Germany have sharpened our focus on the necessity of pursuing economic and fiscal policies that are consistent with the principles of markets and competition—what we call *Ordnungspolitik*. This approach can make crucial contributions to the concrete design of policies and especially institutions. In my view, Germany's 'debt brake' is an institution that lays the groundwork for reliable long-term policymaking and that by itself can counteract undesirable fiscal and economic developments."[9]

While *Ordnungspolitik* provides a mandate for creating an orderly economic and social framework, a second mandate requires that the government ensure a sound and effective structure of the economy. *Strukturpolitik* is a mandate for policies designed to shape and influence the structure of the economy. The goal of *Strukturpolitik* is to facilitate a structure of the economy that is the most conducive to *Wohlstand*, or economic prosperity. As chapter 4 explained, *Strukturpolitik* is implemented at all levels of governments, ranging from regional and city governments to state governments and to the national or federal government.

When David arrived in Berlin in 1985 to start his new job as a research fellow at an economics research think tank, the International Institute of Management (subsequently the Social Science Research Center Berlin or Wissenschaftszentrum Berlin für Sozialforschung, WZB), it was to work in the department of *Strukturpolitik*. He persisted in pestering colleagues about what that actually meant. They would shrug their shoulders and mumble "structural policy." But what did that mean? Nothing from the rigors of a demanding American PhD program in economics provided any guidance as to what was actually meant by "structural policy," or *Strukturpolitik*. Germany apparently undertook policies to ensure that the economy benefited from a structure that would ensure a strong economic performance. American-educated PhDs in economics simply were not, or still are not, prepared or oriented for thinking about structure as a salient feature of an economy.

But for the German economy, as well as society, it all starts with organization and structure. The concept is ubiquitous in policy analyses and political commentary, peppering the debate and criticism with the prognosis of "structural weakness," "structural adjustment," or "structural reform," which to an American audience, untrained and unused to thinking and analyzing the economy in terms of structure and organization, seems mysterious and inaccessible.[10]

Corporate Germany

Paul Helmke had a long and distinguished career stretching over twelve years as the mayor of Fort Wayne and many more in the private sector. When asked how he found his new position as a professor of practice at Indiana University, he shook his head, "The students are great, but I can't figure out who's in charge here." Countless other colleagues at countless other universities who have transitioned from business or government to the university would no doubt share his dismay. How universities are governed, that is, how decisions are made and who participates and has authority in making those decisions, is strikingly different from either the industry or the government context.

Similarly, someone making the transition from a corporation in the United States to one in Germany might also be bewildered about how decisions are made, who is involved in making those decisions, and who has decision-making authority. The governance of companies in Germany is strikingly different from that in the United States.

The structure of decision-making for companies is legally dictated to a considerable degree in Germany, just as it is in other countries. However, the legal mandate is decidedly different in Germany.

One main difference involves who is legally mandated to participate and have voice and influence on advisory and supervisory boards. Representatives from both banks and workers, typically unions, participate in such boards and have a voice in decision-making. Another difference involves the boards of companies that are publicly listed, with shares being traded on a stock market. In Germany the *Aufsichtsrat*, or board of supervisors, is totally separate from the board of directors. Membership of the supervisory board and the size of the board are strictly mandated by legal requirements. Not only is the share of representatives from the employer explicitly mandated, but since 2015 the number and share of female directors serving on the supervisory board are also explicitly mandated.

Another difference in the structure of decision-making is the legal mandate for a *Betriebsrat* or works council. According to the Works Constitution Act, the works council has a legally mandated right to information, consultation, and what is referred to as *Mitbestimmung*, or codetermination.[11] Through the legally mandated structure of decision-making that includes a works council, the views, perspectives, and interests of workers have voice and are represented in the decision-making process—codetermination.

Seen from the perspective from North America, or indeed much of the rest of the world, legally forcing companies to include workers in the decision-making process seems to be counterintuitive. After all, wouldn't workers simply always advocate for shifting more resources toward them in the form of higher wages? That is, wouldn't codetermination always erode or destroy the firm's value and ultimately its competitivness by shifting financial resources toward the workers?

This is exactly what happened when workers and employer representatives imposed extreme wage demands in the round of collective bargaining in 1973–74, which became known as the *Kluncker Runde*,[12] and resulted in an increase in wages of 11 percent.[13] German companies responded defensively, substituting automation and machinery for labor, which sabotaged the dream of full employment for years to come.

Workers, their representatives in the unions, companies, and the entire society learned from the collatoral damage inflicted by excessive wage increases resulting from the *Kluncker Runde*. Works councils and their counterparts in industry subsequently learned to focus more on employment effects, which shifted the focus and negotiations toward targeted investments enhancing workers' skills, qualifications, and capabilities.

Yet another difference in the legally mandated structure of Germany involves the banking and financial system. As the title of an article in the *Economist* observes, "Old-Fashioned but in Favor."[14] The *Economist* points out that "Europe's biggest economy has its bittiest banking system."[15]

The financial institutions and system of finance in Germany are considerably different from what can be found in their counterparts in either the United States or Great Britain. The German financial system is characterized by a complex network of financial intermediaries, which may actually be better equipped to provide liquidity to the Mittelstand than is the case in other countries. There is compelling empirical evidence that the superior access to finance and financial resources has enabled the Mittelstand to drive competitiveness in Germany to a greater degree than in most other developed industrialized countries.[16]

In particular, the banking system in Germany differs from that in other countries in a crucial way. The country has a three-pillar banking sector consisting of banking services, which are divided among the private banking sector, the saving and loan banks (*Sparkassen*), and the mutual or cooperative banks (*Genossenschaften*). Two of the pillars—the 423 savings banks and 1,116 cooperative banks—made it through the global economic crisis with barely a scratch.[17] These financial institutions already have a system of joint liability, which means that no individual member bank is allowed to go bust. Neither the *Sparkassen* nor the *Genossenschaften* want to become part of a wider European banking union, where guarantees would extend to weak peripheral banks.

These two types of banks typically have close relationships with their local clients, and in particular the small and medium-sized companies comprising the Mittelstand, acting as their *Hausbank*, or their main provider of debt. The savings banks and cooperative banks provide about two-thirds of all lending to Mittelstand companies and 43 percent of lending to all companies and households.[18] The *Landesbanken*, which act as wholesale banks for the savings banks, DZ Bank, and WGZ Bank, and do the same for the cooperative banks, step in to provide more sophisticated services, such as hedging and offshore financing. Although these close banking relationships tend to generate higher interest rates for procuring credit and loans, they also provide a type of insurance and safety net in the case of financial distress.[19]

An example of a particularly German institution charged with the mandate to provide finance to the Mittelstand is the Kreditanstalt für Wiederaufbau (KfW). Originally established following World War II to facilitate rapid reconstruction, the KfW has the explicit mission to provide finance for the development of technological capabilities of the German Mittelstand. The Kreditanstalt für Wiederaufbau is actually the leading source of finance for the Mittelstand. In particular, the KfW provides long-term investment loans as well as working capital loans for SMEs in Germany. The Kreditanstalt für Wiederaufbau serves as an important institution implementing government policies. Recent policy priorities of the Kreditanstalt für Wiederaufbau include the promotion of green technologies. The KfW supports loans and finance to SMEs with the targeted purpose of increasing investments in the energy-efficient refurbishments of buildings or enhancing energy-efficient production methods. Loans for these purposes are partly subsidized by federal budget funds and are therefore provided at particularly favorable terms. The Kreditanstalt für Wiederaufbau acts as complementary partner to the other types of banks such as the *Sparkassen, Genossenschaftsbanken*, and private banks. The Kreditanstalt für Wiederaufbau makes its loans through these regular banks and thus facilitates the process of making and approving loans and credit to the Mittelstand.[20]

Beyond the banking relationships, firm managers, owners, and executives from the local *Sparkassen* and *Genossenschaftsbanken* are members of regional social networks with their mutually beneficial relationships. Executives from *Sparkassen* and *Genossenschaftsbanken* together with the owners of the local companies typically provide key leadership in the local networks, serving as a local representative of the municipal council. They also serve as directors of the local *Vereine*, the sport clubs, the *Heimatvereine*, and other local committees. They have to pull together as a great local family, since the distress of a Mittelstand company can easily trigger problems for everyone in the community. Mutual relationships with the local banks provide a safeguard for the local economy.[21]

Unlike in other countries, banks are highly involved in the decision-making of companies. *Deutschland AG* is synonymous worldwide with the interrelationship of the German banking sector and the large public companies listed on the stock market.[22] Herman Abs, the former CEO of Deutsche Bank, served as a member of the *Aufsichtsrat*, or the board of directors, on twenty-three companies—all at the same time!

Scholars in economics, law, and political science have generally taken a dim view of the efficacy of the governance of corporations and the system of finance in Germany. Alexander Dyck, a professor at the Rotman School of Management of the University of Toronto, scrutinized the literature in finance and economics and concluded that scholarly research generally characterizes Germany as a country "with weak protection for investors . . ., very limited equity markets, an almost complete absence of takeovers, and an overwhelming influence of the banking sector, among both listed and unlisted firms."[23]

Given this rather dire assessment by scholars, Germany's strong economic performance and resilience, particularly at a time when most other developed countries and European neighbors succumbed to the despair of the great recession, poses something of a paradox. If the decision-making and governance structure legally imposed on German companies along with a banking and financial system that flies in the face of global realities are so detrimental, what accounts for such a sterling economic performance?

Dyck ponders, "Why didn't this [structure] change over time, as it did in countries like the United States and Britain, and how could such corporate structures not lead to significant inefficiency rather than the positive indicators described"?[24] The secret is in the structure. Corporate Germany is less a shareholder than a stakeholder society. Balancing out the interests of groups either in the political or the economic decision process is more important than the protection and interests of any single group, regardless of how important they might be.

Infrastructure

Perhaps it is not at all surprising that a country that takes structure and organization as the starting point for virtually every endeavor would also make infrastructure a priority. Provision of infrastructure, ranging from transportation to healthcare and other social services, is simply assumed to be necessary for quality of life. It is *selbstverständlich*, or a matter of fact. It is infrastructure that binds citizens and other residents together to comprise the fundamental Gemeinschaft, or community. *Gemein* means "common," and the infrastructure is generally accessible to and can be used by virtually every one. If it is not a public good, in the sense that economists mean,[25] then it no doubt is a common good. Community and society, Gesellschaft, are such fundamental values woven into the fabric of German culture and reflected in its institutions and policies, that investment in infrastructure of all types is understood and widely valued. For example, Professor Dr. Michael Hüther, who serves as the director of the Institute for the German Economy, Cologne, succinctly explains that "an effective infrastructure is the basis of a healthy economy, both for manufacturing and for services."[26]

When the country was reunited in October 1990, one of the highest priorities was to get the remnants of the decrepit infrastructure in the new five eastern Länder up to speed. This involved massive investments financed through, among other things, the generous *Solidaritätszuschlag*, nicknamed the "*Soli*," or the solidarity tax, paid by people living in the western part of the country, resulting in a massive redistribution of income from the western Länder to the Eastern Länder. It is telling that equipping the new five East Länder with state-of-the art infrastructure was almost taken for granted and *selbstverständlich* in those heady years following the fall of the Berlin Wall in 1989.

By contrast, for a country where structure and organization are not part of the policy concepts and vocabulary for thinking about the economy, such as the United States, it stands to reason that infrastructure would also not be valued highly or be a policy priority. In "Infrastructure Cracks as Los Angeles Defers Repairs," the *New York Times* reports, "The scene was apocalyptic: a torrent of water from a ruptured pipe valve bursting through Sunset Boulevard, hurling chunks of asphalt 40 feet into the air as it closed down the celebrated thoroughfare and inundated the campus of the University of California, Los Angeles. By the time emergency crews patched the pipe, 20 million gallons of water had cascaded across the college grounds."[27]

According to the *New York Times*, the failure of the nearly century-old water main "was the latest sign of what officials described as a continuing breakdown of the public works skeleton of the second-largest city in its nation: its roads, sidewalks and water system."[28] In short, the infrastructure.

The cost of undertaking the deferred maintenance is estimated at $8.1 billion, which is just under one-third of the city's annual budget. And it's not just happening in Los Angeles. All across the country, Americans complain of a crumbling infrastructure, ranging from imploding bridges to dysfunctional rail service. As the journalist Fareed Zakaria warns, "Infrastructure [in the United States] is ranked 23rd in the world, well behind that of every other major advanced economy."[29]

The journalist John Nichols writes in *The Nation* that the decaying of American infrastructure has spread so far that it has infected the ability of citizens to participate in basic functions inherent to democracy.[30] In an article titled "The Infrastructure of American Democracy is Dysfunctional," Nichols warns that inadequate investment in the technology, personnel, and processes have resulted in an unacceptable performance in terms of voter participation.[31]

In fact, there is a view prevalent in the United States that infrastructure does not matter as much as it used to. According to this view, knowledge and entrepreneurship have pushed aside investments in physical capital as the engine of economic growth, job creation, and competitiveness in global markets. For example, an article in *Foreign Affairs*, "How to Fix America," argues that "in the contemporary knowledge-based economy, innovation is the linchpin of growth, not physical infrastructure. . . . It is unlikely that building new physical infrastructure would do as much for growth in today's knowledge-based economy as it did in the two decades following World War II."[32]

But not in Germany.

A number of leading and highly respected international assessments comparing national infrastructure and its contribution to competitiveness, such as the IMD's *World Competitiveness Yearbook*, consistently rank Germany among the world's leaders. For example, in its *2011–2012 Global Competitiveness Report*, the World Economic Forum ranked Germany as the second leading country in the world in terms of quality of infrastructure, following only Hong Kong (SAR). Germany's stellar ranking reflects an outstanding quality of roads and airports, the rail and port infrastructure, and the country's outstanding communications and energy infrastructure.[33]

However, the secret is not only the existence of a broad portfolio of infrastructure, but also the maintenance. Infrastructure in Germany is operated by public companies with the government as a main shareholder. This guarantees at least a minimum standard of quality, which could not be guaranteed under a private and market system. Otherwise, partial privatization and the public listing ensure a market pressure and prevent management from behaving as they might if it were a purely public and state-owned enterprise.

Companies providing infrastructure in Germany typically ensure that quality and safety standards are adequately met. Examples of such companies publicly listed as blue chips on the stock market include Deutsche Lufthansa, where 68 percent of the shares are owned by the German government, and another 11 percent owned by the United States;

Deutsche Telekom, which as a global player in the telecommunication industry has its American subsidiary, T-Mobile; Fraport AG, a leading international airport company, operating Frankfurt Airport; and the two energy companies E.On and RWE. Since its privatization in 1996, Deutsche Post DHL has become a global player and is the world's largest courier company, with 79 percent of the shares free floating and 21 percent owned by the Kreditanstalt für Wiederaufbau (KfW), which is a state-owned bank. Only the Deutsche Bahn still remains a purely state-owned enterprise, although an IPO was considered a few years ago. However, the market share of the privately-owned railway companies has been increasing over the last decade, from less than 7 percent in 2003 toward 33 percent in 2013.[34]

Most of the production, services, and wholesale and retail trade in Germany depend upon, and enjoy considerable efficiency and productivity gains from, accessing the highly effective, modern, and reliable infrastructure. It would be erroneous, however, to conclude that Germany hosts the largest airports, highways, railroad networks, harbors, and shipping lanes in the world. Rather, at least part of the competitive advantage bestowed from the German infrastructure emanates from the rich diversity of different types of infrastructure and how they provide complimentary inputs for production. Because companies can rely on the state-of-the-art infrastructure, they can deploy strategies that split their value chains but maintain some of the production within Germany, and often within close geographic proximity. Just-in-time production requires close relationships and short distances. This is afforded by inputs and intermediates that are transported on the autobahn. The autobahn network has a total length of about 12,917 kilometers, which ranks it among the densest and longest systems in the world (after China with 97,355 km and the United States with 75,932 km). But Germany's small size in square meters compared to China and the United States yields considerable cost advantages in transportation and time enjoyed by German industry.

Connecting people, goods, and services is also facilitated by railroad infrastructure. With about 33,000 km of tracks, Germany's railroad system is by far the longest in Europe, with over thirty-nine thousand trains moving more than 14 million passengers per year. Munich hosts the second largest railroad station in the world, after the Grand Central Terminal in Manhattan, and is the largest in Europe. Hamburg is home to the second largest railroad yard in the world, behind Bailey Yard in Nebraska.

Important centers for production, wholesale and retail trade, and people are all connected by the various modes of transportation involving air, water, or land. Metropolitan areas such as Munich, Stuttgart, the Ruhr Valley, Hamburg, and Berlin also serve as hubs for the thousands of medium-sized Mittelstand firms and hidden champions, which, as chapter 2 explains, are typically located in the more isolated and peripheral regions. Thanks to the rich and ample infrastructure prevalent throughout Germany, the closest airport, railway station, or autobahn is often only a stone's throw away from the Mittelstand company, so that its geographic location in a remote or isolated region does not impose locational cost disadvantages.

Despite the stellar performance in high-profile international comparisons ranking infrastructure, there is also considerable concern, or even angst, simmering in Germany about the current state of its infrastructure. In order to address this very question, the Institute for the German Economy, Cologne (Institut der Deutschen Wirtschaft, Köln) released a report in February 2014 titled "Infrastructure between Source of Competitive Advantage and in Need of Investments."[35]

This careful study highlights a number of strengths with the German infrastructure, but at the same time exposes several uncomfortable and even glaring weaknesses. In terms of the transportation network and infrastructure, worrisome weaknesses were uncovered in several geographic regions, as well as aging bridges, requiring an investment of at least 40 billion euros for renovations. In terms of broadband, the overall condition was rated adequate, with the greatest challenge consisting of a need to modernize technology and equipment, which could require an investment of around 40 billion euros over the next decade. The energy network was evaluated as "good," but the transition away from fossil-based fuels to solar and wind-powered energy, or the *Energiewende*, will require an investment of 40 billion euros to maintain the quality of the infrastructure.[36]

In his statement accompanying the report, the director of the Institute of the German Economy, Professor Dr. Michael Hüther, admitted that "Germans disagree about the condition of their infrastructure. Some say that it is a model. Others say it is broken. It is a case of all is good versus all is bad." Professor Dr. Hüther went on to suggest that the state of infrastructure in Germany is somewhat ambiguous, with some compelling strengths but also some concerning weaknesses. In summing up its findings, the Institute for the German Economy, Cologne, concludes, "*Immer Noch ein Standortvorteil*," or "Still a Source of Competitive Advantage."

Concerns about the traditional stalwart of German competitiveness, the infrastructure, have received considerable attention in the media and in policy discussion. For example, the highly visible weekly magazine *Der Spiegel* warns in a title story, "Ailing Infrastructure: Scrimping Threatens Germany's Future."[37] Because of a decline in the investment rate from 20 percent in 1999 to 17 percent in 2013, "Year after year, tens of billions of euros have been missing for the sorely needed maintenance of highways, railways and machinery."[38]

In "Germany's Ailing Infrastructure: A Nation Slowly Crumbles," *Der Spiegel* reports that "Germany has long had a reputation for excellent infrastructure. Despite its shiny façade, the German economy is crumbling at its core."[39]

Concern about the low levels of investment in the infrastructure has prompted the president of the highly influential Institute of German Economic Research Berlin (DIW Berlin), Professor Dr. Marcel Fratzscher, to proclaim in his 2014 book, *Die Deutschland Illusion*, or *The German Illusion*, that the prosperity generated in Germany over the past seven years is attributable largely to living off the investments made by previous generations in infrastructure.[40] The illusion, according to Professor Dr. Fratzscher, is that German prosperity is sustainable with inadequate investments in infrastructure and in isolation from the rest of Europe.[41]

German Efficiency

Infrastructure in the form of highways, railroads, harbors, airports, and ports is generally considered to be a form of physical capital. In an earlier era, corresponding to the economic growth model of Robert Solow,[42] it was widely held that physical capital was the key to efficiency. Adding additional physical capital, in the form of factories, machines, tools, or infrastructure, would enhance the productivity of a given amount of labor. As the great Harvard University scholar Alfred Chandler pointed out through meticulous examples and case studies, access to physical capital was the key strategy to becoming the most efficient producer in an industry.[43] Efficiency would, in turn, reduce the costs of production to the firm, enhancing its competitiveness vis-à-vis other producers not having access to that same factor of production.[44] Therefore, firms having access to the relevant state-of-the-art infrastructure will enjoy greater levels of efficiency and productivity, which in turn will enhance competitiveness. Careful research studies have identified a consistent and systematic link between infrastructure investments, efficiency gains, and the economic performance of places.[45]

There is also compelling evidence suggesting that, at least in Germany, infrastructure plays a crucial role in shaping the competitiveness of business in a globalized economy. According to a study undertaken at the Institute for the German Economy, Cologne, 92 percent of surveyed firms indicated that infrastructure ranks among the most important sources generating competitiveness for them.[46] Having access to stable and reliable sources of energy is a key source of competitiveness to 92 percent of the firms. Over 85 percent of the responding firms identified viable roads and highways as being important in generating their competitive advantage. Similarly, 82 percent of the surveyed firms named communications infrastructure as important in generating their comparative advantage. While infrastructure is highly heterogeneous and has many faces, it is clear that it is one of the secrets of Germany in bestowing competitive advantage and success in regional and global markets.

Talent

Another way in which infrastructure can contribute to economic performance involves a very different type of input or factor of production—human capital, or talent. The competitive advantage of a highly developed European country such as Germany is clearly based on human capital, or what is increasingly referred to as talent.[47] It's not just about the number of years in school and universities, but rather what the person can do to leverage that education and training along with his or her wealth of experiences to contribute to decision-making and ultimately innovative activity.

Richard Florida, who is a professor of business at the University of Toronto, introduced a slightly different view of human capital, which he termed as *the creative class.*

Florida provides compelling examples, case studies, and empirical evidence linking the performance of cities to his measures of the creative class.[48] The measurement that Florida developed to identify the creative class involves job categories. Specific job categories, ranging from engineers to teachers and musicians, are classified as belonging to the creative class. Other job categories, ranging from assembly line workers and fast-food workers, do not belong to the creative class. While there is considerable overlap, Florida's concept of the creative class is decidedly different from and broader than—in that it includes people without high levels of formal education—the more traditional concept of human capital.

Cities and regions in Germany have actively adopted Florida's creative class approach in devising policies and strategies to attract talent to their *Standort,* or place. The "creativity and culture" economy in Germany, which includes sectors like theaters, movies, music, movies, the media, architecture, and design, encompasses over 248,000 firms, over 1.5 billion employees, with a gross value added of around 65 billion euros. The creativity and culture industries recently ranked fourth place in terms of importance and size, lagging behind automobile manufacturing, machinery, and financial services, but ahead of energy and the chemical sector.[49] While the magnitude of the creative sector in Germany is impressive, its contribution to other aspects of the economy and society, such as entrepreneurship and new venture creation, often remains hidden and underestimated.

An article titled "Activists in Hamburg Resist Creative Class Policies"[50] documents how Hamburg has developed a strategy of policies to attract the creative class through targeted instruments to enhance competitiveness, jobs, and growth. However, as the article suggests, there is no consensus among people actually living in Hamburg about the efficacy of policies to attract talent to the city. One critic of Hamburg's *Standortpolitik* targeting the creative class complains that "Richard Florida's ghost roams throughout Europe these days. We live in a world of global cities that are involved in interurban competition to attract investors and the so-called international knowledge worker. Keynesian economic policy has made a shift to an entrepreneurial and managerial approach to metropolitan governance. The inevitable rise of city branding and Florida's creative class theory are direct derivatives from these developments."[51]

Despite such resistance, there is no shortage of compelling examples, case studies, and even systematic empirical evidence confirming that places can contribute to economic performance by attracting talent and human capital to that place. Analyzing the interrelation between creativity and entrepreneurship is complex in that direct and indirect relationships between both exist. The link between creativity and entrepreneurship could be, at least, threefold. First, there is a direct link between entrepreneurship and creativity by new venture creation in the creativity sector. The second link is that creativity is shaped by endowment factors where new venture creation is one determinant. The third link is that creativity and entrepreneurship are interrelated, in that creativity shapes new venture creation by attracting creative people who are also attracted by a creative environment. Which policy instruments can actually be deployed to attract and retain the creative class is far from certain. Numerous hypotheses, anecdotal evidence and even "urban myths" pervade the media and popular policy debates. Florida has his own view. He advocates that a place develop policies and strategies focusing on what he terms as the three T's—tolerance, technology, and talent. Tolerance characterizes the acceptance of heterogeneity in the types of people living and working at a place. This diversity can reflect a heterogeneity of races, backgrounds, ethnic groups, ages, and lifestyle choices. Technology reflects the primacy of knowledge and ideas as a driving force for innovative activity. Florida's point is that a place rich in knowledge and ideas generally serves as a magnet for the creative class. According to Florida, talent seeks out other talent, so that policies attracting the creative class tend to be self-reinforcing. Music, theater, museums, and sports and recreational facilities are examples of cultural amenities that can serve as policy instruments to attract the creative class. There is rich empirical evidence from a plethora of studies suggesting that cities and regions deploying these instruments by investing in cultural amenities and quality of life tend to exhibit superior economic performance.[52]

Another important policy instrument identified by Florida to attract and retain the creative class is investment in research universities: "By attracting eminent researchers and scientists, universities in turn attract graduate students, generate spin-off companies and encourage other companies to locate nearby in a cycle of self-reinforcing growth."[53]

Infrastructure also serves as a key policy instrument for attracting and retaining the creative class. There is little doubt that the strong attraction of major German cities to talent and human capital, both domestic and foreign, reflects the state-of-the-art infrastructure accessible to residents. For example, the *Wall Street Journal* reports, "After Allied bombing during World War II, and subsequent rebuilding by two regimes (East and West) whose architectural aesthetic no one would describe as lovely, Berlin cannot boast the beautiful public spaces of other European capitals."[54]

Nonetheless, since the Wall fell in 1989, Berlin has become a major destination for students and young people, especially artists, emanating an allure that is hard to explain. Part of the answer has to do with infrastructure. Berlin, like the rest of the country, offers public transportation infrastructure, ranging from trains to subways, trams, and buses, providing virtually unlimited access to everywhere in the city at a very low price. In addition, great attention and detail is placed on the use of public spaces. For example, when the airport of Göring's prized Luftwaffe, Tempelhof, was finally closed, Berliners voted not for commercial development or additional housing but to keep the space as an experimental urban park. What used to serve the most terrifying air force in the world is now the playground for "couples strolling, children learning to ride bikes, teenagers playing soccer and even windsurfers cruising down its vast runways, from whose cracks crabgrass now grows."[55]

The priority placed on investments in culture, public infrastructure, and a climate of tolerance and diversity has played a significant role in generating Berlin's new image.[56] There is evidence that it is working: A 2012 survey of adults under thirty years old reports that nearly two-thirds of young Germans would prefer to live and work in Berlin.[57] Perhaps most telling, the survey suggests that Berlin is considered to be the best place in Germany to become an entrepreneur and start a new business. As Henrik Berggren, an entrepreneur from Sweden, who came to Berlin to develop his e-book start-up ReadMill exclaims, "I got sucked into Berlin. It became clear that this was the place to be."[58]

Berlin, "on this Island in Germany," as described in the famous song "Berlin" by the British New Wave band Fisher-Z in the 1980s,[59], has emerged as a special hot spot for the creative class: "Young faces new ideals / in search of paradise / They merge into the history / the theater of memories / that make up the feel of / Berlin / Berlin / Berlin / Berlin." Without an official closing hour, or *Sperrstunde*, Berlin has become a city that doesn`t sleep. Bars, discotheques, and clubs often open for twenty-three hours a day—the remaining hour is reserved to clean up, people joke. The military governance by the Allies during the post-war era has also led to another curiosity that made Berlin "sexy" for young and creative people—the ban of the German military. During this era when West Berlin was occupied by the allies – England, France and the United States – Germans living in Berlin were not allowed to join the compulsory military service. Instead of spending at least fifteen months (*Wehrpflicht*) in military service, youngsters flocked from the unoccupied parts of West Germany to Berlin to become a *Berliner*. Studying in one of the two universities in West Berlin, either at the Technical University or at the Free University, could be viewed as a choice of a lifestyle. All these made Berlin a magnet for the creative class, stimulating songwriters to dedicate their music to the city of Berlin. For example, David Bowie moved from Los Angeles to Berlin in 1976. In his favorite song, "Heroes," Bowie raised a memorial to Berlin in the Cold War:

> I can remember
> Standing
> By the Wall
> And the guns
> Shot above our heads
> And we kissed
> As though nothing could fall
> And the shame
> Was on the other side
> Oh we can beat them
> For ever and ever.

"Heroes" still remains an unofficial anthem of the creative class in Berlin.

As another famous song celebrates, *Berlin bleibt doch Berlin*, or Berlin remains Berlin. And so it does—sexy as always. This is illustrated by the emergence of a vibrant fashion industry in Berlin. The Berlin Fashion Week was created to bring together both the established and the newly emerging talent in the industry.[60] Provocative newcomers, such as

Michael Michalsky, are drawing celebrities and stars. His vision combining fashion with sustainability and social responsibility has resonated with both celebrities and global companies like Sony and Adidas. Similarly, Guido Maria Kretschmer not only creates professional clothing for companies like Emirate Airlines and the Hotels Kampinski and Maritim, but also for Hollywood stars like Oscar winner Charlize Theron, who wears his collections.

In no other city in Germany are so many people employed in the fashion industry: As of 2014, 15,300 people were employed by over 3,700 companies and fashion labels. While entry barriers for young and unknown creators are dauntingly prohibitive in the traditional established fashion clusters of New York, Paris, London, and Milan, opportunities to start a new label are accessible in Berlin. According to Sivia Kadolsky, who had previously lived and worked in Paris and New York, not only is the cost of living in general and housing in particular considerably lower, but the vast infrastructure of Berlin is a strong appeal to newcomers.[61]

Thus, one important way that infrastructure contributes to economic performance is by serving as a magnet attracting and retaining human capital, talent, and the creative class. Because Germany is rich in infrastructure, an inward flow of talent and the creative class to German cities has taken place, providing those cities and the entire country not just with the crucial factor and resource of infrastructure, but enhancing the stock of human resources as well.

Social Capital

Infrastructure contributes to economic performance in a very different way as well, through enhancing social capital. Social capital generally refers to linkages, networks, and interactions among people, firms, and other organizations. Such linkages and networks facilitate the spillover of knowledge across people, firms, and other organization within a city or region.[62]

Michael Piore and Charles Sabel, both professors of political science at MIT at the time, identified the key role played by what today would be termed social capital in explaining the strong economic performance of Emilia Romania in Italy. In their highly influential book *The Second Industrial Divide*,[63] Piore and Sabel explained that the secret to the impressive economic performance of Emilia Romania was in the way the people of the region, even with a paucity of human capital and physical capital, interacted and interfaced with each other. The authors identified a broad set of unique networks, linkages, and interactions among the people of Emilia Romania. For example, a rich web of organizations, institutions, and cultural traditions provided dense linkages and interconnections among people and small businesses. These linkages enhanced economic performance of the region by facilitating a high flow of knowledge, ideas, and best practices.

Social capital is explained by the Harvard professor of political science Robert Putnam in his bestselling book, *Bowling Alone*: "Whereas physical capital refers to physical objects and human capital refers to the properties of individuals, social capital refers to connections among individuals—social networks and the norms of reciprocity and trustworthiness that arise from them. In that sense social capital is closely related to what some have called 'civic virtue.' The difference is that 'social capital' calls attention to the fact that civic virtue is most powerful when embedded in a sense network of reciprocal social relations. A society of many virtues but isolated individuals is not necessarily rich in social capital."[64]

Just as economists had identified the importance of physical capital in shaping economic performance, Putnam argued that the relationships individuals have with each other and in a social context also play an important role: "By analogy with notions of physical capital and human capital—tools and training that enhance individual productivity—social capital refers to features of social organization, such as networks, norms, and trust, that facilitate coordination and cooperation for mutual benefits."[65]

Considerable empirical evidence has been accumulated by a minor army of scholars confirming that social capital tends to have a positive impact on economic performance.[66] Just as firms with greater access to social capital tend to exhibit higher rates of performance, cities, regions, and countries with a greater degree of social capital also tend to generate higher rates of economic growth.[67]

The linkages, networks, and interactions among people characterized by social capital can be enhanced by infrastructure. Such human interactions don't just happen in a vacuum. Rather, people need to meet and interface, and a viable infrastructure, ranging from subways and buses to cultural amenities such as parks and theaters, facilitate such human interactions, which form the basis of social capital.

Alfonso Martinez Cearra, director general of Bilbao Metropoli-30, is effusive in his assessment of the impact that infrastructure can have in promoting social capital: "Cultural infrastructures have an important role to play in cities. They contribute to higher levels of competence, creativity and security, not to mention social cohesion. They promote a better understanding between different cultures and different generations of the society. Likewise, they encourage the citizens to participate more actively in collective development, thereby bringing about a greater awareness of identity and benefiting or creating local traditions."[68]

Social capital and the underlying networks, linkages, and interactions among people, in turn, can serve as a key conduit for the spillover of knowledge and ideas across people and organizations. In her highly influential book, the University of California professor AnnaLee Saxenian describes how such social interactions and linkages are conducive to knowledge flows and spillovers in Silicon Valley, which in turn are a key mechanism driving innovative activity, because people "continue to meet at trade shows, industry conferences and the scores of seminars, talks, and social activities. Relationships are easily formed and maintained, technical and market information is exchanged, business contacts are established, and new enterprises are conceived. . . . This decentralized and fluid environment also promotes the diffusion of intangible technological capabilities and understandings"[69]

Social capital and social embeddedness play a crucial role in German society. What are seven Germans doing when they meet by chance? They establish a nonprofit *Verein*, a society or association. The law requires seven persons to register a nonprofit *Verein*. Over 580,000 nonprofit societies and associations are registered in Germany, and members typically are working on an honorary and unpaid basis.[70] One-half of the German population is a voluntary member of at least one *Verein*, such as sports, culture, or civil services. While Germany could be characterized as a country of strong social ties and close relationships, Germans are rather grumps in the social networks. A recent study published by the Bundesministerium für Wirtschaft und Energie (BMWi), or Federal Ministry for the Economy and Energy, ranks Germany as only fourteenth out of fifteen countries when it comes to using social networks like Facebook and LinkedIn. It is not that Germans are reluctant to use the Internet. In fact, German usage of websites for e-commerce and downloading music, podcasts, and videos is robust and growing. Rather, it is about social networks on the Internet.[71]

When it comes to strong networks and relationships within companies, in particular the Mittelstand, or the small and medium-sized companies discussed in chapter 2, Germans are very active and involved. For example, the owner and his or her family are typically deeply involved in nonprofit clubs, societies, and associations, or *Vereine*, which reflects the importance of deep and strong relationships within a town, village, city, or region. What is particularly striking, at least from the perspective of a North American, is that this involvement goes beyond financial sponsorship and includes active membership and participation. The owners and families contribute not just their money but also their time, energy, and personal engagement. Such strong and passionate ties and linkages can cement reciprocal relationships between Mittelstand owners, their employees, and the local community, with benefits accruing to all parties.

Thus, an important way in which the impressive infrastructure in Germany contributes to its strong economic performance is by enhancing the human dimension of knowledge spillovers—social capital.[72]

Entrepreneurship

Dietmar Hopp, Klaus Tschira, Hans-Werner Hector, Hasso Plattner, and Claus Wellenreuther were five young engineers employed by IBM in Germany. Because they worked together, they started talking about new product opportunities. As their discussions and ideas grew more serious, they became increasingly passionate about their new idea, which was to create an entirely new type of business software.

IBM itself expressed no interest in their idea. After all, IBM had risen to world dominance in mainframe computers. As Peters and Waterman explain in their widely read bestseller *In Search of Excellence*,[73] IBM had emerged as not just the best of the best among American companies, but was almost universally considered to be the top company in the world. Peters and Waterman celebrated the IBM strategy of "sticking to its knitting" by not diluting its core mainframe computer business with distractions such as the proposed idea for new business software by its five young engineers.

IBM's rejection of their idea did not deter the passion and dreams of the five young engineers. Their own experiences led them to believe in a potentially very lucrative market for their new business software. With start-up finance from a small regional bank near Heidelberg, based on a family connection, they succeeded in founding their new company.[74] And what a start-up it has been! Sales skyrocketed, so that by the end of the first decade of this century, SAP has grown from the handful of engineers to fifty-three thousand employees. It was not just the start-up team of the five engineers that have benefited from founding SAP. The entire region of Baden-Württemberg has reaped enormous benefits from SAP.

But where exactly did the entrepreneurial opportunity come from that fueled that founding and subsequent growth of SAP? Each of the five IBM engineers brought considerable know-how, educational background, and experience with him. But it was in their interactions and interfaces, where they exchanged ideas and tried out new possibilities, that collectively they were able to create what undoubtedly none of them could have created on his own.

Connectivity matters, especially when it comes to creating new ideas, which ultimately provide the opportunities upon which new entrepreneurial ventures are launched. Scholars of entrepreneurship generally focus on opportunities as a critical determination triggering entrepreneurship. But where do such entrepreneurial activities come from?

One answer is that they come from the connectivity of people. Through the interactions and interfaces, new knowledge and ideas do not so much spill over as literally are created by different people interacting and interfacing. Connectivity matters for new ideas, innovation, and entrepreneurship. In the SAP example the interaction among the five young engineers occurred because they happened to work for the same company. Similarly, many the key interactions happened at Harvard University that generated the ideas and knowledge driving the founding of Facebook, just as the students at Stanford were at the same university that facilitated the interactions and interfaces that ultimately served as a catalyst for the start-up of Google.

But what happens if the key people are not, by coincidence, all at the same company or university? The key interactions among people provided by infrastructure play an important role in generating and facilitating opportunities for entrepreneurship by enhancing human connectivity.

Thus, a key way that infrastructure can promote economic performance is by facilitating entrepreneurship. A strong and compelling scholarly literature suggests that entrepreneurship responds to the existence of opportunities. Investments in infrastructure may be particularly conducive to entrepreneurial opportunities because they enhance connectivity. Infrastructure investment typically enhances the ability of people to interact and interface, which, in turn, is beneficial to entrepreneurial activity. Infrastructure can spur entrepreneurial opportunities along with the ability of nascent entrepreneurs to act upon those opportunities in the form of starting a new firm.[75]

There is at least some academic research linking infrastructure to entrepreneurial activity in Germany.[76] Using a unique data set identifying start-up activity and different types of infrastructure availability in Germany, this study is able to provide a link between infrastructure and entrepreneurship. Most generally, infrastructure is found to be positively associated with start-up activity. However, the association is apparently specific to both the particular type of infrastructure and the particular industry context within which the entrepreneurial decision is being considered. Certain specific types of infrastructure, such as broadband, are more conducive to infrastructure than are highways and railroads.

Infrastructure apparently can promote entrepreneurship by providing crucial connectivity among people and firms. Those regions in Germany with more and better infrastructure provide greater connectivity, which in turn facilitates more entrepreneurial activity.

Conclusions

It is difficult to find better, more advanced, and up-to-date infrastructure in the world than in Germany. That is hardly a secret, especially to anyone who has visited Germany and experienced the wonders and joys of the high-speed, long-distance railroad system, sleek autobahn, reliable and comprehensive system of inner-city trams, subways and buses providing complete access to the city at low prices, and breathtaking parks along with the stunning array of museums, galleries, theaters, and operas.

But does any of this matter, especially in terms of economic growth, jobs and competitiveness in global markets?

The answer is a resounding yes. In the zeitgeist of the contemporary era, infrastructure has gotten a bad, or at least rather worn-out and tired, reputation. Everyone knows that in the knowledge economy, people and ideas matter, not buildings and heavy-handed industrial structures such as railroads.

But for people to matter, they have to be connected. They have to interact, interface, and network with each other. And that's where the infrastructure comes in. Infrastructure is all about connectivity. In Germany, people are able to easily meet, interface, and connect, thanks to a highly viable and functional infrastructure. Yes, infrastructure matters, and Germany's got it in spades. Germany shows that it still pays to invest in infrastructure, at least in terms of economic performance.

What invariably catches the eye in Germany, the infrastructure, may reflect only the most visible and superficial aspect of a more fundamental and underlying strength—structure and organization. If the zeitgeist is characterized by the advent of the SMS texting generation, with creativity, ideas, and spontaneity as its trademark, structure and organization may seem to be an outdated, onerous, and weighty impediment to what really matters.

Perhaps the real secret is that structure and organization provide a compelling platform liberating the human spirit for highly coveted creativity and spontaneity. As the American playwright Henry Miller once reflected, "I know that to sustain those true moments of insight, one has to be highly disciplined, lead a disciplined life."[77] Miller's sentiment was not lost on W. H. Auden, who concurred: "Routine, in an intelligent man, is a sign of genius. . . . A modern stoic knows that the surest way to discipline passion is to discipline time; decide what you want or ought to do during the day, then always do it at exactly the same moment every day, and passion will give you no trouble."[78]

6 Laptops and Lederhosen

AT THE DEPTHS of economic stagnation and dismal employment prospects in 1998, Germany hungered for any glimmer of success and resilience. It was the president of the country at that time, Roman Herzog, who spotted an exciting development with the promise of something the entire country could latch onto. President Herzog's home state of Bavaria was gaining economic momentum and had become something of an economic anomaly in a country otherwise bogged down by negligible growth and double-digit unemployment. The rest of the country was struggling to come to terms with the new challenges posed by the post–Berlin Wall globalization.

But not in Bavaria. In Bavaria something was working. The state of Bavaria, and in particular, the city of Munich, was showing signs of economic vigor and impressive growth. In explaining what exactly Bavaria was doing right, when the rest of the country seemed to be doing everything wrong, President Herzog's insight was "Laptops and Lederhosen."[1] What Herzog had latched onto was the paradoxical and surprising dichotomy of maintaining traditional cultural, political, and social values but combining them with cutting-edge ideas, knowledge, and technology. It seemed to be working.

The advent of globalization following the fall of the Berlin Wall had taken Germany, like most of Europe, by surprise. The old tried-and-true formulae, strategies, approaches, and even values that had guided the country for nearly half a century to prosperity and a high *Wohlstand*, or standard of living, no longer seemed able to deliver.

While the rest of the country languished, Bavaria managed to generate the highest growth rates in Germany along with a welcome reduction of unemployment. What

President Herzog had latched onto was the insight that under the astute political stewardship of the Christian Social Union (CSU), Bavaria seemed to be the only place in Germany that was able to sustain its traditional cultural, political, and social values while at the same time moving into and even thriving in the new, brave world of globalization. As Andreas Kiessing, a political scientist explains, "The secret of success lies in a combination of economic modernization and the keeping alive of tradition."[2]

Few would have foreseen that it would be Bavaria soaring while the rest of the country struggled with stagnant growth, increased unemployment, and diminished prospects. Most of the country, indeed Europe along with the rest of the world, had grown accustomed to thinking of agriculturally based Bavaria as the poor cousin in Germany. The Bavarian image of *Lederhosen* and "oompah" music played by brass bands reflected a predominately rural, but certainly breathtaking landscape along with decades of relatively tepid economic development and a low standard of living when compared to the mighty factories of the Ruhr Valley and the manufacturing force of the state-of-the art plants operated by the scores of nimble companies populating the hills of Baden-Württemberg. For years, the growth rates and standard of living in Bavaria had lagged far behind that of the rest of the country. To West Germans, Bavaria was *selbstverständlich* (that is, as a matter of fact) the poor, rural region that had to be subsidized through the *Ausgleich*, or cross-subsidization, from wealthier to less fortunate Länder, as mandated by the *Grundgesetz*, or Basic Law.

But not anymore. The emergence of Bavaria as the prominent economically successful and increasingly prosperous region of Germany came as something of a shock to more than a few Germans. As the *Guardian* explains, "Its leaders have done a remarkable job in transforming Bavaria from one of the poorest, most agriculturally dependent regions in the country into one of the richest and most technologically advanced. A state associated mainly with Alpine chalets, brass bands and beer halls is today a center for high-tech industries that employ 12.4 percent of the workforce—the highest percentage in Europe."[3]

President Herzog's characterization of laptops and lederhosen depicts the cognitive dissonance created from seemingly inherent contradictions fueling Bavarian's improbable economic emergence. In a tradition-rooted culture and economy, Bavaria had managed to leapfrog into the most advanced technologies and markets. In accomplishing this remarkable economic development, Bavaria led the way in providing a role model, or at least a path or blueprint, for transforming globalization from a burden impeding economic growth and destroying jobs to an opportunity for generating new levels of *Wohlstand*.

Flexibility is not a word that most people would associate with Germany. Just as the key to the Bavarian turnaround was flexibility and adaptability to change, the key to the recent impressive economic resilience of Germany lies in its capacity for flexibility and adaptability to change. The underlying mechanism is the same—flexibility and adaptability in a rapidly changing world. The purpose of this chapter is to explain how that flexibility, which President Herzog characterized as laptops and lederhosen, has served

Germany well by enabling it to shift from what has been characterized as the managed economy in the era of industrial production to an entrepreneurial society in the era of globalization.[4]

The next section of this chapter examines the surprising capacity that Germany exhibits for flexibility and adaptability. The third section explains how that flexibility and adaptability have resulted in a shift in Germany as a country characterized by homogeneity to one celebrating heterogeneity and diversity. How and why this flexibility and diversity have enhanced the economic performance in Germany is explained in the fourth section. Finally, a summary and conclusions are provided in the last section. In particular, this chapter finds that, in sharp contrast to the conventional wisdom and prevailing stereotypes about Germany, its economy is built on the cornerstones of flexibility and diversity, which in turn have contributed significantly to a strong economic performance, standard of living, and economic resilience.

Flexibility

The movie *Schindler's List* was released in Germany on March 1, 1994. The film triggered instant acclaim and resonance throughout the country.[5] In a front-page article, the widely read and influential daily newspaper *Frankfurter Allgemeine Zeitung* advised its readers, "Everybody should see this film. It forces the viewer to ask why others didn't try to do what Oskar Schindler managed."[6] *Der Spiegel* ran a cover story featuring the movie, exclaiming, "'Schindler's List' is great beyond all expectations."[7]

At the same time, the movie elicited surprise and confusion. Not about the story of Oskar Schindler, or how his saving countless Jews from a doomed fate, or even how the concentration camps and German guards were portrayed. All of this was known, understood, and widely accepted. Rather, the surprise was about the director of the film, Steven Spielberg. Spielberg was, of course, known by everyone in Germany, as throughout the world. His Hollywood blockbusters such as *E.T., Back to the Future*, and *Jurassic Park* had riveted enormous audiences in Germany, just as elsewhere.

But this film was different. The cultural, historical, and political sensibilities involved in making *Schindler's List* simply did not square with the view of Spielberg as a brilliant director for first-rate entertainment involving flights of fantasy about extraterrestrial aliens, cars transporting across time, or reviving dinosaur DNA.[8]

What they underestimated was Steven Spielberg's flexibility.

It is perhaps not surprising that people in Germany would pigeonhole Spielberg and the kind of films he makes. After all, the country may be known for many things, but flexibility is not one of them. As the American novelist Mark Twain, noted, what the German language offers in precision it sacrifices in flexibility. In his widely read "The Awful German Language," Twain complains that "every noun has a gender, and there is no sense or system in distribution; so the gender of each must be learned separately and by heart. There is no other way. To do this, one has to have a memory like a memorandum-book."[9]

In terms of economics, the capacity to engage in several or different activities at the same point in time is considered to constitute static flexibility. By contrast, the capacity to engage in several or different activities at different points in time constitutes dynamic flexibility.[10]

Anything other than flexibility comes to mind when thinking about the static context of Germany. One of the dictates of daily life remains *Ordnung muss sein!* or Preserve order! A society with the priority of preserving order does not seem to embrace flexibility.

However, when one considers how Germany deals with problems, challenges, and issues over time, a very different picture emerges. For example, for decades, *Ladenschluss* provided a legal mandate dictating that stores and shops must close by 5:00 p.m. on weekdays, 2:00 p.m. on Saturday, and remain closed all day on Sunday. With no exceptions.

Similarly, beer could only be brewed and sold in accordance to the strict *Reinheitsgebot*, or law ensuring the purity of the brewing process.[11] During those same years, smoking was widespread and accepted as a right for the smokers, just as restrictions and regulations concerning behavior and what is permissible or not permeated daily life in Germany.

Any public discussion or debate proposing changes in modifications of *Ladenschluss*, the *Reinheitsgebot*, or the right to smoke anywhere and everywhere would meet immediate and rigid opposition: "That simply is not the way we do things in Germany."

But the funny thing is, fast-forwarding to today, none of the practices are around anymore. Just as store hours have become remarkably more flexible, beer can be imported and sold containing all kinds of nasty preservatives and artificial ingredients, and smokers have been relegated to tiny restricted booths and designated smoking areas. It's not just about smoking, brewing, and shopping. Rather, these examples illustrate a particularly German paradox—stubborn rigidity in the static context combined with remarkable flexibility in the dynamic context.

We know older Germans who have been citizens of four different political regimes, indeed countries, without ever leaving their hometown or village. The Federal Republic of Germany is still younger than the expected lifetime in the OECD countries. Less than three decades ago the country was reunified. The current currency was introduced only thirteen years ago. We have friends, acquaintances, and colleagues who have experienced three different currencies in their lifetime, and some from the eastern part of the country have experienced four different currencies.

Meanwhile, in America there has been one political regime, or a single nation, for nearly two and one-half centuries. David still recalls the day in kindergarten when the children were marched into the school auditorium to recite the Pledge of Allegiance, because two new stars had been added to the flag to represent the two new states—Alaska and Hawaii—admitted to the United States. Since then, it has been the same flag with the same number of stars for exactly the same states. No one alive has ever used a different currency in the United States.

It seems that United States is the country of stability and constancy, while Germany is the country of change and transition.

There is a difference of how change, and certainly economic change, is manifested between the two countries. In the United States change has been driven considerably more through the entrepreneurial impulse by breaking away from existing organizations to create new ones, forcing the incumbent corporations and organizations to confront new ideas and innovations through the discipline of market-driven competition. *Disruptive technologies* is a buzzword in the United States articulating what scholars from previous generations termed the process of *creative destruction*.

The giant of a scholar Joseph Schumpeter created the concept of creative destruction to describe the process by which the economy and society changed.[12] According to Schumpeter, change was achieved only at the price of what he termed creative destruction. Just as the factory wiped out the blacksmith shop and the car superseded the horse and buggy, Schumpeter argued that it takes newly founded companies to introduce and develop new ideas, technologies, inventions, and ultimately innovations, which displace the static and tepid incumbents. As the Harvard business historian Thomas McCraw, explains, "Schumpeter's signature legacy is his insight that innovation in the form of creative destruction is the driving force not only of capitalism but of material progress in general. Almost all businesses, no matter how strong they seem to be at a given moment, ultimately fail—and almost always because they failed to innovate."[13]

McCraw goes on to point out that Schumpeter "knew that creative destruction fosters economic growth but also that it undercuts cherished human values. He saw that poverty brings misery but also that prosperity cannot assure peace of mind."[14]

Where did this creative destruction come from? Again, Schumpeter had an answer. It was the entrepreneur who triggered the creative destruction underlying positive change and was the driving force for innovation, upon which economic development, growth, and progress rested. Schumpeter argued that what made the entrepreneur different from other agents in the economy was his high valuation of change: "The function of entrepreneurs is to reform or revolutionize the pattern of production by exploiting an invention, or more generally, an untried technological possibility for producing a new commodity or producing an old one in a new way. . . . To undertake such new things is difficult and constitutes a distinct economic function, first because they lie outside of the routine tasks which everybody understands, and secondly, because the environment resists in many ways."[15] Without the entrepreneur, new ideas would not be implemented and pursued. The status quo would tend to be preserved at an opportunity cost of forgone innovative activity, growth, and economic development.

As the IBM executive penned in his now-famous memo in 1986 writing off the offer by Bill Gates to sell his fledgling start-up Microsoft for a paltry sum: "Neither Gates nor any of his band of thirty some employees have anything approaching the credentials or personal characteristics required to work at IBM."[16]

Certainly the metaphor of creative destruction wonderfully describes the disruption, both organizationally and personally, needed to move forward into the future in a positive way, or to change for the better. America is enamored with examples such as Apple Computer emerging and crowding out the less technically gifted DEC Computer, just as Microsoft has pushed aside IBM as the dominant computer company.

But Germany is different. The system of *Konsens*, or consensus, combined with a rich institutional landscape of organizations designed to engage and facilitate interorganizational and intersectoral thinking and ideas is more conducive to incremental change.[17] One resolution to the paradox of German rigidity in the static context but flexibility in the dynamic context is that institutions, organizations, behavior, and habits seem to be inextricably rooted and anchored beyond the hope of reform or change—in the static context.

However, in the dynamic context, the very nature of German institutions and governance facilitates institutional change. As a team of leading German labor economists concludes, "The remarkable transformation of the German economy from the 'sick man of Europe' to a lean and highly competitive economy within little more than a decade is rooted in the inherent flexibility of the German system of industrial relations. This system allowed German industry to react appropriately and flexibly over time to the demands of German unification, and the global challenges of a new world economy."[18]

One of the leading economists in Germany and former president of the German Economics Association (Verein für Socialpolitik), Professor Michael C. Burda of Humboldt University, has pointed out that the institutional mechanisms of employer associations, along with the involvement of trade unions in company decision-making, resulted in wage concessions as a strategy to combat global competition. Viewed over longer periods of time, Germany seems to exhibit not only more change than many of its neighbors, but more changes in a direction conducive to a positive economic performance.[19]

Germany mirrored its European neighbors in its economic despair throughout the decade of the 1990s. In fact, the economic performance in terms of growth and unemployment was generally worse and more discouraging in Germany than it was in its European counterparts such as France, Sweden, Finland, the Netherlands, and the United Kingdom, but also Italy, Ireland, and even Spain. It certainly started to seem that Germany might no longer be in the Champions League.

How did the country manage to break away from the pack as the continent descended into the economic despair of the first decade of this century? What sets Germany apart from other European countries, indeed from many of its OECD counterparts, is the ability to change and adapt to a changing world.

A country rooted in inflexibility and rigidities does not seem a likely candidate to champion change.

But change is exactly what the country did. In 2003, under the leadership of Chancellor Gerhard Schröder, a series of labor reforms, referred to as the Hartz Reforms,[20] were implemented to inject a considerable degree of new flexibility into the labor markets.[21] Among other things, the Hartz Reforms attacked a number of what had been considered the "sacred cows" of German labor policy. For example, the generous long-term unemployment benefits, which had clearly become an assumed entitlement, were drastically trimmed. Other labor reforms loosened prohibitive restrictions against part-time work to enable more temporary work and increased flexibility in hiring and firing practices.

While the Hartz Reforms were the focus of public and media scrutiny, many other aspects of Germany changed along with the labor market regulations. In the first rigorous comparison of educational outcomes within Europe, the Pisa study, the educational system of Germany was exposed as being deficient and ineffective. Under Chancellor Schroeder's leadership, the educational system was fundamentally reformed, so that in subsequent years the international performance of education in Germany has improved considerably. The Exzellenz Initiative was introduced to upgrade Germany's university and research prowess, as a cornerstone of transforming the economy into one driven by knowledge, research, and innovation.

Diversity

Deutschland literally means "land of the Germans".[22] A country consisting of and open to immigrants and a broad spectrum of ethnic nationalities might be fine for Australia or the United States, but they are both inherently melting pots. Germany is different. Or at least used to be different. In recent years, Germany has charged ahead in allowing and even encouraging immigration of many types, so much so that it has become a melting pot nation itself. Deutschland is no longer a country exclusively for ethnic Germans.

It would be inaccurate to think of contemporary Germany as anything but a country with high immigration. For example, in 2012, Germany ranked second in number of immigrants among OECD countries with 399,900, placing it only behind the United States, with 1,031,000 immigrants, but ahead of the United Kingdom, with 282,600 immigrants. As *Der Spiegel* concludes, "Look at Germany now: It has indisputably become a nation of immigration."[23]

Living with high levels of immigration and the resulting diversity is anything other than easy or *selbstverständlich*. Like almost all countries that are dynamic and welcoming to an inflow of people from a broad spectrum of countries and nationalities, the country struggles with integration and a new identity. As *Der Spiegel* ponders, "Who is German? And who should be allowed to become German? Are we a country that allows dual citizenship? Do we prefer citizenship that is based on the concept of *Jus sanguinis*, the right of blood passed down only from family members who are citizens of a state, or *Jus soli*, the right of citizenship for anyone born on German territory? And are we a country that should encourage Green Cards for immigrant workers or should we promote ethnic German children? These are debates that for years made it difficult for people who weren't born with 'German blood' to become part of our society or even citizens. If you're not like us, then you don't belong. Those kinds of ideas are the source of considerable tension."[24]

The extent to which Germany has become a country far more diverse than just ethnic Germans became clear when the President of Germany, Christian Wulff, pronounced in 2010 that "Islam is now a part of Germany."[25] The diversity of Germany is reflected in its soccer *Nationalmannschaft*, which has exhibited an increasing degree of diversity in recent years. The World Cup–winning team included Mesut Özil, who has Turkish origins, Jérôme Boateng, whose father is from Ghana, Sami Khedira, who has Tunisian origins, and Miroslav Klose, who was originally from Poland.

Not only is Germany a destination for the inflow of people from other countries, but there is considerable evidence that those people feel comfortable and are happy to be in Germany. In 2014 the Ministry of Migration and Refugees in Germany undertook a survey of immigrants, which revealed that those with a high degree of human capital feel comfortable and positive about living in Germany.[26] In particular, 68.6 percent of immigrants in Germany with high human capital and 75 percent of those immigrants from outside of the European Union with a higher-education degree aspired to remain in Germany for at least a decade.

Widespread acceptance and integration of foreigners in Germany is new. The American journalist Peter Ross Range returned to Germany fifty-one years after he had been an exchange student in Bremerhaven.[27] Looking back to his days as an exchange student, he recalls seeing and meeting almost exclusively Germans. There was hardly anyone other than Germans around. In the subsequent half century, things have changed considerably. While he reports that "once there, it feels like a second home," he also notices some striking differences that have changed with the passage of time. Perhaps most notable is the shift from being a country comprised almost exclusively of Germans, to now being a melting pot consisting of a great variety and diversity of peoples with a wide range of ethnic, national, and geographic backgrounds: "Right in the Frankfurt airport, I notice big changes. Lots of dark-skinned people working in the airport, more than I've ever seen before. Some of them speak with accents; others speak German like school kids in a Hessian village. They all seem to fit right in."[28]

Immigration and diversity are certainly not new topics or themes in Germany. The Wirtschaftswunder of the 1950s was so successful in wiping out unemployment that Germany began to face labor shortages. Thanks to its stronger and more dynamic economy, East Germans migrated with increasing numbers to West Germany, where unfilled jobs were in abundance.[29] Estimates place the number of Germans switching from the German Democratic Republic in East Germany to the Federal Republic of Germany in West Germany between the end of World War II in 1945 and August 1961 at 3.8 million people.[30]

Confronted with such an exodus of labor, the pressure grew in East Germany to do something to close the floodgates. The response was to erect the Berlin Wall in August 1961. East Germany had simply become fed up with investing in the labor skills, training, and human capital of its people only to have its western counterpart reap the benefits from those costly investments. With the erection of the Berlin Wall in 1961, the labor spigot was turned off. As a result, labor shortages in West Germany became that much more acute as thousands of people who lived in the East but had been attracted to commute daily to their better-paying jobs, or even migrate to the West, were suddenly trapped behind the Iron Curtain.

To alleviate the chronic shortage of labor, West Germany created the legal category of *Gastarbeiter*, or guest worker. The *Gastarbeiter* was the result of specific bilateral recruitment agreements that Germany signed with other countries, beginning in 1955 with Italy, followed by Greece and Spain in 1960, Ireland and Turkey in 1961, Portugal in 1964, Tunisia in 1965, and Yugoslavia in 1968.[31] Typically workers from those targeted countries would be given the legal right to work at particular jobs in particular industries for a specific period of time, ranging between one and two years.

Prior to the Berlin Wall being erected, in 1960, only 1.2 percent of the total German population consisted of Gastarbeiter, largely from Italy, or 686,000 people.[32] By 1973, the number of Gastarbeiter had reached 2.6 million, which accounted for nearly 7 percent of the country's total population. The origin of the Gastarbeiter had shifted away from Italy, which accounted only for 17 percent of the Gastarbeiter, to Turkey, which accounted for well over one in five of the Gastarbeiter.[33]

The number of foreigners with the status of legal residents increased to 7.3 million by 2003, which accounted for 8.9 percent of the population. The country of origin most prevalent was Turkey, which had 1.9 million Turkish citizens living in Germany, of which 654,000 were born in Germany. An additional 575,000 people had Turkish origins but had been naturalized as German citizens. In addition, there were over one million foreigners from the former Yugoslavia. Around four-fifths of all foreigners living in Germany had European origins, while another 12 percent came from Asia.[34] By 2010 the number of people of Turkish descent living in Germany had increased to four million.

The Wirtschaftswunder of the 1950s and 1960s was fueled by industrial production in manufacturing industries. The chronic shortage of labor confronting (West) Germany consisted mainly of unskilled workers to man the production lines in assembly factories. Thus, the Gastarbeiter consisted mainly of unskilled workers who were trained and acquired the requisite labor skills, to a considerable extent, in Germany.[35]

The New Immigrants

Germany's contemporary economic success has once again resulted in a shortage of labor. However, the difference from the earlier Wirtschaftswunder is that this shortage involves a considerably greater share of highly skilled workers and those with high human capital. Thus, a major policy concern confronting Germany has been how to best increase the supply of skilled and high-human-capital workers. One important way is through increased immigration, not just of any type of worker, but with a particular focus on high human capital and skilled labor. As the journalist Peter Ross Range notes, "Germany is desperate to fill a shortage of trained workers, now and especially in the future. The difference between today's labor shortage and the need for guest workers in the 1950s and 1960s is education: The German economy doesn't need coal miners and street cleaners so much as highly-skilled machine operators and computer-savvy information specialists. And it is willing to train them in Germany."[36]

To alleviate the chronic shortage of labor, and especially skilled labor, Germany has had to inject considerable more diversity into the ethnic composition of people living in its cities. However, attracting people with little or minimal labor skills is very different than attracting highly skilled workers with high levels of human capital. They have a choice about where to locate. Success in attracting what Richard Florida characterizes as the creative class means having a city, state, and country that is attractive to foreign people spanning a broad spectrum of nationalities and ethnic backgrounds. As the journalist Fareed Zakaria shares what the former leader of Israel, Shimon Peres, emphasized to him: "You cannot be global and racist. Finished. You cannot be global and even nationalistic."[37]

Germany has done exactly that. Peter Ross Range is amazed at the changes in Germany that have taken place between the *Zeitalter*, or era, of the Gastarbeiter and today's contemporary highly skilled and educated immigrants: "I discovered a new term in the German newspapers: the 'culture of welcome!' It means a kind of official open-arms attitude towards immigrants."[38]

The headline-grabbing opponents of immigration, like Pegida,[39] which began as a reaction of almost exclusively middle-class people in the new eastern *Bundesländer* against recent Islamic attacks, are small in numbers compared to the thousands who participated in the counterdemonstrations that almost immediately took place in response in nearly every large city in Germany. In unusually strong language, Chancellor Angela Merkel used her 2015 New Year's Day address to reaffirm Germany's welcome to asylum-seekers and urged Germans to keep a safe distance from Pegida: "Do not follow people who organize these rallies, for their hearts are cold and often full of prejudice, and even hate."[40]

Der Spiegel considers Germany "a nation of immigration."[41] This is echoed by the greatly respected Swiss newspaper the *Neue Zürcher Zeitung*: "Germany is increasingly becoming a modern country of immigration."[42]

This new welcoming attitude toward immigrants and people of diverse ethnic origins has not been lost on foreigners. Perhaps more striking, people from Israel are also drawn and attracted to contemporary Germany. For example, one report from Berlin suggests that "Israelis have for years been drawn to Berlin's cosmopolitan flair, vibrant arts scene and advanced public transportation. There are already several places in the city where one can have authentic hummus, and there is a bio-monthly Hebrew-language magazine."[43]

Der Spiegel reports official estimates of Israelis living in Berlin ranging between twenty thousand and forty thousand people.[44] This is a sharp contrast to the widespread perception as recently as a decade ago there were "no Israelis around."[45] In what seems like an explosion of Israelis living in Berlin, now it is difficult to leave one's flat "without picking up some Hebrew from the sidewalk."[46] As Gregor Schlosser of the Chamber of

German-Israel Commerce (AHK-Israel) shares, "For many young Israelis, Berlin is the city of dreams, similar to Tel Aviv—free, liberal, and anything goes."[47]

The current economic boom in Baden-Württemberg has resulted in a shortage of skilled labor, which, if unabated, will ultimately serve as a drag on economic performance. According to Norbert Czerwinski, who works in human resource development in Mannheim, "Small and mid-sized companies are desperate for new employees and trainees."[48] As *Der Spiegel*, a leading news magazine in Germany reports, "Unless countermeasures are taken, the Rhine-Neckar region of southwestern Germany could see a shortfall of about 35,000 skilled workers. "[49]

The strategy developed by the state of Baden-Württemberg, as well as the individual cities and towns located in that *Bundesland*, is to try to offset the shortage of skilled workers by attracting workers with similar skills level from southern Europe, which is suffering a plague of unemployment. This strategy, however, poses a number of daunting challenges. As *Der Spiegel* reports, "Workers from Southern Europe are in demand in booming towns like Villingen-Schwenningen and Schwäbisch Hall. Unfortunately, these places have names that mean almost nothing to people in Spain and Portugal."[50] In addition, there is the obvious language barrier, as well as significant cultural differences.

Representatives from the region—from the private, nonprofit, and government sectors—have given talks at schools and universities in cities such as Barcelona and Lisbon. Journalists from southern Europe have been invited to visit the region. As *Der Spiegel* observes, "Advertisements have been taken out in Greek newspapers to tout the benefits of living and working in smaller German cities and rural areas. The Confederation of German Employer Associations (BDA) even published a guideline for business owners on the subject of creating a 'welcoming culture,' while municipalities have studied ways to integrate the new arrivals from the south."[51]

The point to be emphasized here is that the region of Baden-Württemberg is not simply waiting for the lure of a job at a comparatively high wage rate to induce workers to move away from the high unemployment at home. Rather, through its targeted and strategic *Standortpolitik*, highly skilled and high-human-capital workers from other countries are actively being courted and encouraged to relocate to Baden-Württemberg.

In his penetrating look at contemporary Berlin, the German novelist and critic Peter Schneider describes the diversity of types of people, in every sense of the word, found in Berlin: "Standing in line at the legendary club Berhain, where the doors open at midnight on Friday and the party continues into Sunday, Mr. Schneider finds himself in the company of Japanese, Australians, Portuguese, Americans—and even a few Germans."[52] Schneider goes on to wonder about Israeli Jews who have fallen in love with Berlin: "What is it that could attract people back to the country in which their parents and grandparents were so viciously persecuted?"[53]

Some of the flexibility prevalent in Berlin is derived from its twisted and onerous history, or what Schneider refers to as the city's "mutability."[54] Everyone knows, of course, that Berlin serves as the capital of Germany. What is less known, and certainly startling, is that the same city has served as the capital of five distinct Germanys. A sixth could be included if Prussia is also counted. Berlin has served as the capital of Bismarck's Reich, the Weimar Republic, the Third Reich, the German Democratic Republic, and the Federal Republic of Germany after the capital was moved from Bonn to Berlin in the early 1990s.

As the *Wall Street Journal* reports, "Berlin has been many different things to many different Germans, and this gives the city a feeling of unlimited possibility. If New York is the city where anyone can make it, Berlin is the city where anything can happen. A bar can sprout up, seemingly overnight, in a disused industrial space on the banks of the Spree and transform, as the famous Bar 25 did in the 2000s, into an all-purpose recreation center for the young and underemployed: nightclub, art gallery, yoga studio and gourmet restaurant, all rolled into one."[55]

Country of origin, ethnicity, and cultural background are only one dimension of diversity. A very different dimension of diversity, and way to enhance the amount of human capital and skilled labor in the workforce, involves gender. Expanding the participation of females in all aspects of the labor force, but particularly in highly trained and high-human-capital occupations has been a top policy priority.[56] For example, most organizations and firms now include a *Frauenbeauftragte*, or representative of female employees, on many boards and official committees.

The focus on increasing the participation of females is evidenced by the CEO of Fischer, Klaus Fischer. He has created a special event, "Girls Day," with a specific focus on recruiting females: "We must train more females for technical work."[57]

The labor force participation rate of females has increased drastically over time. In 1970, the (West) German female participation rate of 38.4 percent ranked among the lowest in Europe and among OECD countries.[58] However, since then the labor force participation of females has risen considerably, to nearly 58 percent by 2010.

Most striking, the Bundestag, or parliament, unanimously passed a new law in March 2015 requiring a *Frauenquote*, or female quota, for the board of directors on the leading publicly traded companies.[59] While the top hundred publicly traded companies are required to have 30 percent women on their board of directors starting in 2016, this will be expanded to around 3,500 companies. Similar appointments in government and other public agencies and institutions will also be affected, along with the goal of having one-half of *Beamter*, or civil service positions be comprised of females.

The increased ethnic and gender diversity has increased the *quantity* of skilled and unskilled labor in Germany. But it has also enhanced the *quality* in an important way. A focus on quantity considers labor to be interchangeable or fungible within any skills category or level of human capital.

Richard Florida, in *The Rise of the Creative Class*, sees it differently.[60] In particular, Florida, drawing on the great scholar of urban issues Jane Jacobs,[61] argues that differences among people, or diversity, can actually spur creativity and innovation. In a world of perfect homogeneity, or where everyone was a perfect clone of each other, there would be no gains from interaction. Everybody would react to any particular situation, or information set, in an identical way. However, in a world of heterogeneity, it is the differences across people that lead to gains from interaction. Florida[62] argues that the degree of diversity reflected by the population and workers in a place contributes to the tolerance and acceptance of new ideas. Essentially, diversity of population and workforce translates into a diversity of ideas and ultimately innovative activity. Thus, while the more traditional argument involving diversity referred to the industrial or economic structure, Florida's more contemporary version refers to the people and workforce at the place. According to Florida, "The key to success today lies in developing a world-class people climate. By this I mean a general strategy aimed at attracting and retaining people—especially, but not limited to, creative people. This entails remaining open to diversity and actively working to cultivate it, and investing in lifestyle amenities that people really want and use often, as opposed to using financial incentives to attract companies, build professional sports stadiums or develop retail complexes."[63]

Similarly, Carlos Haertel, director of General Electric Global Research Europe, shares the strategy of General Electric: "In research based business, the one thing that is crucial for growth is talented people."[64] According to Haertel, General Electric originally conducted research and development only at its headquarters in New York State. Then, in 2000, it realized that "inputs to innovation come from outside of the firm—proximity matters. To be able to connect is crucial for innovation. You have to go to where the people are"[65] in order to access the best talent. Subsequently, General Electric opened research facilities in Munich. As Haertel concludes, "If you want to get the best and brightest you have to go where people like to live."[66]

Haertel's observation implies that locational choice is not just a key strategic variable for firms but also for individuals as well, "especially people who have choices. The environment has to be attractive to them and their families."[67] In particular, educated people with high levels of human capital will consider how location will enhance their human capital.[68] Individuals tend to locate at places that enhance their human capital, skill, or talent, ultimately making them more valuable. Horace Greely's "Go west, young man," to access the frontier and its natural resources, reinterpreted for the modern youth might be "Go to the place that accepts you, fosters your talent, and enhances your knowledge," in order to not just survive in the contemporary globalized economy, but to thrive.

Increasingly that place has been Germany – not just the land of Germans, but a land that is home to a broad group of people spanning diverse ethnic backgrounds and nationalities. As the former president of the country, Roman Herzog, insightfully observed, Germany may be a land of lederhosen, but thanks to its dynamic flexibility, it has made room for laptops as well.

Conclusions

The euphoria triggered by the fall of the Berlin Wall on November 9, 1989, did not last long. Along with the newfound freedom in Eastern and Central Europe, which quickly spread throughout China and the rest of Asia, came a more sobering realization. The post–World War II structure of comparative advantage that had served as a bedrock for Western stability had been fundamentally shaken by the sudden inclusion of almost all countries into an increasingly integrated global economy.

Much of Europe, not the least Germany, spent the subsequent decade fending off what was widely perceived to be the intrusive and unwelcome impact of a destructive globalizing economy triggered by that very same fall of the Berlin Wall, with the opening up of Eastern Europe and ultimately the rest of the world. As the Nobel Prize winning economist Michael Spence, writing in *Foreign Affairs*, explains, "Globalization is the process by which markets integrate worldwide."[69]

Spence goes on to point out that "globalization hurts some subgroups within some countries, including the advanced economies."[70] Europe gloomily realized that globalization is a double-edged sword confronting the West with what is characterized in *Foreign Affairs* as "the big tradeoff."[71] On the one hand is the goal of preserving traditional values, culture, institutions, and indeed, an entire way of life. However, this seems to come at the cost of succumbing to an inevitable economic decline in the face of more competitive, lower-cost competition elsewhere in the world.

On the other hand is the prospect of taking advantage of the opportunities afforded by globalization to ensure sustainable prosperity and a high standard of living into the future. But this can seemingly be attained only at the cost of sacrificing many of the traditions, institutions, values, and culture upon which the foundation of Europe is based.

Germany has defied this assumption. Few other countries, certainly not in Europe, have been able to defy the seemingly ironclad trade-off between cultural, political, and social integrity on the one hand, and economic viability on the other. France, for example, considers globalization to be the root of such an untenable and unacceptable policy trade-off. In "France Demonizes Globalization," Pascal Lamy, the French former director-general of the World Trade Organization, worries that "what the French have as a specificity is that they are the only one on this planet to demonize globalization."[72]

Germany has found a way to make globalization work. The secret is not to abandon its lederhosen in favor of laptops, but by embracing flexibility in key areas, such as labor markets, Germany is able to leverage its strongly rooted traditions to generate competitiveness in the globalized economy.

7 Made in Germany

MANUFACTURING IS WHAT made America rich. It enabled President Abraham Lincoln to fend off the agrarian-based rebels in the South to persevere in the American Civil War. It fueled the emergence of all of the great cities of the previous century. David's grandfather, Don Lochbiler, was a newspaperman much of his adult life with the *Detroit News*. After retiring, he published his sole book, *Detroit's Coming of Age*, which celebrated the emergence of not just a world-class automobile industry proudly shipping its products to the rest of the world, but also one of the most prosperous and wealthy cities of its day, Detroit.[1] As Martin S. Hayden, who served as the editor of the *Detroit News*, wrote in the preface to *Detroit's Coming of Age*, "In the story of urban America it would be difficult to parallel the evolution of the city of Detroit from a localized hub of Michigan and Great Lakes commerce to the 1973 sprawling giant known worldwide as the birthplace of the industrial mass production."[2]

But it wasn't just Detroit. Rochester, New York, similarly provides an example where the performance of a city was inextricably linked to that of a dominant manufacturing corporation, Kodak. As Kodak emerged as the leading company in the photography and film industry, its strong economic performance was leveraged by Rochester to ensure that the city enjoyed its share of wealth and prosperity. Similarly, the impressive ability of Cleveland, Ohio, to generate jobs, growth, and wealth a century ago was linked to the dominance of Standard Oil, just as the strong economic performance of Akron, Ohio, stemmed from the dominant US tire companies.

Economic success meant manufacturing. Ralph Gomory, the former IBM vice president of science and technology reflects, "Manufacturing was once widely recognized as the outstanding strength of America and the basis of its prosperity."[3]

As Barbara Streisand sings in the film in which she costars with Robert Redford, that is "The Way We Were." But no more. In 1950, over 16 million Americans were employed in manufacturing.[4] Employment in manufacturing in the United States continued to rise until its peak in 1978 at around 19 million. And then the decline started. Today, employment in manufacturing is around 12 million people.[5] Over that same time period the share of the labor force employed in manufacturing has dropped from one in three to fewer than one in ten.

One reaction is simply to accept the massive decline in manufacturing as inevitable but not consequential. In an article titled "Why Manufacturing Doesn't Matter," *Forbes*, the magazine for the finance community, explains, "We all know the factors that have led to economic success in the industrial era: access to land, labor, raw materials, capital, machinery, and (in many cases, anyway) a good idea. Today, all of those traditional advantages are falling away except one: the good idea. We are leaving the industrial era and entering the innovation economy, where manufacturing is a commodity and the idea, a.k.a. intellectual property, trumps all."[6]

Bloomberg Business Week concurs in an article titled "Factory Jobs Are Gone: Get Over It."[7] The article argues that the "factory obsession is based on flawed economics," and backs up its view by referring to an economist at the prestigious Brookings Institution, Justin Wolfers, who ponders, "What's with the political fetish for manufacturing? Are factories really so awesome?"[8]

N. Greg Mankiw, who at the time served as chair of the Council of Economic Advisors under President George W. Bush, lectured an audience in Washington, DC, in 2003 "that the more recent fall in manufacturing jobs was an 'inescapable' consequence of rapid productivity growth."[9] Mankiw argued that "the long-term trends that we have recently seen in manufacturing mirror what we saw in agriculture a couple of generations ago."[10] Similarly, the professor of economics at the University of Chicago, Austan Goolsbee, who served on the Council of Economic Advisors under President Obama, made exactly the same point. The decline in manufacturing jobs was not only inevitable, but also unproblematic: "Employment in the [manufacturing] sector and the share of spending in the sector get smaller and smaller almost as proof of how productive it has become. It is exactly the same process that agriculture went through."[11]

According to this *Why worry, be happy* view, "Manufacturing is better left to others. The nation is actually fortunate to be losing manufacturing and aiming to replace it with design, research, and services."[12]

However, not everyone is willing not to worry. Other scholars and thought leaders, as well as policymakers, express considerable concern about not just the decline of manufacturing, but the erosion of the economy and society that seems to go along with it. A visit to Detroit, Cleveland, or Gary, Indiana, illustrates what happens when manufacturing is lost and little else is generated to take its place.

And not just in the United States. Nicolas Sarkozy, the former president of France, declared that France would stop being a great nation "the day we don't build trains, airplanes, automobiles and ships."[13] He has reason to be concerned. The share of the labor force employed in manufacturing has been cut in half in France since 1970, from 28 percent to less than 14 percent. The French experience mirrors the loss of manufacturing sweeping throughout Europe as well as the rest of the OECD. An article in one of the world's most influential daily newspapers, *The Guardian*, wonders, "Why Doesn't Britain Make Things Anymore?" and warns that "in the past 30 years, the UK's manufacturing sector has shrunk by two-thirds, the greatest de-industrialization of any major nation. It was done in the name of economic modernization—but what has replaced it?"[14]

But not in Germany. Manufacturing continues to provide the vital economic backbone of the country. As Charles W. Wessner, the former director of the Board on Science, Technology and Economic Policy of the National Research Council at the United States National Academies of Sciences and Engineering, points out, "The 2008 financial crisis left most industrialized nations reeling. Yet Germany, especially its manufacturing sector, has done exceedingly well."[15] The numbers back up Wessner's claim. While manufacturing accounts for only 13 percent of GDP in the United States and 12 percent of GDP in the United Kingdom, the manufacturing share of GDP in Germany is nearly twice as high, at 21 percent.

As Wessner explains, "While other industrialized nations have buckled under Asian competition, Germany has increased exports to China and the rest of Asia."[16] He then goes on to wonder, "How is Germany doing this? How is a highly regulated, high-wage country with a strong currency increasing its share of the global market in the face of low-cost Asian competition?"[17] He is not alone in wondering. In fact, much of the developed world would like to know how and why *Made in Germany* still resonates, even in the era of globalization. The purpose of this chapter is to explain why *Made in Germany* matters even today and, just as importantly, why this is one of the secrets to Germany's economic resilience.

The German Difference

The decline of manufacturing in the developed countries is broadly attributed to globalization, and in particular to the advent of lower-cost competition from Asia. In his bestselling book, *The World Is Flat*, Thomas Friedman explains how the process of globalization triggered the decline of manufacturing in the developed countries, including the United States.[18] Friedman explains that countries of Asia, along with Eastern and Central Europe, had previously been left on the sidelines, unable to participate in the great trading and economic integration that had been developed in the OECD countries. It was that openness to trade and the mobility of factors of production, such as capital and people, that had contributed greatly to the astonishing growth of the West, along with Japan and the Asian Tigers, after World War II.

The fall of the Berlin Wall changed all that. With the opening up of Eastern Europe and the massive countries of China and India, the structure of comparative advantage was fundamentally shaken up. It became possible to trade with these countries and to build plants and open up facilities accessing lower-cost resources, and in particular labor, that had previously been inaccessible. Friedman provides colorful examples of the outsourcing and offshoring of production from the high-cost developed countries to these new low-cost entrants into the world economy.[19]

However, America's trouble with manufacturing actually started considerably earlier. A decade prior to the fall of the Berlin Wall, by the end of the 1970s the crisis of manufacturing in the United States had already started. As Japan and Europe recovered from the devastation of World War II and gradually regained their own manufacturing prowess, lower-cost automobile and steel imports surged dramatically in the United States, causing devastation of its domestic production, employment, and ultimately the viability of the products of manufacturing-based Midwestern cities, ranging from tires in Akron to steel in Pittsburgh and Gary to automobiles in Detroit, along with many smaller communities dependent upon suppliers. Economic growth stalled, and unemployment skyrocketed.

Economists, thought leaders, and policymakers branded this economic misery the "competitiveness crisis." American manufacturing companies simply were not able to compete against their more efficient overseas rivals enjoying state-of-the art factories, which had been built after the war, and access to lower-cost labor.

So began the long decline of manufacturing in the United States. In the United Kingdom it was hardly different. As in the United States, the decline of manufacturing activity started at the end of the decade of the 1970s and early 1980s. As the *Guardian* recalls, "When Thatcher came to power, manufacturing accounted for almost 30 percent of Britain's national income and employed 6.8 million people. By the time Brown left Downing Street last May, it was down to just over 11 percent of the economy, with a workforce of 2.5 million."[20]

However, just as in the United States, no single political party can be blamed for the decline of manufacturing. It may have started under Prime Minister Margaret Thatcher, but continued to gain momentum even as the party in office changed. "It was with Tony Blair that the argument for moving from industry to services shifted from one of dire necessity to being an altogether more optimistic vision about Britain's place in the world. The architects of New Labour were convinced that the future lay in what they called the 'knowledge economy.' Mandelson declared Silicon Valley his 'inspiration'; Brown swore he would make Britain the e-commerce capital of the world within three years."[21]

The *Guardian* explains that this economic strategy revolved around abandoning manufacturing for economic activity that could not be outsourced and offshored so easily, such as knowledge and services: "Again, the theme was simple: most of what could be manufactured could be done so more cheaply elsewhere. The future lay in coming up with the ideas, the software, and most of all, the brands. Once the British had sold cars and ships to the rest of the world; now they could flog culture and tourism and Lara Croft."[22]

The loss of manufacturing has been devastating in France, as well. As *Der Spiegel* reports, "Sarkozy was unable to stop the dismantling of factories in France. The number of jobs in the auto industry declined by more than half between 1980 and 2010."[23] However, *Der Spiegel*, goes on to point out that "this was not an inevitable development, as evidenced by the situation in neighboring Germany, where VW, Daimler, BMW and the like employ more people now than they did three decades ago."[24]

Why has Germany been impervious to the twin symptoms afflicting manufacturing in the developed countries, outsourcing and offshoring, enabling it to maintain its competitiveness? The answer is not a low-valued currency, as has been the case for China. Almost since its introduction in 2001, the euro has had a high value relative to the other major currencies, such as the US dollar. In any case, Germany and France, along with all of the other countries included in the eurozone, all have the same currency; yet somehow manufacturing in Germany continues to thrive, while it fades to worrisome levels in many of the neighboring countries. Rather, a number of policies and institutions have contributed to enabling German companies to access highly productive factors in the manufacturing process, which in turn has made *Standort Deutschland*, or the location of Germany, attractive and competitive for manufacturing.

These policies and institutions include the nurturing of key translational institutes and agencies and organizations, facilitating the application of new technological developments at universities and technical colleges (*Fachhochschule*), a highly skilled labor force that, to a large extent, is trained through government-subsidized training and apprentice programs, a willingness among workers and their unions to accept modest wage increases in order to maintain employment levels, an excellent infrastructure, a unique Mittelstand with its own qualitative advantages, and cities that are so vibrant, attractive, and diverse that highly skilled foreign workers are not deterred from joining the workforce in Germany.

In particular, a key factor underlying Germany's manufacturing prowess is the rich and diverse set of research institutes that provide key knowledge, technology, and human capital inputs for German manufacturing companies. Most notable are the sixty-seven institutes comprising the Fraunhofer Society. While the institutes comprising the Max Planck Society are perhaps more famous and receive their share of world attention, not to mention Nobel Prize winners, the focus is on fundamental research, or "knowledge for its own sake" that moves a research or academic discipline forward.

By contrast, the Fraunhofer Institutes focus is on applied research, with the goal of providing solutions that have a commercial value. In particular, Fraunhofer Institutes provide a bridge between basic research and commercial applications by business.

There is nothing comparable to the Fraunhofer Institutes in the United States—other than the handful of Fraunhofer Institutes that are actually located there. One of the most striking examples of successfully bridging the gap between basic research and manufacturing innovative products was the development of the MP3 digital audio format by the Fraunhofer Institute for Integrated Circuits, which has its headquarters in Erlangen.[25] The compression algorithm was invented and patented by the Fraunhofer Institute for Integrated Circuits, which had reaped 100 million euros in licensing revenues as of 2005.[26]

The Fraunhofer Institutes can best be characterized as a public-private partnership. One-third of the funding comes directly from the German government. Another third of the funding also comes from the government, but is indirect in that the funding is for government-contracted applied research. The final third of the Fraunhofer budgets comes from contracts for applied research from the private sector. In 2014 the total budget for the entire Fraunhofer Society was $2.75 billion, which was used to employ over twenty-three thousand people, many of them scientists and engineers. In 2012, the Fraunhofer Society had six thousand active patents and pending patent applications. Licensing revenue generated by the intellectual property created by the Fraunhofer Society totaled $160 million in 2012.[27]

The institutes comprising the Fraunhofer Society have contributed considerably to German manufacturing prowess by serving as an institutional conduit for the spillover of knowledge from basic research to a commercializable technology for manufacturing, and by facilitating the competitive advantage of German manufacturing companies through both process and product innovations. This has enabled German companies, especially the small and medium-sized companies, or the Mittelstand, to develop high-quality technologically advanced product niches. As Sujai Shivakumar, who is the senior program officer of the Board on Science, Technology and Economic Policy at the National Research Council of the National Academies, points out, the participation and contribution of the Fraunhofer Institutes has resulted in coupling the manufacturing process to the innovation process at the same location, or *Standort*: "The knowledge crucial to innovation falls apart if you're not actually producing stuff yourself."[28]

Similarly, Charles Wessner points out that "one source of German success is its concentrated efforts to support research relevant to small- and medium-size enterprises that are less likely to move production offshore. Through Fraunhofer, Germany offers skills, equipment and services that those companies could not afford on their own. As a result, Germany has strengthened its export-oriented manufacturing base and retained good manufacturing jobs, even though its workers' wages are among the highest in the world."[29]

For example, the Fraunhofer Institute for Applied Informatics in St. Augustin has worked closely with German companies to develop data-management tools and scanning technology at the level of molecules. Similarly, the Fraunhofer Institute for Building

Physics, which is located in Stuttgart, has worked together with construction companies to develop new noise-canceling materials and to design buildings more efficiently using hygrothermal analysis, or the analysis of how heat and moisture move through a structure.[30]

The Fraunhofer Institute for Applied Optics and Precision Engineering in Jena leverages a century-old competitive and technological advantage in optics. Together with Carl Zeiss AG and the Friedrich Schiller University of Jena, the Fraunhofer Institute has developed new technologies in optical lenses and precision cutting, such as applications for lasers for measurement and new materials resistant to light and lasers.[31] These new technologies have contributed to the cluster of optics in Jena, which includes over forty companies in a city with a population around one hundred thousand. For example, Mahr GmbH, which manufactures precision instruments, contracted the Jena Fraunhofer Institute to develop a new product that provides rapid measurement in 3D. After the technology was successfully developed, the company purchased the licensing rights and began manufacturing the new product.[32]

The Fraunhofer Institutes also inject an entrepreneurial edge in German manufacturing by encouraging employee entrepreneurship through spin-offs. For example, the Fraunhofer Institute for Applied Informatics in St. Augustin has generated five new start-ups recently based on technology developed at the institute. The former member of the Bundestag, or parliament, Ulrike Flach, reflects, "It's the most market-friendly approach to government-led research there is."[33]

The Fraunhofer Institutes embody a key mechanism in the triad of institutions comprising a virtuous circle for German manufacturing—knowledge creation and spillover institutions, local companies, typically the German Mittelstand, and a committed local policy, or *Standortpolitik*.

Perhaps more than anything, however, the secret is that Germany has remained committed to manufacturing. Such a commitment means finding policies that work and are effective in sustaining the viability of manufacturing. While other countries have been quick to abandon any hope of retaining a large share of manufacturing, Germany has purposefully and methodically created conditions to generate a global competitive advantage.

At the heart of this strategy has been a relentless focus on innovation and quality. According to Michael Shank, who is the vice president at the Institute for Economics and Peace in the United States, and Thorben Albrecht, who is head of the Strategy ad Policy Department of the Social Democratic Party (SPD) in Germany, "Here's how they did it: Instead of trying to outcompete global markets in cheap goods, German industry specialized in high-quality products and kept its share in a growing global markets, as other European countries, Japan and the U.S. lost shares to China."[34]

The American journalist Peter Ross Range, recalls, "When I was a child growing up in America, 'Made in Germany' was a sign of solidity and workmanship. Cameras, machine tools, and BMW motorcycles were the obvious examples. Often the products were of such high quality that only the rich or the professional could afford them: Mercedes cars, Leica cameras (Volkswagen was a different matter: the Beetle was a cheap, simple car for students, teachers, hippies; I drove a Volkswagen bus). These brands are known everywhere. So is Siemens, the technology giant. But for a while, during the 1990s and 2000s, 'Made in Germany' lost its luster. Volkswagen had practically abandoned the American market. Daimler-Benz made its curious merger with Chrysler, a failed marriage that lasted from 1998 to 2007."[35]

Range goes on to point out that "today 'Made in Germany' is resurgent. Once again, German products are seen as champions at the top of the market. Germany has wisely stayed out of the mass market, leaving low-cost products and price wars to China and other low-wage producers. . . . Germany's business community refused to fall for the conventional wisdom that industrial manufacturing was dead and gone to China. Germany builds the machines that China needs to build the products that dominate world consumer markets."[36]

Perhaps the greatest difference between Germany and the countries that have lost their share of manufacturing is the institution of *Standortpolitik*. As chapter 4 makes clear, *Standortpolitik* provides a mandate for every city, region, and state in Germany to implement strategies to sustain a strong economic performance. The recent resurgence of Dresden is in no small way attributable to the strategies crafted at the local level to foster a high-technology cluster in the region. In particular, out of the shadow of four decades of communism, Dresden has sprouted a vibrant microelectronics industry. As of 2014 there were something like fifteen hundred companies and research facilities in microelectronics generating over forty-eight thousand jobs, making Dresden one of the focal points for microelectronics in Europe.[37]

The astonishing economic turnaround from the communist era to a thriving, globally competitive manufacturing success reflects a well-considered *Standortpolitik*: "Economic success is a result of courageous economic investment and development. After the communist centrally-planned economy was replaced at the beginning of the 1990s, the opportunity arose for Dresden to be restored to its former splendour—and Dresden took it with both hands. The city invested with great vigour and courage in advanced technology and its associated research. And this has paid off. Today, Dresden is considered to be one of the most dynamic and forward-looking cities with a strong economy, characterized by medium-sized businesses."[38]

In particular, this meant creating the key inputs and resources that drive competitiveness and economic success in the microelectronics industry. A dense network of non-university research institutes was created and nurtured. As of 2014 there were twelve Fraunhofer Institutes, three Leibnitz Institutes, and three prestigious Max Planck Institutes, all with a focus on developing new technologies and materials for application in the microelectronics industry. The Helmholtz-Zentrum Dresden-Rossendorf is engaged in developing devices that offer unique experimental opportunities for international research collaboration.[39]

Productivity

It is pretty clear that Germany has succeeded where others have failed—in sustaining economic activities, both employment and production—in manufacturing. How has it been able to fend off the daunting challenges posed by a globalized world economy in the form of outsourcing and offshoring, not to mention an erosion of market share due to foreign competition in low-cost countries?

The simple answer is productivity. Germany ranks among the most productive countries in the world. What is not so simple is what exactly is meant by productivity.

Labor productivity generally refers to the output per unit of labor within a certain time dimension. According to the Deutsche Bank, which provides statistics on productivity for Germany, "Productivity is the real value of output produced by a unit of labor during a certain time."[40] This is where comparisons in productivity across countries can become more nuanced. A year is, of course, identical in every country. There is nothing confusing about that. If the output is measured by GDP, then the productivity of labor is simply the value of GDP divided by the number of workers.

Productivity is what enables German companies to offset high labor costs without sacrificing competitive advantages. Thus, unit labor costs—the ratio of labor costs and productivity—reveal how a high-labor-cost country like Germany is able to attain and sustain competitiveness in global markets. Labor productivity in terms of the workforce, as shown in table 7.1, reveals that Germany ranks among the highest countries in Europe. Where the confusion starts, however, is that people do not work the same number of hours in a week or in a year in different countries. For example, it is well known that in Germany, as elsewhere in Europe, the average work week is relatively short. There are more official holidays, and workers are guaranteed six weeks of vacation each year. Productivity in table 7.1 is thus calculated as GDP at production costs per working hour. Mean value is the arithmetic mean of all countries excluding Germany, and weighted by the percentage of world exports (2010–2012).

Based on one exchange currency (row 1 of table 7.1) the international comparison of productivity provides a valuable insight into how Germany is able to main competitiveness in global markets. No large industrial country, other than the United States, shows such a high level of productivity. France, Italy, Japan, Canada, and the United Kingdom lag behind Germany.

The large differences in productivity across countries are reflected in labor costs. Norway, as an example, a country with a high level of productivity, also has to bear the highest labor costs (table 7.1). Poland is the country with the lowest level of productivity, only one-fifth of the level in Germany, but has only about 14 percent of the labor costs compared to Germany. As table 7.1 reveals, high levels of productivity do not necessarily compensate for high labor costs. This is also reflected in a comparison of the level of unit labor costs in various countries (see figure 7.1).

TABLE 7.1

Productivity and Unit Labor Costs

	Currency level	Purchasing power parity	unit labor costs (Germany = 100)
Norway	128	85	137
United States	**112**	**113**	**90**
Sweden	104	82	93
Netherlands	101	96	92
Germany	**100**	**100**	**100**
Denmark	100	76	110
Belgium	99	93	113
Austria	95	90	87
Mean value	**85**	**81**	**81**
Canada	84	70	77
Finland	83	70	90
France	81	75	93
Japan	81	62	73
Spain	73	83	62
UK	71	69	86
Italy	60	61	71
Slovenia	44	55	45
Greece	41	48	31
Slovakia	33	49	24
Lithuania	31	n.a	17
Cyprus	31	n.a	30
Czech Republic	29	43	26
Portugal	29	38	25
Latvia	24	n.a	16
Hungary	22	39	16
Estonia	21	30	19
Poland	19	33	14

Source: Christoph Schroeder, "Produktivität und Lohnstückkosten der Industrie im internationalen Vergleich," Institut der deutschen Wirtschaft, *IW Trends*, 4, 2013.

Note: Productivity is calculated by GDP at production costs per working hour. Mean value is the mean value of all countries excluding Germany, each weighted by the percentage of world exports (2010–2012).

As the comparisons of productivity and labor costs across countries show, Germany exhibits high levels of both. The seven secrets highlighted in this book, however, provide insights to two questions about productivity and economic performance. The first question is why the level of productivity is so high in Germany. The second question is how the German economy can exhibit so much resilience in an era of global turbulence. In fact, productivity levels after the global financial crisis in 2007 and in 2012 are not strikingly different.

One of the main reasons productivity is so high in Germany is the quality of labor deployed in manufacturing. The German apprentice and training system, discussed in chapter 3, ensures that manufacturing firms have access to workers with the requisite skills to maximize efficiency and productivity. The localized nature of both production and the apprenticeship program, which was the focus of chapter 3, means that the skills needed by the companies in a region are those emphasized in the apprentice and training programs. Not only do young people learn highly valued skills that are needed by local manufacturing companies, they are also taught softer skills, such as reliability and communication, needed to successfully contribute to a company.

Everyone understands the phrase "Garbage in, garbage out." In Germany, thanks in no small measure to the apprentice and training system, it's the opposite—high quality of labor in, high quality of product out.

Part of the German productivity advantage may stem from cultural differences reflecting a different sociology of work and the workplace in Germany than in, say, the United States. In Germany there is a sharp separation of the workplace and working life from the personal sphere. Most notably, Germans typically refer to each other using the formal *Sie* form in a work or office environment.

The separation of personal or private life from the *Arbeitsplatz* or work life reflects a greater degree of work-life balance in Germany. Germans simply spend less time at work than do their counterparts in the United States. Time spent at work is clearly not a reason accounting for the roughly equal output per worker between the two countries. The mean number of hours worked per worker in Germany in 2013 was 1,388.[41] By contrast, in the United States, the mean number of hours worked per worker was 1,788.

This leads to the observation that "with those numbers it would be easy to conclude that Americans *do* more and would be more productive in the workforce. It seems many Americans are born hard-wired with the belief that productivity requires *time*. There are no shortcuts for a good, Puritan work ethic. It's the American Way, after all. We love stories of companies who started with nothing and worked like dogs to become massive successes. The Sam Waltons, the Bill Gateses—these are true American heroes."[42]

By contrast, there is considerably more interface between one's work life and personal life in the United States. Consider the world-popular television series dominating the ratings for years, *Friends*. The main characters would inevitably congregate at their favorite coffee shop, where Rachel was actually on duty in many episodes. In the American workplace, people tend to interact in a familiar manner and would use the *du* form if it existed in English.

One comparison considering the structure of work between the two countries observes, "In the U.S., hanging out by the coffee machine and having a few minutes to talk while you drink your coffee is normal. So yeah, the workday is longer in the U.S., but it is also more relaxed. Longer, however does not mean more productive. About the same amount of productive work gets done in either case."[43]

Not only do Germans work fewer hours per week than do their American counterparts, they also work fewer weeks in the year. The average German worker is entitled to six weeks of vacation. By contrast, in the United States, the concept of vacation is almost disappearing. As *Der Spiegel* points out, "Much of Europe closes up shop in August. From steelworkers in Spain to technology consultants in Germany, the European Union's workers head for the coast or other vacation hot spots, forgoing the sweltering heat of Europe's cities for some rest and relaxation."[44]

Wages

The penetrating analysis of the post–World War II Wirtschaftswunder, or economic miracle, by Herbert Giersch, Karl-Heinz Paqué, and Holger Schmieding attributed both the rise and the demise of the Wirtschaftswunder largely to wages.[45] They painstakingly document that the modest wage increases in the 1950s and 1960s, even while productivity was surging ahead, greatly enhanced the competitiveness of German manufacturers vis-à-vis their international trading partners. However, as the title of their book, *The Fading Miracle*, suggests, as wage increases outstripped the growth in labor productivity, the competitiveness of German manufacturing began to fade.

A more recent study by an equally prominent team of economists, Christian Dustmann, Bernd Fitzenberger, Uta Schönberg, and Alexandra Spitz-Oener, finds that it is exactly the same force of moderate wage increases that has fueled the restoration of Germany, "From Sick Man of Europe to Economic Superstar."[46] As figure 7.1 shows, the growth of German wages over the first decade of this century was restrained, especially when compared to that of key European neighbors and trading partners.

The average annual percentage change in hourly compensation (measured in US$) from 1997 to 2013 in Germany was 3.3 percent, considerably lower than in France (3.5 percent), Italy (4.0 percent), and Spain (4.5 percent), but greater than in the United States (2.9 percent) and the United Kingdom (3.0 percent).[47]

Figure 7.2 shows that about 60 percent of hourly wage costs in Germany are payments for work time. This includes direct salaries and wages, overtime, and night work premiums. Compared to France, Italy, Austria, and Spain, pay for work time is the highest in Germany. Otherwise, costs of social insurance, which comprises retirement and disability pensions, health insurance, income guarantee insurance, pay for sick leave, life and accident insurance, occupational injury and illness compensation, unemployment insurance, and severance pay, among others, are rather low in Germany, compared to the other key

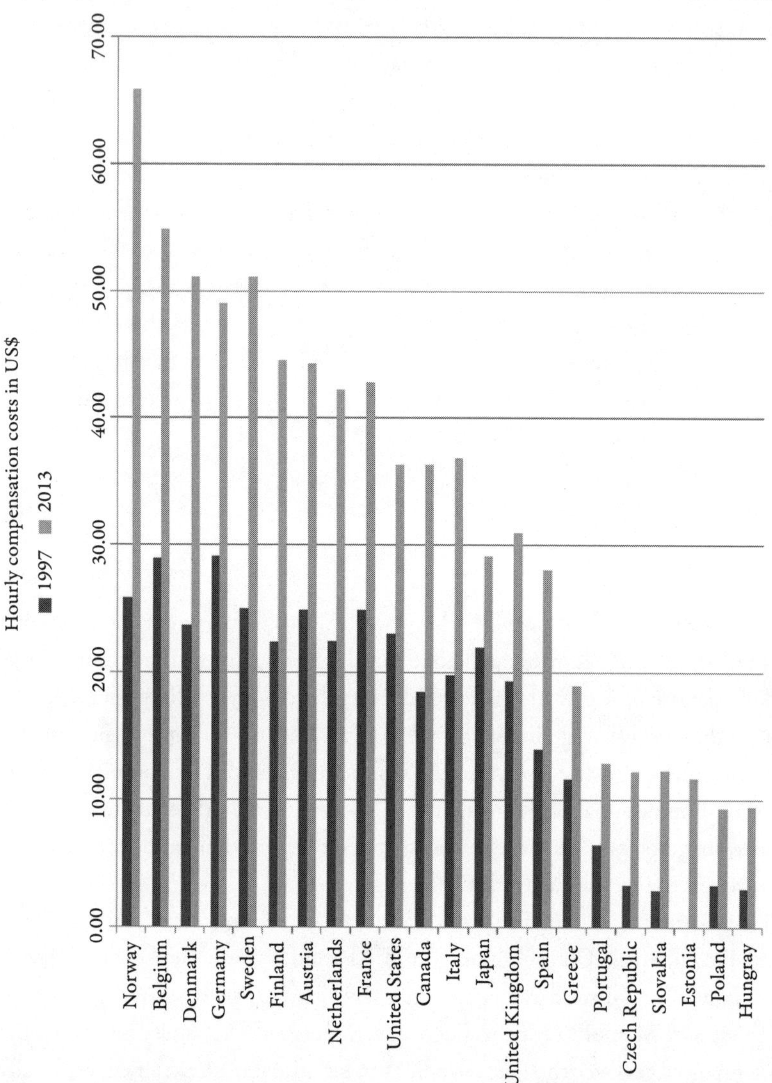

FIGURE 7.1 **Hourly Compensation Costs in Manufacturing (in US$)**
Compensation costs include direct pay, social insurance expenditures, and labor-related taxes. Data from "International Labor Comparison," Conference Board, December 2014, 1, www.conference-board.org/ilcprogram/compensation/datatables, accessed January 4, 2015.

countries in Europe, but also lower than in the United States. Also, directly paid benefits, like seasonal and irregular bonuses or pay for time not worked for vacations and holidays, are exceptionally high in Germany—because of the relatively high number of holiday and vacation days.

Dustmann and coauthors not only show that wage increases remained fairly modest relative to the growth in productivity and to wage increases in key European neighbors and OECD trading partners. In addition, they document how wages have become more

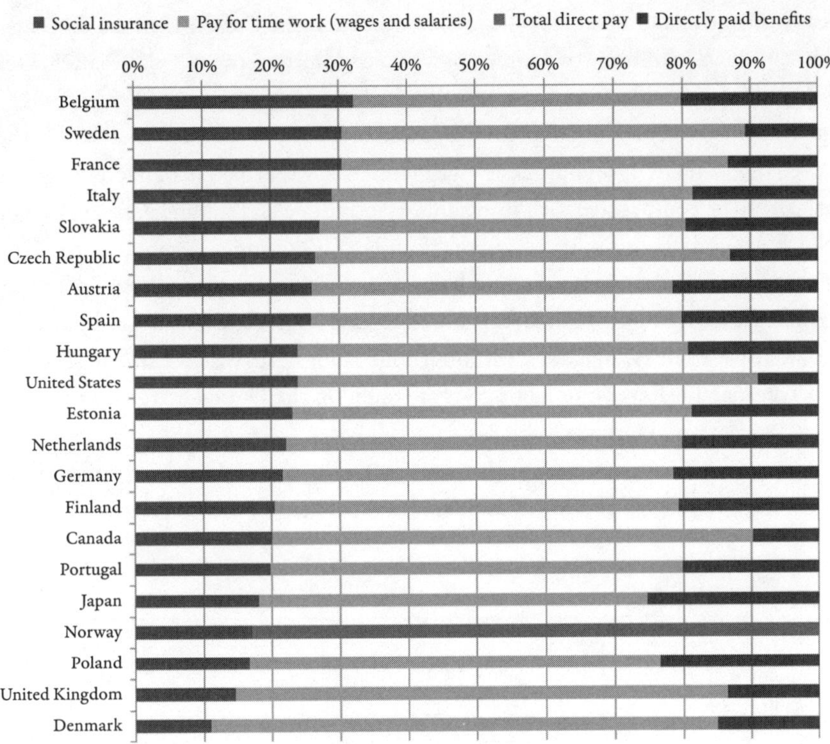

FIGURE 7.2 Components of Manufacturing Hourly Compensation

Costs as a percentage of total compensation. Social insurance expenditures are legally required, private, and contractual social benefit costs, and labor-related taxes minus subsidies. Directly paid benefits are primarily pay for leave time, bonuses, and pay in kind. Pay for time worked is primarily base wages and salaries, overtime pay, leave time, bonuses, and pay in kind. Pay for time worked is primarily base wages and salaries, overtime pay, regular bonuses and premiums (paid each pay period), and cost-of-living adjustments. Data source: "International Labor Comparison," Conference Board, December 2014, 1, www.conference-board.org/ilcprogram/compensation/datatables, accessed January 4, 2015.

heterogeneous within the German economy. Wage levels have tended to diverge within the labor force, resulting in a considerable increase in wage inequality. Their study shows that lower wages in service employment, a key input into the manufacture of goods and products, have fueled the increase in the competitiveness of German manufacturing. As the authors point out, the value added for manufactured goods contributes only about one-third of the total value added to the product sold.[48]

Relative Unit Labor Costs

High manufacturing productivity enhances competitiveness, just as higher wages detract from it. As Giersch, Paqué, and Schmieding made clear for the Wirtschaftswunder, and as Dustmann and coauthors do for the more recent resurgence of the German economy, it is the combination of these two forces, or what economists term the relative unit labor costs, that ultimately influences an economy's competitiveness.[49]

Figure 7.3 shows labor unit costs in Europe and other key countries in the world. The high levels of productivity and modest wage increases have enabled manufactured goods in Germany to be competitive with its neighbors in Europe and trading partners in Asia and North America. Labor unit costs in the three largest European economies after Germany, the United Kingdom, France, and Italy, exceed German costs by about 15–20 percent, while the average European level is lower. Countries like the Netherlands, a rather export-intensive country, operate with lower unit labor costs than Germany. Outside Europe, considerably lower unit labor costs are found in the United States (19 percent), Japan (10 percent), and Canada (9 percent).

Dustmann and coauthors explain that the resurgence of Germany's manufacturing, even as its European neighbors have floundered, is attributable to several factors. The first

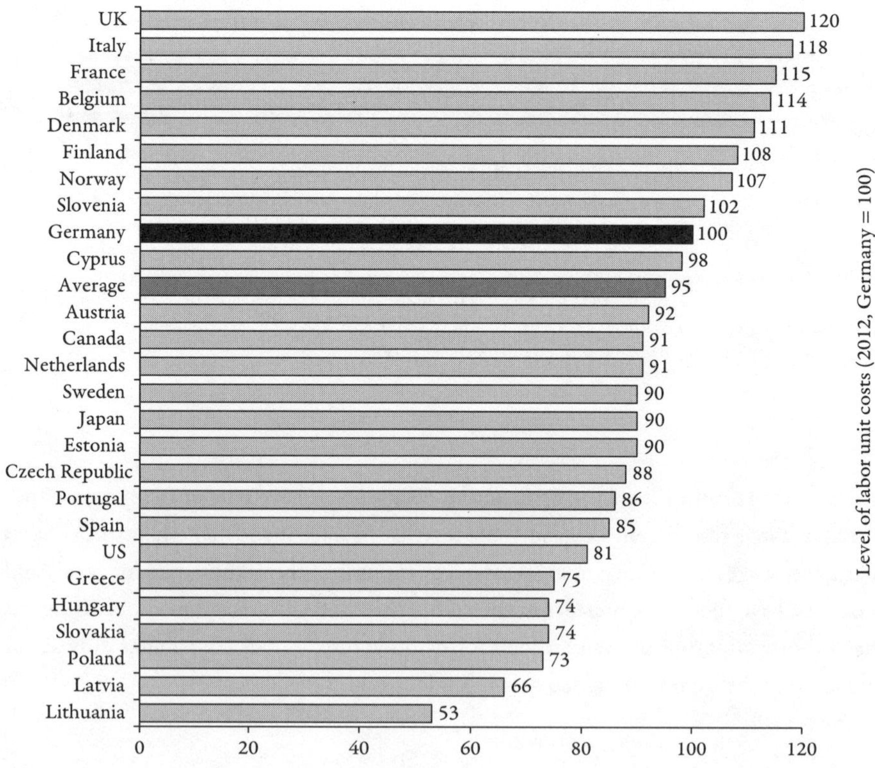

FIGURE 7.3 Unit Labor Costs

Based on currencies and prices in 2012. Mean value calculated as the mean value of the countries, except Germany, and weighted with the percentage on world exports (2010–2012). See Christoph Schroeder, "Produktivität und Lohnstückkosten der Industrie im internationalen Vergleich," Institut der deutschen Wirtschaft Köln, *IW Trends*, 4, 2013, 8.

is the large role that services play as an input in producing manufactured goods. It is in those services that wages have risen the least.

The second reason is that, as discussed above, increases in wages in the manufacturing sector have remained less than the growth in productivity, contributing to the sharp decrease in unit labor costs. The third factor is the expanded integration of trade and production with countries in Eastern and Central Europe, enabling companies manufacturing in Germany to access lower-cost inputs. Since such inputs account for roughly one-fifth of the total value of manufactured goods in Germany, the impact of accessing lower cost inputs from abroad tends to suppress the costs of "Made in Germany," enhancing competitiveness.[50]

Conclusions

Germany has resisted a global trend among the developed industrial nations of losing significant chunks of manufacturing. While not everyone thinks that this loss matters, it certainly has mattered for Germany. The ability to thrive with a manufacturing-driven economy sets Germany apart from its European neighbors and indeed its main trading partners in the developed world.

The prevalent view among scholars and thought leaders in policy and business is that an inevitable trade-off exists between manufacturing and innovation. A city, region, state, or country can choose between the two. Choosing innovation and knowledge carries with it the promise of higher wages and greater prosperity, but at a risk due to the uncertainty inherent in ideas and innovation. Andy Grove, one of the founders of Intel, famously titled his book *Only the Paranoid Survive.*

On the other hand, choosing manufacturing may lead to less uncertainty, but at the same time the prospects for higher wages and a rising standard of living are diminished. Relentless competition from lower-cost countries in Asia and increasingly from emerging economy countries such as Brazil exerts a downward pressure on wages and ultimately the standard of living.

This seemingly inevitable trade-off between innovation and manufacturing has resulted in the divergence between two Americas. Places that have successfully chosen knowledge and innovation provide a striking contrast with those that have continued with manufacturing. That difference is reflected by the incomes on the two sides of that choice. What do Silicon Valley, the Research Triangle in North Carolina, Austin, Fairfax County in Virginia, and Redmond, Washington have in common? Each place has a knowledge- and innovation-based local economy and has been rewarded by high levels of income and rising prosperity.

By contrast, places hanging on to manufacturing, such as Ohio, Michigan, and South Carolina, are struggling to keep their standard of living from declining. Even though Lee Iacocca, the colorful one-time CEO of Chrysler, pleads, "What we really need to do in this country is get back to the factory floors. You've got to stand for making good stuff or you're not going to win,"[51] to many scholars and thought leaders in policy and business, choosing manufacturing is tantamount to accepting a diminished standard of living.

The secret of Germany has been to refute this seeming trade-off between manufacturing and innovation. Rather, Germany has approached manufacturing and knowledge not as substitutes but as complements. Under this approach, knowledge and innovation are key factors that need to be leveraged to enhance manufacturing capabilities, ultimately fueling the competitive advantage of not just companies, but ultimately of the *Standort*, ranging from villages and towns to cities, regions, states, and the entire country. The most prosperous places in Germany, such as Baden-Württemberg, Stuttgart, and Munich, have pursued strategies of investing in knowledge and human capital, not as an alternative to manufacturing, but to enhance the manufacturing capabilities.

Peter Ross Range observes that "looking at Germany's success, President Obama wants to revive the American manufacturing sector. Many American economists believe it is a fool's errand to compete with low-wage countries. They insist that America's future lies in the knowledge economy and the services sector. But Germany has proven the opposite."[52]

Actually, Range has it not quite right. Germany has not proven the opposite. Rather, the secret of Germany is that there is no "opposite." Innovation and manufacturing are not inevitable trade-offs, but different sides of the same coin.

8 It's Good to Be German

IT HARDLY SEEMS odd that at an international sporting event like the World Cup, an enthusiastic show of flags and other national symbols would urge the home team on to victory. But 2006 was anything but normal. The World Cup was hosted by Germany, the country that had inflicted so much pain and suffering on, not just its neighbors, but the entire world in World War II. Visitors to Germany had become accustomed to a nonshow of the traditional symbols of national patriotism and emotional attachment. Germans would simply stand quietly, looking away modestly in embarrassed silence. As the former foreign minister Hans-Dietrich Genscher characterized it, the German stance amounted to a "culture of restraint."[1] One of the leading weekly magazines, *Der Spiegel*, explains: "Until 2006, Germans saw themselves as a brooding society." Everyone understood that thanks to its historical atrocities, Germany was different. Germans were different.

Only at the World Cup, for the first time since 1945, they weren't different. As the games and schedule deepened from the tentative initial matches of early June into the first official days of summer and then moved toward the brutal final rounds in early July, the black, red, and gold flew proudly over German balconies, attached to automobile antennas, and adorned T-shirts on backs and hats on heads. As the journalist Marc Young noted, "The soccer tournament has unleashed a torrent of feel-good vibes from Hamburg to Munich that has stunned the locals probably even more than all the foreign visitors from around the globe. Germans—long shy about expressing positive attitudes toward their country in light of their difficult history—have experienced three weeks of unabashed fun and pride decked out in the national colors." Young went on to ponder:

"The Germans are positive. The Germans are friendly. How can that be? For years, commentators both at home and abroad have derided the Germans for their pessimism and often glum or crabby manner."[2]

The contemporary attitudes, actions, and values of Germans have earned the respect of not just European neighbors but the larger world. As *Der Spiegel* reflects, "Germany . . . is a very different country than it was in 1984, not to mention 1994 or 2004. One gets the sense that two different aspects are converging to change the country: a new lightness of being and growing importance in the world."[3] This change in Germany involves not just the way that Germans think of themselves, or their identity, but also the way that others in the world view the Germans, or their image. As Young explains, "The soccer spectacle has already altered the way the world sees the Germans and even how the Germans see themselves."[4]

Despite such attention-grabbing headlines, it takes more than a few lads kicking around a soccer ball, combined with enthusiastic fans and celebrations, to change a country. It takes work, lots of work. Patient, meticulous, dedicated, backbreaking work. This work was done by people such as Richard von Weizsäcker, who, as president of Germany, uttered a sentence on May 8, 1985, at the Bundestag that echoes to this day. He referred to the end of World War II exactly four decades earlier not as a defeat for the German people but rather as *Befreiung*, or liberation. The *Bundespräsident* and former Wehrmacht officer declared "Der 8. Mai ist ein Tag der Befreiung," or "May 8 is a day of liberation."[5]

The American journalist Tom Brokaw earned countless accolades with his portrayal of the heroic Americans who fought and won that war as the "greatest generation."[6] Perhaps Germany's greatest generation came a little later. Because their approach was humble, devoted, dedicated but persevering, they may not be as noticed as their American counterparts. It was not just Richard von Weizsäcker, but an entire generation that undertook the hard work of first clearing away the rubble and ultimately clearing away a new path for the country. Erik's professor in economics and mentor at the University of Nuremberg, Professor Dr. Manfred Neumann, was just such a man. In his quiet, unpretentious way, Professor Neumann dedicated his life to lifting Germany up and paving the way for not just Erik, but for subsequent generations.

Thus, while the celebrations may have come in 2006 and 2014, they would have been vacuous without the generation of Germans, like Richard von Weizsäcker but also Professor Dr. Manfred Neumann, who through meticulous steps, mostly small but a few giant, did the hard work that ultimately would enable such celebrations to become a reality for subsequent generations.

The next section of this chapter explains the challenge to Germans in overcoming the angst inherited from a past that, increasingly, they had not themselves created. The chapter then examines how the identity of Germans has evolved, along with the image of Germans and Germany as seen by people in other countries.

That Germans have a considerably more positive identity, as well as image in the eyes of others, is fine and good, but why should it matter? Recalling the ironclad economic models of growth and standard of living, image and identity seem to be pretty extraneous. But matter they do. The fifth section makes explicitly clear why new theories and insights about how people view themselves, as well as the view held by others, can have a strong impact on economic performance. The chapter ends with a conclusion that is as simple as it is startling.

Overcoming the Angst

By May 1945 Hitler was dead. The nightmare of National Socialism was over. Germans clearing away the rubble from the streets of the devastated cities generally had nothing, but no doubt considered themselves lucky. At least they were alive. They had survived.

But moving forward, they quickly discovered the burden that they had inherited. Postwar Germans had inherited a record of cruelty and atrocities committed by the Nazis in the name of the *Deutsches Volk*. The numbers were, and remain, staggering. Eight million Jews. By the time MacArthur accepted the Japanese emperor's unconditional surrender, over sixty million people had been killed in World War II, or about 2.5 percent of the total population on earth.

In finding its way back to the rest of Europe and the world as an ally and partner, Germans set upon an explicit course of *Versonnenheit*, or atonement. A visit to one of the historical sites at a former concentration camp was expected of each class in school. From an early age, students were required to read solemn diatribes such as *The Burden of Guilt: A Short German History, 1914–45*.[7]

The legacy of two world wars and annihilating targeted groups of people left the question posed by *Der Spiegel*, "Will Hitler ever leave?"[8]

The weight of the question left a palpable scar on the German psyche, "the country of *Weltschmerz* and *Angst*, a nation constantly terrified of pending nuclear doom and haunted by memories of hyper-inflation, a joyless people."[9] The *Guardian* reports that the former prime minister of Britain, Margaret Thatcher characterized Germans as "a joyless people prone to egotism, inferiority complex, sentimentality."[10]

The historical legacy of Germany has led to a type of self-imposed reticence toward international affairs along with a suppression of "normal" values and sentiment of nationalism and patriotism: "The problem for Germans is that they have become numbed into believing that they cannot speak up for the rest of the world. Since World War II, they have been keen to demonstrate to themselves as much as to international onlookers that they despise the traditional, inherited values of nationhood which led to the great disaster of the Nazi era."[11]

The post–World War II identity of Germans seemingly precluded a self-confidence that is normal among neighboring countries in Europe and elsewhere in the world. There was always the underlying, and generally unspoken, issue of the centuries-old *Deutsche Frage*, or question concerning the unification of the German people.[12] As Günter Hellman, professor of political science at the Goethe University of Frankfurt am Main, observed shortly after reunification, "The only people calling for a 'self-confident nation'" were a scattered group of intellectuals from the "new democratic right" who bemoaned Germans' "broken" national consciousness."[13] Similarly, *Der Spiegel* points out that "for years, Germans as a people were extremely tense and inhibited, partly because they lived in a divided country. They had trouble determining their own identity. Were they German? Somehow they were, but were they different from the Germans on the other side of the Berlin Wall? Many West Germans just described themselves as Europeans."[14]

The impact of the historical burden on Germans was articulated by *Der Spiegel*: "Up to the present, they have lived with a forbidden identity. The unresolved loneliness of being German forced them to live beyond spontaneity, beyond sadness, beyond any collective self-awareness other than their perpetrator status."[15]

Identity

Shedding the old identity of the burdened Germany has given way to an unabashed positive sense of what it means to be German. This new attitude and identity was unmistakably apparent at the 2014 World Cup hosted by Brazil but won by Germany: "Germans discovered a new lightness in the run-up to their World Cup victory. It's a shift apparent not only in football. Increasingly, confident and content, Germany is emerging from the dark shadows of its past."[16]

Der Spiegel reports that this new German attitude first emerged during the 2006 World Cup in an interview of Christine Meier: "We wear necklaces and hats with the colors of the German flag, some paint the colors on their face. There is cake, antipasta and sometimes I make a noodle salad in black, red and yellow."[17] Meier adds, "People abroad are watching us. They want to know how we live and who we are. We are an uncommonly good people."[18]

Still, as *Der Spiegel* wonders, "But is that what it means to be German?"[19]

The former foreign minister under Chancellor Gerhard Schröder and member of the Green political party Joschka Fischer has an answer: "Today it is clearer what we Germans actually are. When seen collectively, Germany is a wonderful country. That someone with my history would say this says something."[20]

According to Professor Hellman, "Today, who 'we' are and what 'we' are (supposedly) entitled to is defined differently by Germans than 20 or 40 years ago."[21] One reason that the identity of Germans has evolved considerably is that the perpetrators, either actively or passively, have now passed retirement age. The entire generation that had firsthand experience with the Third Reich is now retired, leaving the question, "Can Germans born after the war still be blamed for it? Should those born decades or even a half century later still be made to feel the burden of guilt?"[22] Similarly, in his book *Stranger in My Own Country: A Jewish Family in Modern Germany*, the Harvard scholar Yascha

Mounk poses the penetrating question, "Are Today's Germans Morally Responsible for the Holocaust?"[23]

In fact, the contemporary identity of Germans is considerably different than it had been for the first decades following World War II, or even for the decade following German reunification. As *Der Spiegel* points out, "The Germans have become one again—they've become Germans. Prefixes are no longer needed. That significantly reduces inhibitions and contributes to the new lightness of being."[24] According to *Der Spiegel*, "Remembering today no longer means that you can't laugh or be happy. The Germans have already learned to shed part of their collective depression, a development that first became visible at the World Cup in 2006, which provided the world with a fantastic party. Today we can remember the past with anger and with sadness, but without becoming overly uptight about it."[25]

The question of German identity has been controversial and widely discussed for decades. According to *Der Spiegel*, "The German self-image is a complex, painful mess of contradictions which is often misunderstood, even by themselves. Sixty years after the end of the war, five times the duration of the Third Reich, the signs are that this has begun to change. The pangs of reunification, the economic downturn, the rediscovery of their own wartime trauma, as well as the larger European issues of multiculturalism and integration, have all contributed to a new kind of self-awareness. All those life-essential ingredients of identity such as language, home, belonging and nationhood are back in focus."[26]

Der Spiegel goes on to pose the intriguing question, "What does it mean to be German in the 21st century?" One answer is, "Many of [Germany's] neighbors might still harbor animosity with origins rooted in the war. But Germany has clearly become more and more a normal country in recent decades and less and less burdened by the guilt over its horrific past."[27]

The new German identity can be described: "A strong feeling of self-confidence is bound up in Germany's lightness. Let's call it: We Are Somebody Again."[28] What used to be a nation of pessimists has evolved into a country of remarkably positive people. According to the *Guardian*, Germany has as a "new identity as Europe's optimists."[29] This observation is backed up by a 2014 survey undertaken by the German Economic Institute in Cologne, which revealed that the majority of Germans are "extremely satisfied with their lives." In fact, only a miniscule 2 percent characterized their level of contentment with life in Germany as being "low."[30]

The survey is based on 1,106 interviews, including 694 (63 percent) Germans and 412 (37 percent) foreigners.[31] The German respondents confirmed that traditional characteristics such as *Gründlichkeit*, thoroughness, *Zuverlässigkeit*, reliability, and *Fleiss*, hard-working are still core characteristics of how Germans view themselves. These traits would hardly surprise anyone and are consistent with traditional German values.

Perhaps more surprising is that Germans now also view themselves as being innovative, creative, and with somewhat less conviction, flexible. Equally surprising, at least considering the more traditional German identity, is that the contemporary identity of Germany includes *Gastfreundlichkeit*, or being hospitable to foreigners, friendly, and tolerant.[32]

The study identified three key characteristics that Germans associate with the country's *Standortqualität*—infrastructure, nature, and quality of life.[33] The study also uncovered how Germans feel about three dimensions of German identity involving *Gesellschaft*, or society—sport, culture, and *Solidarität*, or social solidarity. In addition, the survey found that German identity includes three key dimensions involving the intellectual and scientific aspects of life—science, state of the medical and health system, and the education system.[34]

The identity of Germans and Germany today is markedly different than just a few years earlier, let alone the years following World War II. It would be wrong to conclude that the stigma and burden of history have been overcome. They certainly have not been forgotten. But at the same time, a new German identity has been forged, accentuating positive and optimistic aspects.

Image

Standing in a sea of black-, red-, and gold-adorned and cheering fans in Berlin's famed fan mile at the end of June 2014, it would have been difficult to imagine that any German could be anything other than euphoric about the *Nationalmannschaft*, whose victories continued to mount in that summer's World Cup. There seemed to be nothing but smiling, happy faces among the four hundred thousand fans from around the globe who had come together in a celebration centered on soccer. But it was also, and perhaps more importantly, a celebration for Germans and Germany. Germans and Germany had a new image.

Something had changed. Being German was no longer a burden. More than a few colleagues and friends would wonder what it must be like to be, say, French, Italian, or Canadian. Anything, really, to be free of a *Last*, or burden created and perpetuated by earlier, older generations. The burden, the *Last,* was named by the historian Hagen Schulze, the *Geschichtsfelsen des Nationalsozialismus*, or historical rock of National Socialism.[35] As *Der Spiegel* observes, "But that changed after Germany hosted that year's brilliantly successful World Cup [with the official slogan *Die Welt zu Gast bei Freunden*, the world as a guest among friends]."[36]

Such a dramatic change of identity, of course, didn't just happen. Rather, it was the result of decades of *Versonnenheit* and *Nachdenklichkeit*, or atonement. Like no other country, Germany and the Germans confronted their past, discussed it, and engaged in numerous activities in coming to terms with a horrible and inescapable past.[37] Television programs, lectures, books, and magazine articles made it virtually impossible for even the most isolated in society not to know about the atrocities committed by the Third Reich.

Because it has been a required part of the school curriculum (in West Germany), every young student is exposed to the horrible and inescapable past history. While the 2006 World Cup may have been the tipping point, it would not have been possible without decades of the hard work of confronting and living with the past—*Versonnenheit.*

But it didn't stop there. There is considerable evidence suggesting that the image of Germany in the world has improved. A 2013 poll by the Pew Foundation asked citizens of eight European countries who they thought was the most trustworthy. Germany was the choice of every country, with the sole exception of the Greeks, who named themselves.[38]

To shed light on what, exactly, foreigners think of Germans, the Cologne Institute for Economic Research conducted a survey at the Hannover Messe trade show, in 2012 asking both foreign and domestic participants whether they would recommend Germany as a place to live and work.[39] The response was resolute—76 percent of the foreign visitors would recommend working and living in Germany. In particularly, the *Lebensqualität*, or quality of life, was named as its strongest asset. The assessment of Germans themselves was only slightly higher—82 percent of the interviewed Germans said that they would recommend Germany as a place to live and work.

A considerably broader survey revealed even more compelling evidence confirming the positive identity of Germans and Germany in the world. In 2013 the BBC announced the findings from its annual Country Ratings Poll by announcing that Germany was ranked as the most popular country in the world.[40] The survey consisted of 26,000 respondents from twenty-five countries, who were requested to rank countries in terms of their image. Germany had the highest image, with 59 percent of the respondents assigning it a positive rating.

Peter Ross Range, writing in the German daily newspaper *Handelsblatt*, characterizes the rapid alteration in Germany's image: "Germany is a super-power today—a new kind of super-power in Europe, an economic and even political powerhouse, even if others are stronger militarily."[41] Range goes on to add that, along with this new image for Germany also comes the expectation and responsibility: "Germany is expected to solve everything. All roads to Europe run through Berlin—and Frankfurt."[42]

The image of Germany has evolved from being a belligerent and aggressive country to that of a highly respected nation. People throughout the world not only respect Germans, but like them.

Why It Matters

The image and identity of North Carolina couldn't have been worse in the 1950s.[43] While most of America boomed, North Carolina seemed to get poorer and poorer. Not only was North Carolina the poorest state in 1952, but the view from the rest of the country was that it was inhabited by rednecks. The level of education, or what we today would term human capital, was low, in the lowest tier in the United States. The main industries were in tobacco and textiles, which generally utilized unskilled labor working with only a modicum of machinery and technology.

As they watched educated and talented youth flee North Carolina, state leaders knew that something had to change. It started with identity and image. North Carolina had to fundamentally change its identity as well as the way other people viewed the state.

In his masterful and insightful book *A Generosity of Spirit*, Albert N. Link, the Virginia Batte Phillips Distinguished Professor at the University of North Carolina at Greensboro, meticulously explains how the state did exactly that—changed its identity and image.[44] It wasn't easy. The state had to create what today has become the famous Research Triangle Park, which shifted the entire focus of what mattered for economic prosperity away from the traditional stalwarts, tobacco and textiles, to high-technology products and services, such as computers, software, pharmaceuticals, and biotechnology.

Slowly but surely the rest of the country, and ultimately the rest of the world, began to view North Carolina as a state valuing creativity, science, engineering, ideas, and entrepreneurship. Through a series of targeted and conscious strategies, which Link meticulously documents, the state radically improved not only its identity and image, but ultimately its economic performance. As the identity and image began to change, the best and the brightest workers not only stopped leaving the state in hordes, but actually began to leave other places, such as Silicon Valley, to locate in North Carolina.

The same holds for high-technology firms and foreign direct investment. North Carolina became a magnet attracting some of the world's top technology companies. The extent to which the image of North Carolina was transformed is evidenced by a study identifying what corporate executives how they view metropolitan areas in the United States: "A lot of brainy types who made their way to Raleigh/Durham were drawn by three top research universities. . . . U.S. businesses, especially those whose success depends on staying at the top of new technologies and processes, increasingly want to be where hot new ideas are percolating. A presence in brainpower centers like Raleigh/Durham pays off in new products and new ways of doing business. Dozens of small biotechnology and software operations are starting up each year and growing like kudzu in the fertile climate."[45] Today, the Research Triangle region is one of the most technology-oriented and prosperous regions in the United States and in the world.[46]

Compelling examples, case studies, and empirical evidence garnered by careful scholars confirm that the identity and image of a *Standort*, or place, are inextricably linked to its economic performance and ultimately standard of living. In his highly influential book *The Rise of the Creative Class*, Richard Florida develops the theory that how people in a place view themselves, or their identity, and how others view that place, or image, can have a considerable impact on how well that place does. In particular, Florida argues that the "creative class," a concept he developed to identify people with human capital who are creative and work with ideas, is attracted by the twin magnets of identity and image. According to Florida, "The key to success today lies in developing a world-class people climate. By this I mean a general strategy aimed at attracting and retaining people—especially, but not limited to, creative people. This entails remaining open to diversity and actively working to cultivate it, and investing in lifestyle amenities that people really want and use often, as opposed to using financial incentives to attract companies, build professional sports stadiums or develop retail complexes."[47]

The image of a place is, of course, influenced by numerous factors and dimensions. Florida highlights the key role that cultural amenities play in luring the creative class to move to a place. Florida offers the case study of Austin, Texas, which transformed its identity and image as a rather isolated state capital of lowbrow cultural tastes, to a rich cultural scene, which ultimately attracted software engineers into relocating from Silicon Valley. As the motto written on thousands of T-shirts exclaims, "Keep Austin Weird!"

The policies implemented by Austin transformed the city from a sleepy town to a technological powerhouse. According to the former mayor of the city, Kirk Watson, "Austin has benefited from a convergence between technology and our laid-back, progressive, creative, lifestyle and music scene. The key is that we continue to preserve the lifestyle and diversity, which enables us to lure companies and people from places like Silicon Valley."[48]

The impact of Austin's image on attracting scientific, engineering, and entrepreneurial talent has been undeniable. Joel Kotkin, a Distinguished Presidential Fellow in Urban Futures at Chapman University, points out in *Forbes* that "brains are flocking to Austin for good reason.... Along with Raleigh-Durham, Austin is emerging as the next Silicon Valley, luring lots of brains who would have previously headed toward the West Coast. Its vibrant cultural scene certainly helps in attracting college-educated millennials."[49]

In addition to case studies, such as Silicon Valley, a rich body of systematic studies provides ample empirical evidence linking the positive image of a place to its economic performance.[50] A strong and positive identity and image pay off in terms of economic performance and standard of living.

The contribution that identity and image make in attracting the creative class and human capital, in addition to companies and foreign direct investment, is not specific to North America but applies in Germany too.

The new identity and image of Germany, and especially Berlin, was certainly not lost on the city's former mayor, Klaus Wowereit. His now famous depiction of the country's capital city as "arm aber sexy," or "poor but sexy," may sound like self-deprecation but was actually a celebration of the city's emerging identity and image.[51]

"Sexy" is not the way anyone would have described Berlin given its near total destruction in May 1945. The identity of the city was subsequently shaped by losing its status as the capital of the country. When its basic survival was threatened by the Soviet blockade of the city in 1949, prohibiting the transport of people and goods from and into the city, and then by the erection of the Berlin Wall, which divided the city into two separate parts, the city's identity and image struggled. To give the city a boost, the American president John F. Kennedy visited the city in 1962, when he famously proclaimed, "Ich bin ein Berliner."

Even President Kennedy's moving declaration of allegiance, loyalty, and support for the city was not enough to retain much of the private industry previously located in Berlin. Companies fled the divided Berlin in droves. It took substantial subsidies from the government to convince those remaining to stay in West Berlin. More than a few experts thought that it was only a matter of time until West Berlin succumbed to the inevitable.

However, events have a way of surprising even the experts. The identity and image of Berlin changed quickly and fundamentally after the Berlin Wall fell in November 1989. The existentialist threat that was only an international crisis away simply vanished, along with the remnants of the Berlin Wall. The city once again resumed its role as the nation's capital following the reunification of Germany in October 1990.

The identity and image of the city also evolved, albeit considerably less heroic and exotic. As the waves of *Beamter*, or civil servants, poured into Berlin, the city seemed doomed to an identity and image of economic stagnation resulting from a business-hostile local government and rigid bureaucracy. The historical legacy of Prussian bureaucracy, heavy-handed regulations, combined with the more recent episodes of National Socialist control, followed by the Allied occupation of a divided city under perpetual threat, did little to alleviate the not entirely inaccurate view that the city could not help but be antibusiness, overly burdened by heavy handed government and bureaucracy. For the first decade following the fall of the Berlin Wall, the economic performance of Berlin ranked among the worst in the country.

Melanie Fasche, a postdoctoral fellow at the Martin Prosperity Institute of the Rotman School of Management at the University of Toronto, explains that a priority for former mayor Wowereit and the entire Berlin government was to transform the economy and standard of living of Berlin by transforming its identity and image. In particular, this new strategy involved shifting Berlin's image away from a colorful but not particularly productive past, toward a new, contemporary image that inspires and connects with the young, creative generation as "the" place to be.[52] Along with the new century came a new identity and image for Berlin, which, while certainly acknowledging and confronting its difficult past, celebrated the freedom, creativity, and opportunities for a new generation.

The drastic and positive change in Berlin's identity and image has made an impression on the German novelist and critic Peter Schneider: "When natives of New York, or Rome, ask me where I am from and I allude to Berlin, their eyes instantly light up."[53] The *Wall Street Journal*, noting that the devastation of the city in World War II led to a hastily thrown up hodgepodge of buildings, wonders, "If Berlin is not beautiful why is it so beloved?"[54]

Schneider suggests an answer—Berlin has succeeded in shedding its old identity and image for one that resonates with a multitude of diverse people from many backgrounds.[55] Nicholas Stang, writing in the *Wall Street Journal*, attempts to characterize Berlin's new identity and image: "This Berlin, the Berlin of improvisation amid the wreckage of history, of making something out of almost nothing, is the Berlin that many of us love and keep coming back to."[56]

Armed with such a positive image and identity, it is not surprising, that creative and talented people from around the world are flocking to Berlin. As *Der Spiegel* reports, "It is a growing trend in the German capital. With the economy struggling across Southern Europe as a result of the euro crisis, increasing numbers of young Italians are moving to Berlin to start their own businesses or to work at one of the city's many established start-ups."[57] Berlin's new identity and image provide a magnet attracting the creative class.

The creative class does more than just be creative. Among other things, it starts new businesses. Thus, as talent and human capital have flocked to Berlin, the city has emerged as one of the most entrepreneurial places in Germany, perhaps even in all of Europe. The University Industry Innovation Network (UIIN) refers to Berlin as "The entrepreneurship and innovation hub of Europe."[58]

Berlin's contemporary identity and image as an entrepreneurial hub is, in fact, backed up by data. The 2012 start-up rate in Berlin was the highest in Germany. Nearly 3 percent of the working-age population had a start-up company. By contrast, the start-up rate was somewhat lower in Hamburg, at 2.5 percent, and in Bremen, at 2 percent. The high start-up rate in Berlin is reflected in the total amount of finance in start-up activity, which exceeded that in the state of Bavaria, which until Berlin's emergence had been the perennial leader in attracting entrepreneurial finance.[59]

What did the city actually do to so fundamentally transform its identity and image? In a meticulous study, Fasche[60] documents the targeted strategies and polices implemented, such as investments in culture and public infrastructure, to transform the image of Berlin and ultimately attract talent and human capital.

As Richard Florida makes clear, identity and image serve as a beacon for attracting talent, especially entrepreneurial talent. For example, Caitlin Winner, who is from Williamsport, Pennsylvania, and graduated with distinction from Wellsley College with a dual major in art and economics, had an entire globe full of places where she could choose to live and work. She chose Berlin, where she helped to found an Internet company, Amen.[61] What attracted Caitlin to Berlin? "Berlin is the coolest place in the world. Especially for people in the community of Internet start-ups."[62] Caitlin doubts that her entrepreneurial idea and new firm could have happened in some other high-technology cluster, such as Silicon Valley. She points out that the idea for the company is a platform for a social network featuring opinions and discussions that mirrors the unique and compelling culture prevalent in Berlin bars, or *Kneipen*.

Caitlin is not alone in her discovery of Berlin as a hotbed of creative ideas and entrepreneurial buzz. The image of Berlin that pulled Caitlin away from her native country is making a similar siren call to an entire generation of young, dynamic people pursuing their entrepreneurial dreams and aspirations. To those young, aspiring, creative entrepreneurs, "Berlin is the best city ever."[63] As the *New York Times* notes, "More than two decades after the fall of the Berlin Wall, the German capital has gone from a cold war relic to one of the fastest-growing start-up communities. Engineers and designers have flooded into Berlin in recent years, attracted by the underground music scene, cutting-edge art galleries, stylish bars and low rent."[64]

Not surprisingly, one of Caitlin's cofounders, Felix Petersen, who was born and raised in Berlin, sees the identity of the city in a longer and more historical context: "Berlin itself is a type of start-up. The entire city is in a constant state of change."[65] A cover feature of the biweekly magazine *TIP Berlin* highlighted the three founders of the Internet start-up with the headline, "Revenge of the Nerds: How Berlin is Becoming the Next Silicon Valley."[66] *TIP Berlin* explains how the city emerged as an entrepreneurial hub: "Berlin is known around the world for being cool. But it is an underdog type of cool, not like New York, Paris or London, but rather like Portland or Seattle. In Berlin there are clubs and bars, artists, students, designers, bloggers and musicians."[67]

It takes more than talent to start a new company. It also takes money. Caitlin Winner and her cofounders were able to leverage Berlin's new image as an entrepreneurial hub by attracting a million-dollar investment from the Hollywood film star Ashton Kutcher. Apparently Kutcher was so fascinated by the pulsating Berlin scene that he wanted to be a part of it, and the investment followed.[68] The venture capital firm Sunstone Capital followed up Kutcher's investment with additional funding.[69] Berlin's status as "poor but sexy" already seems outdated. The city is well on its way to being "sexy and rich."

Conclusions

A popular weekly television series in Germany back in the 1980s had the main characters on a bus tour of the American Southwest. In a scene that was constantly repeated in a wide variety of tourist destinations—the Grand Canyon, Las Vegas, Bryce Canyon, the Snake River—upon reboarding the tour bus following a visit to a historical site, the American tour leader would invariably announce, "It's time to board the bus—Germans to the rear!" This pretty much summarizes not just how Germans viewed themselves but also how the rest of world viewed them as well. They understood that a historical burden from a past, not of their making, relegated them to the back of the bus.

That identity and image is gone, if not forgotten, and is a relic of the previous century's foibles. Germans now see themselves and their country very differently today, and in a much more positive and optimistic light, and so too do people throughout the rest of the world. As the journalist, Marc Young provides perspective, "Just as Germany was never as bad a place as many foreigners thought, it was certainly much nicer than many Germans were willing to admit."[70]

The new identity and image of Germans and Germany comes with benefits. As human capital, talent, and the creative class flock to Germany, so too do the world's leading companies rush to invest in Germany.

It's good to be German.

9 Conclusions: The Right Zeitgeist for the *Zeitalter*

IT WOULD BE wrong to conclude from this book that Germany has managed to reach the unattainable—the *end of history*, as Francis Fukuyama famously declared at the end of the Cold War.[1] One secret that still eludes Germany is how to free itself from the onerous dictates and downturns of the business cycle. Unfortunately, this secret remains exactly that—a secret, indecipherable to Germany, just as it remains for every country.

However, while the seven secrets may not have exempted Germany from economic slowdowns, downturns, and full-blown recessions, they have provided considerable resilience in a turbulent global era when many of its neighbors and partners among the developed countries seem to have lost their way. Simply look how Germany rapidly vaulted from its status as the sick man of Europe to pulling away from its European neighbors.[2] The European Union was built on the pillar of a Franco-German partnership. For decades the two countries stood side by side, shouldering the burdens of Europe, spurring on their smaller, somewhat overshadowed neighbors. As Germany descended into its fifteen-year stagnation following the fall of the Berlin Wall, many wondered whether the sick man of Europe was still up to the task of sharing the heavy lifting with its French partner.

The sick man got better. This book has been about what happened to turn the German economy around. In fact, it is now Germany that has, for nearly a decade, diverged not just from France, but from many of its other European neighbors, such as Italy, Spain, and Portugal. As *Der Spiegel* notes, it is France that has suffered from "zero growth, vanishing competitiveness, climbing unemployment and years of budget deficits that exceed three percent of gross domestic product, the maximum allowed by EU rules. Merkel believes that France has become what Germany was ten years ago: the Sick Man of Europe."[3] In fact, considerable consternation has been expressed at "the pain felt at the nationwide belief that Germany has left France behind."[4] According to the minister of economics, Emmanuel Macron, France is "in danger of becoming a Cuba without the sun."[5]

The point of this book is not to express schadenfreude toward any particular country, but rather to highlight one country, Germany, that within the span of a remarkably short period of time vaulted from being the sick man of Europe to a viable economy that has learned how to leverage the opportunities afforded by globalization, rather than succumb as a victim.

Thus, our purpose in revealing the secrets underlying Germany's resilience in a turbulent global economy is not to instruct Germany on how best to move forward into the future. After all, the premise of the book is that Germany is doing fine without us. This is not a book to instruct Germans and Germany. Rather, the point of this book is to provide insights for people in other countries and national contexts that can benefit from understanding that economic resilience in the era of globalization is, in fact, possible, and what it is exactly that Germany has been doing to generate such economic resilience.

One important lesson is that austerity has little to do with it. We contest the broadly popular characterization of the German "secret" as a policy of austerity. We do not find that austerity is a valid characterization of what Germany has done to achieve economic success in an era of global turbulence. The problem with the label of austerity is a focus exclusively on a single side of the great equation created by economists to portray the underlying economic forces in a market economy—the demand side. In fact, all of the seven secrets are about the other side of the equation—the supply side. Most of them revolve around the capacity of the country to produce goods and provide services in a manner that makes *Standort Deutschland*, or locations in Germany, highly productive, innovative, and attractive.

Most of the secrets, ranging from labor skills and human capital to key knowledge creation and transfer institutions, such as the Fraunhofer Institutes and the Max Planck Society, the stout and functional infrastructure, and investments in culture and amenities to fuel flourishing cities attracting a diverse and talented workforce, are based not on belt tightening, but the opposite—spending and investment. Not just spending and investment on anything, as the theoretical Keynesian-based economic models would have people believe. The German approach is not only systematic and determined, it is also from the largely forgotten side—the supply side.

Supply-side economics was first popularized by President Ronald Reagan.[6] However, rather than being characterized as strategic investments to enhance the productive and innovative capacity of the economy, it instead suffered from caricature as trickle-down economics with the sole mantra of reducing taxes, particularly on the wealthiest people in society.[7] Because Americans understood supply-side economics to mean "the wealthy won't work more because they earn too little as a result of high taxes, and the poor won't work more because they already earn too much through unemployment benefits, welfare and high minimum wages," it largely fell into disrepute.

Certainly the heated debates about climbing out of the Great Recession in the United States revolved around the best way to deliver a stimulus to the economy. Even the word "stimulus" reflects the vocabulary of Keynesian, or demand-side economics, suggesting that, perhaps thanks to the twin legacies of the Keynesian and Reagan revolutions, the supply side remains the blind spot of the economy and economic policy.

The problem was, and remains, that there is a lot more to supply-side economics than just the trickle-down theory, with its exclusive focus on the tax incentives influencing the willingness to work. Our examination of Germany is ultimately a validation of the supply side's importance for the economy. Enlightened policies and institutions enhancing that supply side will ultimately pay rich dividends.

Whether certain German political leaders and parties have attempted to inflict austerity on countries within the European Union is beyond the scope of this book. It certainly seems to be a characterization of the German approach pervasive in the international press. For example, as the minister of the economy in France, Arnaud Montebourg, complained to one of the most influential newspapers in Europe, *Le Monde*, "Germany is caught in a trap of austerity that it is imposing across Europe."[8] Reaction to Montebourg's demand that the French government abandon its policy of austerity abruptly triggered the collapse of the French cabinet in August 2014.

Similarly, the *New York Times* warns that "as Europe confronts new signs of economic trouble, national leaders, policy makers and economists are starting to challenge as never before the guiding principle of the Continent's response to six years of crisis: Germany's insistence on budget austerity as a precondition to healthy growth. France this week stepped up what has become an open revolt by some of the euro zone's bigger economies against Chancellor Angela Merkel's continued demands for deficit reduction in the face of slowing growth. Italy has warned against too rigidly following Germany's preferred approach. Even the president of the European Central Bank, Mario Draghi, is pushing for Germany to loosen up."[9]

What we can be sure of is that Germany's remarkable economic success was not the result of austerity but rather a strategic approach to the supply side of the economy. The German approach has not been to "starve the beast" of public spending.[10] Instead, strategic investments have been made by governments at all levels through the fundamental principle of *Standortpolitik*. Without these investments, it is doubtful that there would be any secrets to tell.

What exactly should anyone learn from Germany's seven secrets? There are, in fact, two distinct interpretations. The first is the literal interpretation, where the takeaway is to clone a particular secret in another country. For example, with Germany's vaunted apprenticeship system in mind, the American journalist Range reacts to this first, literal interpretation: "It seems frankly, like a no-brainer. But can it be copied?"[11] In fact, Spain has committed itself to trying to reproduce this secret.

Spain is not alone. In his 2012 State of the Union Address, the president of the United States, Barack Obama, clearly had in mind the German dual education system with its emphasis on worker training through a formal program of apprenticeships, as he held up an example of a worker who graduated from a joint training program sponsored by the German company, Siemens, along with a community college in North Carolina.[12]

The second is the broader interpretation, suggesting that what is important is not duplicating the exact secret that has worked for Germany, but rather finding an analogous process of identifying and then nurturing particular country-specific strengths. This might suggest that while the German apprentice system is exactly that—German—other countries, such as the United States, certainly can find ways to enhance labor skills through training and hands-on internships through institutions and policies that are specific to that country. However, simply cloning what works in one country, for example the German apprentice system, may be less effective than focusing on the underlying function, which in this case involves equipping young people with key labor skills.

In this spirit, one of Germany's top daily newspapers, the *Handelsblatt*, wonders, "What exactly can America learn from this country?"[13] According to Steven Rattner, who is in the finance industry on Wall Street and spearheaded the bailout of the American auto industry in 2009, "We need to learn from the German model."[14]

Similarly, the chairman of General Electric, Jeffrey Immelt, argues, "We need to be more like Germany."[15] Perhaps most poignantly, the president of the United States, Barack Obama, wonders, "Why is Germany so successful at running a high-wage industrial sector?"[16]

Paul Volcker, who had served as chairman of the Federal Reserve Board, simply asked his German counterparts, "How do you do it?"[17]

We know how they don't do it. It is certainly no secret that the German economic approach is not to leave decisions and outcomes entirely up to the market. Rather, the concepts of *Ordnungspolitik* and *Standortpolitik* dictate that the place—cities, regions, and states, as well as the entire country—proactively implements strategies to sustain a strong economic performance, or what we would term the strategic management of place.[18] The focus is not on waiting for global markets to generate the best products and services for consumers at the lowest prices but rather to ensure that the place, or *Standort*, is able to compete in global markets to ensure a strong economic performance and prosperity—not just prosperity for vaguely defined consumers but rather for the people who actually live and work at that particular place, or *Standort*.

Every city, region, state, and country in the developed world should take notice of the fundamental importance of *Standortpolitik*, or the strategic management of place. The characterization by the media, but also by numerous scholars and thought leaders in policy and business, of the economic challenges confronting Europe as a "euro crisis" suggests a focus on the symptom rather than the underlying cause, which is a lack of competitiveness in many European cities, regions, and in some cases, countries. There are places in Europe that have exhibited considerable competitiveness in global markets. Such competitive places include Vienna, Stockholm, the Basque region, and Copenhagen, as evidenced by continued low levels of unemployment and positive growth rates.[19] At the same time, much of Europe, especially the Mediterranean countries, is not competitive. A strategic approach to enhance the competitiveness of such places through both lowering the costs of production and increasing product quality and degree of innovation in production would certainly be consistent with the approach Germany has undertaken.

Karl Marx may have been prescient in suggesting that a specter is haunting Europe. He was less prescient about the exact nature of that specter. In fact, a growing tension is dividing Europe, less on a national basis than on the growing divide separating competitive places from those that are less competitive.

For example, the Spanish province of Catalonia exhibits a high degree of competitiveness. Maria Calleon, who is a professor of economics at the University of Barcelona, carefully explains how this competitiveness was attained, meticulously analyzing the key strategic investments undertaken by Barcelona, the region, and the province.[20] The current movement demanding autonomy is in no small way attributable to the divergence in competitiveness between Catalonia and much of the rest of the country. In particular, Catalonia has devised a strategic approach based on knowledge-based entrepreneurship to generate competitiveness and a strong economic performance in the global economy. The drive for autonomy reflects the sense that having to prop up some of the less competitive neighboring provinces is eroding Catalonia's own strategies at the cost of diluting its own competitiveness.

Similarly, even while southern Italy has struggled economically, reflecting a general lack of competitiveness, the northern provinces, and in particular the Lomardy region, have exhibited a considerable degree of competitiveness, reigniting calls for independence. The solution may have less to do with imposing austerity in less competitive regions than with implementing a strategic approach for each region, along the lines of *Standortpolitik*.

As any observer of all things human surely knows, secrets revealed lead only to more secrets. So too it is with this book. Having posited, introduced, and explained the seven secrets of Germany, we discover additional secrets. As the great classical composer Ludwig van Beethoven shared, "Don't only practice your art, but force your way into its secrets; art deserves that, for it and knowledge can raise man to the Divine."[21]

An additional secret needed to understand our seven is that each of them may not be sufficient on its own, but becomes really effective only when they are taken together. For example, chapter 7, "Made in Germany," explains that manufacturing has contributed to economic resilience in Germany. However, that manufacturing success would not be possible without the key role placed by what is the focus of chapter 2, "Small Is Beautiful"—Germany's small and medium-sized firms, the Mittelstand. While all developed countries have a large population of SMEs, as chapter 2 makes clear, there is a qualitative difference in the German Mittelstand that has fostered higher levels of quality, productivity, and innovative activity, enabling at least some companies to dominate their global product niches and deliver exceptional inputs to the larger companies, which in turn fuel their productivity and competitive advantage in manufacturing.

However, the Mittelstand would not be nearly as effective without the availability of highly skilled workers, trained by the German apprentice system, which is the topic of "Poets and Thinkers," chapter 3, or the key technological innovations contributed by linking institutions such as the Fraunhofer Institutes, providing a conduit for the spillover of knowledge from fundamental, basic research to innovative activity driving commercial products. As chapter 5 explains, the stout infrastructure in Germany provides a crucial resource enhancing the productivity and competitiveness of manufacturing.

Similarly, without the local roots and decentralized levels of governance and decision-making, and the mandate for *Standortpolitik*, which is explained in chapter 4, Germany's Mittelstand companies might not remain located in their traditional towns and villages, and the next generation of family members might lose interest in dedicating their lives to their company and community. At the same time, without the wings, or orientation toward discovering and creating opportunities beyond Germany's borders, which is also explained in chapter 4, perhaps neither the German Mittelstand nor the entire manufacturing sector would be so extraordinary. How and why being open and aware of developments and opportunities outside of Germany pays off is evidenced by Klaus Fischer, the CEO of the high-performing Mittelstand company, Fischer.[22] When international competition started to threaten the competitiveness of the company, Fischer went to Japan and spent sufficient time there meeting his counterparts in industry to realize that the Kanban method of just-in-time production could bestow increases in productivity.

Thus, each of the secrets is richly interwoven with the others, so that the metaphor for German economic success and resilience is not the high-performing individual superstar but the integrated team, much as each instrument blends together in a world-class symphony. How did the German national soccer team win the World Cup in 2014? Not by fielding a thrilling superstar or two. Rather, their world championship was harvested through the discipline of well-coordinated and carefully crafted teamwork.

Similarly, it is the interdependence and coordination of each of these seven aspects of Germany that is most impressive, rather than any single aspect in isolation. This rich interaction is not lost on Charles Wessner, the former director of the Board on Science, Technology and Economic Policy at the National Research Council of the National Academies of Sciences and Engineering. He asks, "What are the implications for the United States?" His answer begins with the insight that "perhaps the first lesson is that German firms are not 'home alone.' They are supported by a dense network of institutes that help them make the increment improvements that bring long-term commercial success. A second lesson is that this is seen as an important national mission, the way national defense is here in the United States. It requires a steady flow of resources, concentrated effort, well-funded, well-led institutions, and a sense that these are investments that are important for the country's future."[23]

It is also important to remember that most of the secrets reflect a deep-rooted approach to German society and economy that is anything but recent. The deep-rootedness of the secrets combined with the recent economic resurgence poses something of a paradox: How could the same deep-rooted secrets that led Germany to become the sick man of Europe contribute to its now celebrated economic success and resilience?

The answer has to do with how the secrets have been recalibrated to meet the challenges of the contemporary economy—the *Zeitalter*. Across the board, policies and institutions have been changed, modified, reformed, and recalibrated. For example, when David received his first *Aufenthaltserlaubnis*, or residence permission, it explicitly prohibited him from engaging in *selbstständige Arbeit*, or becoming self-employed. More recently, as it dawned on policymakers that they were prohibiting key foreign scientific and high-human-capital talent from becoming entrepreneurial, they simply changed this policy.

Similarly, the once-rigid working hours have been considerably loosened, so that part-time and temporary employment contracts and work now abound and flourish. A country that once stubbornly stuck to its official native language now embraces the widespread use of English, from universities to businesses and research organizations, as a way of linking up with the rest of the world to access key opportunities. As we suggest in chapter 6, few people associate the concept of flexibility with Germany. Yet in rising to the challenges posed by the new era of globalization, Germans have responded with remarkable flexibility. While the secrets are indeed deeply rooted, they have been reformed, modified, and recalibrated to both create and reflect a new spirit, or zeitgeist, in Germany that embraces the opportunities created by globalization rather than cowering and allowing the country to succumb as a victim.

Thus, by modifying, reforming, and recalibrating each of these secrets and the way they interact, Germany has been able to stay true to its roots and fundamental values, along with its basic approach to society and the economy, even as it has embraced the wings to grasp new challenges and opportunities emerging in the contemporary globalized economy. Taken together, the seven secrets bestow Germany with the right zeitgeist for our *Zeitalter*. As the great French novelist Alphonse Karr observed more than a century ago, "Plus ça change, plus c'est la même chose," or "The more things change, the more they remain the same."

Notes

CHAPTER 1

1. Matthew O'Brien, "Spain Is Beyond Doomed," *The Atlantic*, April 26, 2013.

2. Liz Alderman and Alison Smale, "Divisions Grow as a Downturn Rocks Europe," *New York Times*, August 29, 2014.

3. According to a recent study from Ernst & Young; see "Deutschland widerstand dem Krisen-Trend," *Handelsblatt*, January 6, 2015. See also Michael C. Burda and Jennifer Hunt, "What Explains the German Labor Market Miracle in the Great Recession," Working Paper No. 17187, National Bureau of Economic Research, 2011.

4. "Südwesten mit niedrigster Arbeitslosenquote," *Stuttgarter Nachrichten*, January 29, 2015, accessed February 2, 2015, at http://www.stuttgarter-zeitung.de/inhalt.baden-wuerttemberg-suedwesten-mit-niedrigster-arbeitslosenquote.d9bf6b3c-da42-4c34-a719-34b89a5347c6.html.

5. Stephen F. Szabo, *Germany, Russia, and the Rise of Geo-economics* (London: Bloomsbury Academic, 2015).

6. "German Exports: 1950–2014," *Trading Economics*, July 2014, accessed February 2, 2015, at http://www.tradingeconomics.com/germany/balance-of-trade.

7. "Long-Term Interest Rate Statistics for EU Member States," European Central Bank, September 2014, accessed February 2, 2015, at http://knoema.com/ECBIRS2015Jan/long-term-interest-rate-statistics-for-eu-member-states-monthly-jan-1993-to-december-2014.

8. "Division 999," *Die Zeit*, April 18, 1946, accessed January 30, 2015, at http://www.zeit.de/1946/09/division-999.

9. Herbert Giersch, Karl-Heinz Paqué, and Holger Schmieding, *The Fading Miracle: Four Decades of Market Economy in Germany* (New York: Cambridge University Press, 1992).

10. Giersch, Paqué, and Schmieding, *The Fading Miracle*.

11. "The Sick Man of the Euro," *The Economist*, January 3, 1999.

12. Giersch, Paqué, and Schmieding, *The Fading Miracle*.

13. Giersch, Paqué, and Schmieding, *The Fading Miracle.*

14. Giersch, Paqué, and Schmieding, *The Fading Miracle.*

15. David B. Audretsch, "New Firms and Creating Employment," in John T. Addison and Paul J. J. Welfens (eds.), *Labor Markets and Social Security: Wage Costs, Social Security Financing and Labor Market Reforms in Europe* (Heidelberg: Springer, 1998), 130–163.

16. David B. Audretsch, "Innovationen: Aufbruch zur Entrepreneurship-Politik," in Klaus F. Zimmermann (ed.), *Deutschland—was nun? Reformen für Wirtschaft und Gesellschaft* (Munich: Deutscher Taschenbuch Verlag, 2006), 237–250.

17. Gerlinde Sinn and Hans-Werner Sinn, *Jumpstart* (Cambridge: MIT Press, 1994).

18. David B. Audretsch, "Die Entrepreneurial Society im Zeitalter der Globalisierung," in Beatrice Weder di Mauro (ed.), *Chancen des Wachstums: Globale Perspektiven für den Wohlstand von Morgen* (Frankfurt: Campus Verlag, 2008), 91–110.

19. Joseph S. Stiglitz, *The Roaring Nineties: A New History of the World's Most Prosperous Decade* (New York: Norton, 2004); and David B. Audretsch, *The Entrepreneurial Society* (New York: Oxford University Press, 2007).

20. Lester Thurow, *Fortune Favors the Bold* (Cambridge: MIT Press, 2002).

21. David B. Audretsch, "Germany, along with Europe, Is Embracing the New Economy," *European Affairs* 1 (3), 2000, 46–51.

22. Audretsch, *The Entrepreneurial Society.*

23. "Those German Banks and Their Industrial Treasures," *The Economist*, January 21, 1995, 75–76.

24. Thurow, *Fortune Favors the Bold*, 35.

25. "Es kann jeden Treffen," *Der Spiegel*, 5, 1994, 82–83. The original text states, "Der weltweite Strukturwandel hat die deutsche Wirtschaft mit einer Wucht getroffen, die noch vor kurzem unvorstellbar schien: Viele ihrer Produkte wie Autos und Maschinen, Chemikalien und Stahl sind international nicht mehr wettbewerbsfähig. Und in den Zukunftsindustrien—der Biotechnik etwa oder der Elektronik—sind die Deutschen nur unzureichend vertreten."

26. "Some Germans Fear They're Falling Behind in High-Tech Fields," *Wall Street Journal*, April 27, 1994, 1.

27. Lothar Späth and Herbert A. Henzler, *Countdown für Deutschland: Start in der neue Zeit* (Berlin: Siedler, 1995).

28. D. Benjamin, "The Trailing Edge: Some Germans Fear They're Falling Behind in High-Tech Fields," *Wall Street Journal*, April 27, 1994, 1.

29. Hans-Werner Sinn, *Ist Deutschland Noch zu Retten?* (Berlin: Econ Verlag, 2004).

30. Jochen Bittner, "Germany without Angst? That Worries Me," *New York Times*, October 20, 2014, accessed November 16, 2014, at http://www.nytimes.com/2014/10/21/opinion/jochen-bittner-germany-without-angst-that-worries-me.html?_r=0.

31. "Bloc in Europe Starts to Balk over Austerity: In Rift, Nations Want Steps to Ease Slump," *New York Times*, October 17, 2014, 1.

32."One Big Unhappy Economy," *New York Times*, September 18, 2014, accessed November 16, 2014, at http://article.wn.com/view/2014/09/20/One_Big_Unhappy_Economy/.

33. Horst Siebert, *The German Economy: Beyond the Social Market* (Princeton: Princeton University Press, 2005); Sinn, *Ist Deutschland Noch zu Retten?*; Hans-Werner Sinn, *Can Germany Still Be Saved? The Malaise of the World's First Welfare State* (Cambridge: MIT Press,

2009); Hans-Werner Sinn, *Die Bazar-Ökonomie* (Berlin: Econ Verlag, 2005); Thilo Sarrazin, *Deutschland Schafft Sich Ab: Wie Wir das Land aufs Spiel Setzen* (Berlin: Deutsche Verlags-Anstalt, 2010).

34. http://www.bundespraesident.de/SharedDocs/Reden/DE/Roman-Herzog/Reden/1997/04/19970426_Rede.html, accessed April 15th 2015

35. Charles W. Wessner, "How Does Germany Do It?" *ASME*, November 2013, accessed October 30, 2014, at https://www.asme.org/engineering-topics/articles/manufacturing-processing/how-does-germany-do-it.

36. Stiglitz, *The Roaring Nineties*.

37. Romano Prodi, "For a New European Entrepreneurship," public speech, Instituto de Empresa in Madrid, 2002.

38. Audretsch, *The Entrepreneurial Society*.

39. Cited from David B. Audretsch, *Everything in Its Place: Entrepreneurship and the Strategic Management of Cities, Regions and Countries* (New York: Oxford University Press, 2015). National Economic Council, Council of Economic Advisers, and Office of Science and Technology Policy, Washington, D.C.: The White House, February 2011, http://www.whitehouse.gov/sites/default/files/uploads/InnovationStrategy.pdf

40. "A Strategy for American Innovation: Securing Our Economic Growth and Prosperity," National Economic Council, Council of Economic Advisers, and Office of Science and Technology Policy, Washington, D.C.: The White House, February 2011, http://www.whitehouse.gov/sites/default/files/uploads/InnovationStrategy.pdf

41. "Obama's Innovation Agenda," *Forbes*, January 25, 2011,http://www.forbes.com/sites/brianwingfield/ 192011/01/25/obamas-innovation-agenda/.

42. Hermann Simon, *The Hidden Champions of Germany* (Boston: Harvard Business School Press, 1996); and Hermann Simon, *Hidden Champions of the Twenty-First Century: The Success Strategies of Unknown World* (Heidelberg: Springer, 2009).

43. "The Death of Distance," *The Economist*, September 30, 1995, accessed February 2, 2015, at http://www.economist.com/node/598895.

44. Maryann P. Feldman, *The Geography of Innovation* (New York: Springer, 1994); David B. Audretsch and Maryann P. Feldman, "R&D Spillovers and the Geography of Innovation and Production," *American Economic Review* 86 (3), 1996, 630–640; and Maryann P. Feldman and David B. Audretsch, "Innovation in Cities: Science-Based Diversity, Specialization and Localized Competition," *European Economic Review* 43 (2), 1999, 409–429.

45. Paul Romer, "Increasing Returns and Long-Run Growth," *Journal of Political Economy* 94 (5), 1986, 1002–1037.

46. Szabo, *Germany, Russia, and the Rise of Geo-economics*, provides a description and analysis of German policy toward Russia, revealing how unified Germany is finding its global role, and explores the role of German business and finance in the shaping of foreign policy. He investigates how Germany's policy toward Russia affects its broader foreign policy in the region and how it is perceived by key outside players such as the United States, Poland, and the European Union.

47. Hermann Simon, "Unternehmerische Erfolgsgeheimnisse: Deutschlands Staerke hat 13 Gründe," *Frankfurter Allgemeine Zeitung*, October 14, 2012, accessed November 21, 2014, at http://www.faz.net/aktuell/wirtschaft/unternehmen/erfolgsgeheimnisse-deutschlands-staerke-hat-13-gruende-11925735.html.

48. Simon, "Unternehmerische Erfolgsgeheimnisse."

49. Marcel Fratzscher, *Die Deutschland-Illusion: Warum wir unsere Wirtschaft überschätzen und Europa brauchen* (Hamburg: Hanser Verlag, 2014).

50. Bittner, "Germany without *Angst*?"

51. "Germany Put Four Past Minnows Gibraltar but Joachim Löw Wasn't Happy," *Independent*, November 14, 2014, accessed November 16, 2014, at http://www.independent.ie/sport/soccer/european-championships/germany-put-four-past-minnows-gibraltar-but-joachim-löw-wasnt-happy-30746508.html.

52. Bittner, "Germany without *Angst*?"

53. Quoted from Phillip Adler, *Bloomington Herald Times*, October 20, 2014.

54. Bittner, "Germany without *Angst*?"

CHAPTER 2

1. Klaus Ulrich, "Hidden Champions Power Growth," *Deutsche Welle*, October 21, 2012, accessed August 2, 2014, at http://www.dw.de/hidden-champions-power-growth/a-16321468.

2. "Sister Machines Heidi, Sissi, and Gabi Bore for Project of the Century," accessed February 12, 2015, at http://news.eisenwarenmesse.de/en/2011/11/sister-machines-heidi-sissi-and-gabi-bore-for-project-of-the-century/.

3. Jeffrey Fear, "The Secret behind Germany's Thriving 'Mittelstand' Businesses Is All in the Mindset," *The Conversation*, April 28, 2014, accessed at http://theconversation.com/the-secret-behind-germanys-thriving-mittelstand-businesses-is-all-in-the-mindset-25452.

4. Hartmut Berghoff, "The End of Family Business? The Mittelstand and German Capitalism in Transition, 1949–2000," *Business History Review* 80, 2006, 263–295; Institut für Mittelstandsforschung Bonn, "Der deutsche Mittelstand: Ein Konglomerat verschiedenartiger Unternehmen," *IfM Standpunkt* 1, 2013, Bonn.

5. Rose Jacobs, "On Top of the World: This Could Be the Start of Century of German Success," *Newsweek*, July 17, 2014, accessed August 15, 2014, at http://www.newsweek.com/2014/07/25/top-world-could-be-start-century-german-success-259410.html.

6. "German Lessons: Many Countries Want a Mittelstand Like Germany's. It's Not So Easy," *The Economist*, July 12, 2014, downloaded at http://www.economist.com/news/business/21606834-many-countries-want-mittelstand-germanys-it-not-so-easy-copy-german-lessons.

7. Zoltan J. Acs and David B. Audretsch (eds.), *Small Firms and Entrepreneurship: An East-West Perspective* (Cambridge: Cambridge University Press, 1993).

8. David B. Audretsch, *Innovation and Industry Evolution* (Cambridge, MA: MIT Press, 1995); David B. Audretsch, "New-Firm Survival and the Technological Regime," *Review of Economics and Statistics* 73, 1991, 441–450; Michael T. Hannan and John Freeman, "The Population Ecology of Organizations," *American Journal of Sociology* 82 (5), 1977, 929–964; Michael T. Hannan and John Freeman, *Organizational Ecology* (Cambridge, MA: Harvard University Press, 1989); and John Sutton, "Gibrat's Legacy," *Journal of Economic Literature* 35, 1977, 40–59.

9. Audretsch, *Innovation and Industry Evolution*; Audretsch, "New-Firm Survival"; Richard Caves, "Industrial Organization and New Findings on the Turnover and Mobility of Firms," *Journal of Economic Literature* 3, 1998, 1947–1982; and Paul Geroski, "What Do We Know about Entry?" *International Journal of Industrial Organization* 13, 1995, 421–440.

10. "Mittelstand baut Verschuldung ab," *Handelsblatt*, accessed December 12, 2014, at http://www.handelsblatt.com/unternehmen/mittelstand/studie-mittelstand-baut-verschuldung-ab/7622962.html.

11. This is a contrast to conventional thinking but adds to the findings for the United States. See Luigi Zingales, "Survival of the Fittest or the Fattest? Exit and Financing in the Trucking Industry," *Journal of Finance* 53 (3), 1998, 905–938. He shows that not the fittest, i.e., the highly leveraged firms, survive exogenous shocks but those with a lower equity/debt ratio.

12. In 1998, a group of investors working with BC Partners purchased all of the available Grohe shares from the family and delisted the company in the following year, making the Grohe Holding GmbH company, owned by BC partners, into the majority owner of Grohe AG in 1999. It is estimated that BC Partners paid only 100 million euros from their own equity resources and the additional 800 million euros raised by debt financing (leveraged buyout), which led to a high debt and interest burden for Grohe. The company's sales and profitability had been stagnating for years. With the new ownership, cost-saving programs were implemented, and in particular employment cuts at production locations within Germany, while employment at production locations outside of Germany in low-cost countries like Thailand and in particular China were expanded considerably. BC partners sold the company to a consortium of investors from the Texas Pacific Group (TPC) and CSFB Private Equity, a subsidiary of the Swiss Credit Suisse banking group, in 2004, for about 1.5 billion euros. In 1998, when the Grohe family sold their shares, Grohe was the world market leader with a net operating margin of about 10 percent and an equity ratio of 50 percent. Firm growth was always financed by own reserves. In 2005, Franz Müntefering, chairman of the then ruling German Social Democratic party (SPD), sparked a debate on capitalism by designating foreign private equity firms as "locusts." He made TPG-owned Grohe his main target. The "locust" metaphor remained popular in German politics and in the media for years afterward. Since January 2014 Grohe has been owned by the Japanese Lixil Group, an international holding company for building and construction materials. See David B. Audretsch and Erik E. Lehmann, "The Emergence of the Mittelstand Company: A German Perspective," working paper, University of Augsburg, 2015.

13. Ronald C. Anderson and David M. Reeb, "Family Ownership, Corporate Diversification, and Firm Leverage," *Journal of Law and Economics* 46, 2003, 653–684.

14. David B. Audretsch, Marcel Hülsbeck, and Erik E. Lehmann, "Families as Active Monitors of Firm Performance," *Journal of Family Business Strategy* 4 (2), 2013, 118–130.

15. See "Dates, Numbers, Facts," accessed February 15, 2015, at http://www.familienunternehmen.de/en/data-numbers-facts.

16. See www.familienunternehmen.de, accessed December 9, 2014.

17. See www.familienunternehmen.de, accessed December 9, 2014.

18. Frank Maass and Bettina Führmann, "Innovationstätigkeit im Mittelstand," Institut für Mittelstandsforschung, *IfM-Materialien*, 2012, Bonn.

19. http://www.make-it-in-germany.com/en/working/introducing-the-german-mittelstand/, accessed August 25, 2014.

20. http://www.daserste.de/information/reportage-dokumentation/deutsche-dynastien/sendungen/25112013-deutsche-dynastien-das-haus-faber-castell-100.html, accessed July 26, 2014.

21. http://www.make-it-in-germany.com/en/working/introducing-the-german-mittelstand/, accessed August 25, 2014.

22. Ulrich, "Hidden Champions Power Growth."

23. Ulrich, "Hidden Champions Power Growth."

24. David B. Audretsch and Erik E. Lehmann (eds) *Corporate Governance in Small and Medium-Sized Firms* (Cheltenham: Edward Elgar, 2011).

25. Lecture by Wolfgang Grupp at the University of Augsburg, July 4, 2014.

26. Data are taken from *iw-Dienst* 31 (July 31, 2014), 5.

27. Oliver Godart, Holger Görg, and Aofe Hanley, "Trust-Based Work-Time and Product Improvements: Evidence from Firm Level Data," Kiel Working Papers No. 1913, 2014.

28. http://www.dw.de/hidden-champions-power-growth/a-16321468, accessed August 28, 2014.

29. Bundesministerium für Wirtschaft und Energie, "Introducing the German Mittelstand," accessed August 17, 2014 at http://www.make-it-in-germany.com/en/working/introducing-the-german-mittelstand/.

30. http://www.make-it-in-germany.com/en/working/introducing-the-german-mittelstand/, accessed September 1, 2014.

31. http://www.make-it-in-germany.com/en/working/introducing-the-german-mittelstand/.

32. Anja Müller, "Der Stolz der Sieger," *Handelsblatt*, accessed August 3, 2014, at http://www.handelsblatt.com/unternehmen/mittelstand/hidden_champions/weltmarktfuehrer-der-stolz-der-sieger/10258854.html.

33. http://www.make-it-in-germany.com/en/working/introducing-the-german-mittelstand/.

34. http://www.make-it-in-germany.com/en/working/introducing-the-german-mittelstand/, accessed August 23, 2014.

35. Hermann Simon, *Hidden Champions of the 21st Century* (Heidelberg: Springer, 2009), 264.

36. http://www.dw.de/hidden-champions-power-growth/a-16321468, accessed August 28, 2014.

37. Keynote speech by Wolfgang Grupp at the University of Augsburg, July 4, 2014

38. Keynote speech by Wolfgang Grupp at the University of Augsburg, July 4, 2014.

39. "Interview: 'Flexibel und Verrückt' (Flexible and Crazy) with Tobias Groten, CEO Tobit AG," *Wirtschaftswoche*, 42, October 13, 2014, 76–77.

40. Maxwell Wessel, "Why Big Companies Can't Innovate," *Harvard Business Review*, September 27, 2012, accessed December 10, 2012, at https://hbr.org/2012/09/why-big-companies-cant-innovate/. See also Clayton Christenson, *The Innovator's Dilemma: When New Technologies Cause Great Firms to Fail* (Boston: Harvard Business Review Press, 1997).

41. Wessel, "Why Big Companies Can't Innovate"; and Christensen, *The Innovator's Dilemma*.

42. Keynote speech by Wolfgang Grupp, University of Augsburg, July 4, 2014.

43. "Globale Champions," *Wirtschaftswoche* 41 (October 6, 2014), 65.

44. Katrin Terpitz, "Die Orchidee-Kloner," *Handelsblatt*, November 23, 2014, accessed November 25, 2014, at http://www.handelsblatt.com/unternehmen/mittelstand/hidden-champion/hark.

45. Ulrich, "Hidden Champions Power Growth." Originally from: Hermann Simon, "Lessons from Germany's Midsize Giants", Harvard Business Review, March-April, 1992, pp. 115–123.

46. Hermann Simon, *The Hidden Champions of Germany* (Boston: Harvard Business School Press, 1996); Simon, *Hidden Champions of the Twenty-First Century*; and Ulrich, "Hidden Champions Power Growth."

47. Personnel interview with Alexander and Manfred Starnecker, June 15, 2015.

48. Anja Müller, "Der Stolz der Sieger," August 3rd 2014, downloaded at http://www.handelsblatt.com/unternehmen/mittelstand/hidden_champions/weltmarktfuehrer-der-stolz-der-sieger/10258854.html.

49. "Otto wer? Duder was?" *Wirtschaftswoche* 41 (October 10, 2014), 84.

50. Brett Anita Gilbert, Patricia P. McDougall, and David B. Audretsch, "Clusters, Knowledge Spillovers and New Venture Performance: An Empirical Examination," *Journal of Business Venturing* 23 (4), 405–422; Brett Anita Gilbert, Patricia P. McDougall, and David B. Audretsch, "New Venture Growth: A Review and Extension," *Journal of Management* 32 (6), 2006, 926–950. For a review of the literature linking agglomeration to regional growth see Richard Baldwin and Philippe Martin, "Agglomeration and Regional Growth," in J. Vernon Henderson and Jacques-François Thisse (eds.), *Handbook of Regional and Urban Economics*, vol. 4 (Amsterdam: Elsevier, 2004), 2671–2711.

51. "Nanu, sie lebt ja noch," *Wirtschaftswoche* 4 (January 19, 2015), 42–45. See Edward L. Glaeser, *The Triumph of the City* (London: Macmillan, 2011).

52. "Nanu, sie lebt ja noch."

53. See Glaeser, *Triumph of the City*.

54. Audretsch, *Innovation and Industry Evolution*.

55. Zoltan J. Acs and David B. Audretsch (eds.), *Handbook of Entrepreneurship Research: An Interdisciplinary Survey and Introduction*, 2nd ed. (New York: Springer, 2010).

56. Acs and Audretsch, *Handbook of Entrepreneurship Research*.

57. David B. Audretsch, Max Keilbach, and Erik E. Lehmann, *Entrepreneurship and Economic Growth* (New York: Oxford University Press, 2006); David B. Audretsch and Erik E. Lehmann, "Does the Knowledge Spillover Theory of Entrepreneurship Hold for Regions?" *Research Policy* 34 (8), 2005, 1191–1202.

58. Audretsch, *Innovation and Industry Evolution*; Audretsch, "New-Firm Survival"; and David B. Audretsch and Talat Mahmood, "New-Firm Survival: New Results Using a Hazard Function," *Review of Economics and Statistics* 77 (1), 1995, 97–103.

59. Audretsch, *Innovation and Industry Evolution*.

60. Andy Grove, *Only the Paranoid Survive* (New York: Crown Books, 1996).

61. David B. Audretsch, *The Entrepreneurial Society* (New York: Oxford University Press, 2007).

62. "Start-ups: If I Can Make It There . . . Silicon Alley," *Wirtschaftswoche* 27 (June 30, 2014), 42.

63. Audretsch, *The Entrepreneurial Society*.

64. See Julian Franks, Colin Mayer, and Hannes F. Wagner, "The Origins of the German Corporation: Finance, Ownership and Control," *Review of Finance* 10 (4), 2006, 537–585.

65. See "European Entrepreneurs: Les Miserables," *Economist*, July 28, 2012, 2, accessed August 13, 2014 at http://www.economist.com/node/21559618/print.

66. Romano Prodi, "For a New European Entrepreneurship," public speech delivered at Instituto de Empresa, Madrid, February 7, 2002.

67. "Forschungspolititk: Sind wir noch so gut?" *Der Spiegel*, January 5, 2004, accessed February 17, 2015, at http://www.spiegel.de/spiegel/print/d-29610121.html.

68. Marianne Kulicke, "15 Years of EXIST 'University-Based Start-Up Programmes,'" working paper, Fraunhofer Institute, 2014, accessed February 3, 2014 at http://www.exist.de/SharedDocs/Downloads/EN/Entwicklung-Exist-1998–2013-EN.pdf?__blob=publicationFile.

69. David B. Audretsch, testimony on *Spurring Innovation and Job Creation: The SBIR Program: Hearing before the Honorable Committee on Small Business*, 112th Congress, March 7, 2011, accessed September 2, 2014, at http://smallbusiness.house.gov/uploadedfiles/al_link_sbir_testimony_for_4.7.11.pdf.

70. Audretsch, *The Entrepreneurial Society*.

71. "European Entrepreneurs: Les Miserables."

72. "European Entrepreneurs: Les Miserables."

73. Leslie Berlin, *The Man behind the Microchip: Robert Noyce and the Invention of Silicon Valley* (New York: Oxford University Press, 2006).

74. http://de.wikipedia.org/wiki/Br%C3%BCder_Samwer#cite_note-10.

75. "Die Malefiz-Rakete," *Der Spiegel*, 40, September 20, 2014, 64.

76. "Joint Venture mit Roland Berger," Samwer-Brüder gründen Super-Inkubator, http://www.n-tv.de/wirtschaft/Samwer-Brueder-gruenden-Super-Inkubator, December 17, 2014.

77. Audretsch, Keilbach, and Lehmann, *Entrepreneurship and Economic Growth*; David B. Audretsch and Michael Fritsch, "Growth Regimes over Time and Space," *Regional Studies* 36, 2002, 113–124; David B. Audretsch and Max Keilbach, "Entrepreneurship Capital and Economic Performance," *Regional Studies* 38, 2004, 949–959; David B. Audretsch and Max Keilbach, "Does Entrepreneurship Capital Matter?" *Entrepreneurship Theory and Practice*, Fall 2004, 419–429; David B. Audretsch, Werner Bönte, and Max Keilbach, "Entrepreneurship Capital and Its Impact on Knowledge Diffusion and Economic Performance," *Journal of Business Venturing* 23 (6), 2008, 687–698; and Michael Fritsch, "New Firms and Regional Employment Change," *Small Business Economics* 9, 1997, 437–448.

78. David B. Audretsch and Michael Fritsch, "Creative Destruction: Turbulence and Economic Growth," in Ernst Helmstädter and Mark Perlman (eds.), *Behavioral Norms, Technological Progress, and Economic Dynamics: Studies in Schumpeterian Economics* (Ann Arbor: University of Michigan Press, 1996), 137–150.

79. The entrepreneurial ventures spawned from large companies, universities, and research institutions are best characterized in the academic literature in the knowledge spillover theory of entrepreneurship; see Zoltan J. Acs, David B. Audretsch, and Erik E. Lehmann, "The Knowledge Spillover Theory of Entrepreneurship," *Small Business Economics* 41, 2013, 757–774.

80. See "Cluster als Katalysator der Innovation," *Venture Capital Magazine*, "Special Unternehmensfinanzierung in Baden-Württemberg," 3, 2014, 16.

81. "Denkende Hände", *Wirtschaftswoche* 50 (December 8, 2014), 78.

82. "Denkende Hände," 76.

83. "Notorische Neumacher, Deutschlands Pioniere," *Wirtschaftswoche* 29 (July 14, 2014), 64–68.

84. "The Cost of Cool: To Stay Sexy, Must the German Capital Remain Poor?" *Economist*, September 17, 2011, accessed August 19, 2014, at http://www.economist.com/node/21529075.

85. "Der Mittelstand schlägt die Zuckerbergs und Musks," *Handelsblatt*, January 26, 2015, accessed January 29, 2015 at http://www.handelsblatt.com/unternehmen/it-medien/axa-gruendungsstudie-der-mittelstand-schlägt-die-zuckerbergs-und-musks/11280494.html.

86. "Der Mittelstand schlägt die Zuckerbergs und Musks."

87. "Notorische Neumacher, Deutschlands Pioniere," *Wirtschaftswoche* 29 (July 14, 2014), 64.

CHAPTER 3

1. The origin of Germany as *Das Land der Dichter und Denker* remains ambiguous and is typically attributed to two different sources. First, following Jeremy Wasser, "Spätzle Westerns," *Der Spiegel,* April 6, 2006, the expression *Land der Dichter und Denker*, dates back to Wolfgang Menzel (1798–1873), a German philosopher and writer who commented on the drastically greater number of printed pages and the generation and dissemination of knowledge in Germany compared to its neighbors, France, and the United Kingdom; see "Explosion des Wissens," *Spiegel-Online*, August 2, 2010, accessed December 13, 2014, at http://www.spiegel.de/spiegel/a-709761.html. The second source is the French noblesse Anne Louise Germaine de Staël-Holstein (1766–1817), who during her journeys through Germany, frequently met with the famous thinkers, poets, and philosophers, most prominantly Johann Wolfgang von Goethe, Friedrich Schiller, and Friedrich Schlegel. She collected her impressions in her classic book *De l'Allemagne*, and, because Emperor Napoleon Bonaparte banned this book in France, she published it first in the United Kingdom. A few years later, this book served as a starting point for foreign visitors to Germany and led to widepsread fascination with deutsche *Dichter und Denker*, or the poets and thinkers of Germany. See Angelica Goodden, *Madame de Staël: the Dangerous Exile* (New York: Oxford University Press, 2008).

2. http://www.oecd.org/pisa/.

3. "The World University Rankings, 2013–2014," Thomson Reuters, accessed August 15, 2014, at http://www.timeshighereducation.co.uk/world-university-rankings/2013–14/world-ranking.

4. World Economic Forum, *Human Capital Report* (Geneva: World Economic Forum, 2013).

5. "The World's Highest Paid Soccer Players," *Forbes*, May 7, 2014, accessed August 15, 2014, at http://www.forbes.com/pictures/mlh45egml/no-20-luis-suarez-liverpool/.

6. Herbert Giersch, Karl-Heinz Paqué, and Holger Schmieding, *The Fading Miracle: Four Decades of Market Economy in Germany* (New York: Cambridge University Press, 1992).

7. Barry Eichengreen, *The European Economy since 1945: Coordinated Capitalism and Beyond* (Princeton, NJ: Princeton University Press, 2008).

8. Eichengreen, *European Economy since 1945*.

9. Albert Speer (1905–1981), formerly chief architect of Hitlers Germania, was appointed in 1942 by Hitler as the minister of armaments and war production. Until the end of World War II, more than ten thousand managers and engineers, almost all of them younger than forty years old, worked for Albert Speer's ministry. Hitler himself created the expression "Speer's Kindergarten" or "Speer's boys." More than six thousand highly qualified, motivated, and disciplined managers and engineers, all younger than fiffty, worked for the "Endsieg." After the war, they provided the managerial and engineering backbone of the German *Wirtschaftswunder*. See Nina Grunenberg, *Die Wundertäter, Netzwerke der deutschen Wirtschaft* (Munich: Siedler, 2006).

10. Ferdinand Porsche (1875 – 1951), invented the beetle for the Nazis in the mid-1930s. He established the *Dr. Ing. h.c. F. Porsche AG*, usually shortened to *Porsche AG*, which was in 1931 a construction bureau for cars but also tanks. After World War II his son Ferry Porsche began manufacturing his own car, the first Porsche simply because he could not find an existing one that he wanted to buy. Since then, Porsche AG has become one of the most prestigious German automobile manufacturers, specializing in high-performance sports cars. Since 2009 Porsche AG is owned by Volkswagen AG, which is majority-owned by Porsche Automobile Holding SE. P, with the two families of Porsche and Piëch as the stakeholders.

11. Jonathan Wood, *The Volkswagen Beetle* (Buckinghamshire: Shire Publications, 2003) provides a short history.

12. Amity Shlaes explores distinct segments of German society that reflect the memories, traditions, and dreams that will burden and shape the country; see Amity Shlaes, *Germany: The Empire Within* (New York: Farrar, Straus and Giroux, 1991).

13. "Bildung und Kultur, Berufliche Schulen," *Fachserie 11, Reihe 2* (Wiesbaden: Statistisches Bundesamt, 2014), accessed at https://www.destatis.de/DE/Publikationen/Thematisch/BildungForschungKultur/Schulen/BeruflicheSchulen2110200147004.pdf?__blob=publicationFile.

14. "Schult die Meister," *Die Zeit*, December 13, 2014, accessed December 21, 2014, at http://www.zeit.de/2014/49/weiterbildung-meister-echulung.

15. Organization for Economic Cooperation and Development, "Education at a Glance 2013," accessed October 2, 2014, at http://www.oecd-ilibrary.org/education/education-at-a-glance-2013_eag-2013-en.

16. Organization for Economic Cooperation and Development, "Education at a Glance 2013."

17. Robert Solow, "A Contribution to the Theory of Economic Growth," *Quarterly Journal of Economics*, 39, 1956, 312–320; and Robert Solow, "Technical Change and the Aggregate Production Function," *Review of Economics and Statistics* 39, 1957, 312–320.

18. William H. Whyte, *The Organization Man* (New York: Simon and Schuster, 1956).

19. Whyte, *The Organization Man*, 129.

20. See the Presidential Address to the American Association for 1970 by Wassily Leontief, "Theoretical Assumptions and Nonobserved Facts," *American Economic Review* 61 (1), 1971, 1–17.

21. Todd Gitlin, *The Sixties: Years of Hope, Days of Rage* (New York: Bantam Books, 1993), 13.

22. David Halberstam, *The Fifties* (New York: Villard Books, 1993), 116.

23. Subsequently expanded to the Heckscher-Samuelson-Ohlin model; see Edward E. Leamer, *The Heckscher-Ohlin Model in Theory and Practice* (Princeton, NJ: Princeton University Press, 1995).

24. Harry P. Bowen, Edward Leamer, and Leo Sveikauskas, "Multicountry, Multifactor Tests of the Factor Abundance Theory," *American Economic Review* 77, 1987, 791–809; and Harry P. Bowen and Leo Sveikauskas, "Inter-industry Regression Estimates of Factor Abundance," in David B. Audretsch and Michael P. Claudon (eds.), *The Internationalization of U.S. Markets* (New York: New York University Press, 1989), 49–72.

25. Donald Keesing, "Labor Skills and Comparative Advantage," *American Economic Review* 56, 1966, 249–258; T. C. Loweinger, "The Neo-factor Proportions Theory of International Trade: An Empirical Investigation," *American Economic Review* 61, 1971, 675–681; Keith E. Maskus, Deborah Battles, and Michael H. Moffett, "Determinants of the Structure of U.S. Manufacturing Trade with Japan and Korea, 1970–1984," in Audretsch and Claudon, *Internationalization of U.S. Markets*, 97–121; David B. Audretsch and Hideki Yamawaki, "R&D, Industrial Policy, and U.S.-Japanese Trade," *Review of Economics and Statistics* 70, August 1988, 438–447; Bee-Yan Aw, "The Interpretation of Cross-Section Regression Tests of the Heckscher-Ohlin Theorem with Many Goods and Factors," *Journal of International Economics* 14, 1983, 163–167; and Stephen P. Magee, "The Competence Theory of Comparative Advantage," in Audretsch and Claudon, *Internationalization of U.S. Markets*, 11–23.

26. Harry Bowen, Ed Leamer, and Leo Sveikauskas, "Multicountry, Multifactor Tests"; Bowen and Sveikauskas, 1989, "Inter-industry Regression Estimates"; Kirsty Hughes, "The Role of

Technology, Competition and Skills in European Competitiveness," in Kirsty Hughes (ed.), *European Competitiveness* (Cambridge: Cambridge University Press, 1993), 133–160.

27. Hideki Yamawaki, "International Trade and Foreign Direct Investment in West German Manufacturing Industries," in Joachim Schwalbach (ed.), *Industry Structure and Performance* (Berlin: Edition Sigma, 1985), 247–286; Aw, "Interpretation of Cross-Section"; Bowen, Leamer, and Sveikauskas, "Multicountry, Multifactor Tests"; and Bowen and Sveikauskas, "Inter-industry Regression Estimates."

28. Giersch, Paqué, and Schmieding, *The Fading Miracle*.

29. Thomas L. Friedman, *The World Is Flat* (London: Lane, 2005).

30. Gerlinde Sinn and Hans-Werner Sinn, *Jumpstart* (Cambridge, MA: MIT Press, 1994).

31. Lester Thurow, "Losing the Economic Race," *New York Review of Books*, September 27, 1984, 29–31.

32. Lester Thurow, "Healing with a Thousand Bandages," *Challenge* 28 (1987), 23.

33. Paul Kennedy, *The Rise and Decline of Great Powers* (New York: Random House, 1989).

34. Michael L. Derouzos, Richard K. Lester, and Robert M. Solow, *Made in America: Regaining the Productive Edge* (Cambridge, MA: MIT Press, 1989).

35. Joseph S. Stiglitz, *The Roaring Nineties: A New History of the World's Most Prosperous Decade* (New York: Norton, 2004); and David B. Audretsch, *The Entrepreneurial Society* (New York: Oxford University Press, 2007).

36. Stiglitz, *The Roaring Nineties*.

37. Solow, "Theory of Economic Growth"; and Solow, "Technical Change."

38. Paul Romer, "Endogenous Technological Change," *Journal of Political Economy* 98, 1990, 1–102; and Paul Romer, "The Origins of Endogenous Growth Theory," *Journal of Economic Perspectives* 8, 1994, 3–22.

39. This was formalized by Zvi Griliches, "Issues in Assessing the Contribution of Research and Development to Productivity Growth," *Bell Journal of Economics* 10, 1979, 92–116.

40. David B. Audretsch, *Everything in Its Place: Entrepreneurship and the Strategic Management of Cities, Regions and States* (New York: Oxford University Press, 2015); and Tim Bresnahan and Alfonso Gambardella (eds.), *Building High-Tech Clusters: Silicon Valley and Beyond* (Cambridge: Cambridge University Press, 2004).

41. AnnaLee Saxenian, *Regional Advantage: Culture and Competition in Silicon Valley and Route 128* (Cambridge, MA: Harvard University Press, 1994).

42. Zoltan J. Acs and David B. Audretsch, "Innovation in Large and Small Firms: An Empirical Analysis," *American Economic Review* 78 (4), 1988, 678–690; and Zoltan J. Acs and David B. Audretsch, *Innovation in Small Firms* (Cambridge, MA: MIT Press, 1990).

43. Bresnahan and Gambardella, *Building High-Tech Clusters*.

44. David B. Audretsch and Maryann P. Feldman, "R&D Spillovers and the Geography of Innovation and Production," *American Economic Review* 86 (3), 1996, 630–640; Zoltan J. Acs, David B. Audretsch, and Maryann P. Feldman, "Real Effects of University Research," *American Economic Review* 82 (1), 1992, 363–367; Adam Jaffe, "The Real Effects of Academic Research," *American Economic Review* 79, 957–970; and Adam Jaffe, Manuel Trajtenberg, and Rebecca Henderson, "Geographic Localization of Knowledge Spillovers as Evidenced by Patent Citations," *Quarterly Journal of Economics* 63, 1993, 577–598.

45. Gary S. Becker, *Human Capital: A Theoretical and Empirical Analysis, with Special Reference to Education* (Chicago: University of Chicago Press, 1964).

46. "Es ist nicht genug zu wissen, man muss es auch anwenden; es ist nicht genug zu wollen, man muss es tun." Johann Wolfgang von Goethe, *Wilhelm Meisters Wanderjahre*, III, chapter 18.

47. Romer, "Endogenous Technological Change"; and Romer, "Endogenous Growth Theory."

48. Introductory statement of Birch Bayh, September 13, 1978, cited from Association of University Technology Managers, 2004, *Recollections: Celebrating the History of AUTM and the Legacy of Bayh-Dole*, 5. Retrieved from bayhdolecentral.com at http://bayhdolecentral.com/3_DIV_SCAN/B7s023_OCR.pdf.

49. Statement by Birch Bayh, April 13, 1980, on the approval of S. 414 (Bayh-Dole) by the U.S. Senate on a 91–4 vote, cited from Association of University Technology Managers, *Recollections*, 5.

50. David B. Audretsch, Max Keilbach, and Erik E. Lehmann, *Entrepreneurship and Economic Growth* (New York: Oxford University Press, 2006); David B. Audretsch and Max Keilbach, "Resolving the Knowledge Paradox: Knowledge-Spillover Entrepreneurship and Economic Growth," *Research Policy* 37 (1), 2008, 1697–1705; and David B. Audretsch and Max Keilbach, "The Theory of Knowledge Spillover Entrepreneurship," *Journal of Management Studies* 44 (7), 2007, 1242–1254.

51. David Mowery, Richard R. Nelson, Bhaven N. Sampat, and Arvids A. Ziedonis, *Ivory Tower and Industrial Innovation: University-Industry Technology Transfer before and after the Bayh-Dole Act* (Stanford, CA.: Stanford University Press, 2004); and T. Taylor Aldridge and David B. Audretsch, "The Bayh-Dole Act and Scientist Entrepreneurship," *Research Policy* 40 (8), 2011, 1058–1067.

52. Public Law 98–620.

53. Mowery et al., *Ivory Tower*; and Aldridge and Audretsch, "The Bayh-Dole Act."

54. "Innovation's Golden Goose," *The Economist*, December 12, 2002, accessed February 15, 2015, at http://www.economist.com/node/1476653.

55. "Defending the University Tech Transfer System," *Business Week*, February 19, 2010, accessed October 3, 2014, at http://www.businessweek.com/smallbiz/content/feb2010/sb20100219_307735.htm.

56. Testimony of David B. Audretsch to the House of Representatives, Committee on Small Business, March 16, 2011, accessed October 5, 2014, at http://smallbusiness.house.gov/uploadedfiles/david_audretsch_sbir_testimony.pdf.

57. Testimony of David B. Audretsch.

58. Charles C. Wessner (ed.), *National Research Council: An Assessment of the SBIR Program* (Washington, DC: National Academies Press, 2008).

59. Testimony of David B. Audretsch.

60. Robert X. Cringley, *Accidental Empires: How the Boys of Silicon Valley Make Their Millions, Battle Foreign Competition, and Still Can't Get a Date* (New York: Harper Business, 1993); Frank Rose, *West of Eden: The End of Innocence at Apple Computer* (New York: Viking Press, 1989); and Audretsch, *The Entrepreneurial Society*.

61. Audretsch, Keilbach, and Lehmann, *Entrepreneurship and Economic Growth*; Audretsch and Keilbach, "Resolving the Knowledge Paradox"; and David B. Audretsch, *Innovation and Industry Evolution* (Cambridge, MA: MIT Press, 1995).

62. Audretsch, *The Entrepreneurial Society*.

63. Stiglitz, *The Roaring Nineties*.

64. Aw, "Interpretation of Cross-Section"; Bowen, Leamer, and Sveikauskas, "Multicountry, Multifactor Tests"; Bowen and Sveikauskas, "Inter-industry Regression Estimates"; and Audretsch and Yamawaki, "R&D Rivalry."

65. Commission of Experts for Research and Innovation, *Research, Innovation and Technological Performance in Germany: Report 2014* (Berlin: Commission of Experts for Research and Innovation, 2014).

66. Commission of Experts for Research and Innovation, *Research, Innovation and Technological Performance*.

67. Commission of Experts for Research and Innovation, *Research, Innovation and Technological Performance*.

68. R. Steven Turner, "The Prussian Universities and the Research Imperative, 1806–1848," PhD dissertation, Princeton University, 1972, 1, cited in Peter Watson, *The German Genius: Europe's Third Renaissance, the Second Scientific Revolution, and the Twentieth Century* (New York: Harper Perennial, 2011), 225.

69. James F. Tent, *The Free University of Berlin: A Political History* (Bloomington: Indiana University Press, 1988).

70. Watson, *The German Genius*, 233.

71. Daniel Fallon, *The German University: A Heroic Ideal in Conflict with the Modern World* (Boulder: University of Colorado Press, 1980), 5.

72. Turner, "Prussian Universities," 8, cited in Watson, *The German Genius*, 226.

73. Turner, "Prussian Universities," 279, cited in Watson, *The German Genius*, 230.

74. Granville Stanley Hall, "Educational Reforms," *Pedagogical Seminary* (contemporary *Journal of Genetic Psychology*), 1 (1891), 6–8, cited in Fallon, *The German University*.

75. Cited in Fallon, *The German University*.

76. Tent, *Free University of Berlin*.

77. In 1935 Carl von Ossietzky was honored with the Nobel Peace Prize. He was arrested by the Nazis and convicted of high treason and espionage in 1931. He died in 1938 from complications from his treatment at the hands of his captors in various concentration camps. Hitler responded to von Ossietzky's international recognition of his scientific accomplishments by strongly refusing to accept subsequent prizes from the Nobel committee (among them where Richard Kuhn, chemistry, 1938, Adolf Butenandt, chemistry, 1939, and Gerhard Domagk, medicine, 1939). Several scientists and future Nobel Prize winners were able to migrate to the United States after 1933, among them Otto Stern (physics, 1939) and Wolfgang Pauli (physics, 1945).

78. Fallon, *The German University*.

79. The quote dates back to Bernard of Clairvaux (1090–1153) who argued that "There are those who seek knowledge for the sake of knowledge; that is curiosity. There are those who seek knowledge to be known by others; that is vanity. There are those who seek knowledge in order to serve; that is love."

80. Vannevar Bush, *Science: The Endless Frontier* (Washington, DC: US Government Printing Office, 1945).

81. Audretsch, *The Entrepreneurial Society*.

82. David B. Audretsch, "Scientific Entrepreneurship: The Stealth Conduit of University Knowledge Spillovers," *George Mason Law Review* 21 (4), 2014, 1015–1026.

83. Audretsch, "Scientific Entrepreneurship."

84. Zoltan J. Acs, *The Philanthropist: Completing the Circle of Prosperity* (Princeton, NJ: Princeton University Press, 2012).

85. Beth Healy, "Harvard Endowment Posts 15.4 Percent Gain," *Boston Globe*, September 24, 2014, accessed September 26, 2014, at http://www.bostonglobe.com/business/2014/09/23/harvard-university-endowment-posts-percent-annual-gain/Ooi2bqjOcYFjFPPUsXBvCM/story.html.

86. "Harvard's Endowment Is Bigger Than Half the World's Economies," accessed September 26, 2014, at http://www.boston.com/business/news/2014/09/25/harvard-endowment-bigger-than-half-the-world-economies/UAOY9V4lg6fcjArrSyCgWJ/story.html.

87. In an unpublished report, the Expertenkommission Forschung und Innovation of the German government expresses considerable concern and criticism of higher education and university policies that triggered the brain drain of leading scientists and other academics, which has resulted in a high cost of trying to recruit them back. See "Zu Brain Drain: Wissenschaftler Wandern ab," *Der Spiegel*, February 2, 2014, accessed March 19, 2014, at http://www.spiegel.de/unispiegel/jobundberuf/spiegel-zu-braindrain-wissenschaftler-wandern-ab-a-955141.html.

88. "Soziale Einschnitte und Steuerreform sollen Wirtschaftswachstum anregen: Bundesregierung beschließt Aktionsprogramm für Investitionen und Arbeitsplätze," *Der Tagesspiegel*, January 31, 1996, 1.

89. "No Bubbling Brook," *Economist*, September 10, 1994, accessed December 23, 2014, at http://www.highbeam.com/doc/1G1-15816658.html.

90. The actual title of the proposed program was Aktionsprogramm für Investitionen und Arbeitsplätze ("Soziale Einschnitte und Steurreform sollen Wirtschaftswachstum anregen: Bundesregierung beschliesst Aktionsprogramm für Investitionen und Arbeitsplätze," *Der Tagesspiegel*, January 31, 1996, 1).

91. The original text of the Aktionsprogramm states, "Offensive für unternehmerische Selbstständigkeit und Innvoationsfähigkeit" ("Ein Kraftakt zur Rettung des Standorts Deutschland," *Frankfurter Allgemeine Zeitung*, January 31, 1996, 11).

92. See Marcel Hülsbeck, Erik E. Lehmann, and Alexander Starnecker, "Performance of Technology Transfer Offices in Germany," *Journal of Technology Transfer*, 2013, 38, 199–215.

93. Arbeitnehmererfindungsgesetz (ArbNERrfG 2002), German law on employees` invention, 2002, accessed on June 2015 on https://www.bmbf.de/pubRD/arbeitnehmererfindergesetz.pdf

94. Audretsch, *The Entrepreneurial Society*.

95. Klaus F. Zimmerman, "Vorwort," in Klaus F. Zimmerman (ed.), *Deutschland—was nun? Reformen für Wirtschaft und Gesellschaft* (Munich: Deutscher Taschenbuch Verlag, 2006), v.

96. Erik E. Lehmann and Alexander Starnecker, "Introducing the Universities of Applied Sciences," in David B. Audretsch, Erik E. Lehmann, Albert N. Link, and Alexander Starnecker (eds.), *Technology Transfer in a Global Economy* (Heidelberg: Springer, 2012), 99–115.

97. "Standortfaktor Schiller," *iw-dienst* 40 (October 2, 2014), 8.

CHAPTER 4

1. "Karneval und Brotkultur sind deutsches Kulturerbe," *Handelsblatt*, December 12, 2014, accessed February 12, 2015, at http://www.handelsblatt.com/panorama/aus-aller-welt/27-neue-tradition.

2. While the expression *Germanen* was first named by the Roman philosopher Posidonius (about 90 BC), the Roman emperor Julius Caesar introduced this name in the literature in his "De bello Gallico."

3. Peter Arens and Stefan Brauburger, *Die Deutschlandsaga* (Munich: Bertelsmann, 2014).

4. Dirk Nowitzki, "Wenn ich an Deutschland Denke: Dirk Nowitzki über Seine Alte Heimat," *Mobil: Das Magazin der Deutschen Bahn*, August 2014, 32.

5. Nowitzki, "Wenn ich an Deutschland Denke," 32.

6. What Goethe actually wrote was "Zwei Dinge sollen Kinder von ihren Eltern bekommen: Wurzeln und Flügel"

7. David B. Audretsch, "Legalized Cartels in West Germany," *Antitrust Bulletin* 34 (3), 1989, 579–600.

8. David B. Audretsch, *Everything in Its Place: Entrepreneurship and the Strategic Management of Cities, Regions and States* (New York: Oxford University Press, 2015).

9. Vera Linss, *Die wichtigsten Wirtschaftsdenker* (Wiesbaden: Marix Verlag, 2007).

10. Heinz D. Kurz, *Geschichte des Ökonomischen Denkens* (Munich: C.H. Beck, 2013), 120.

11. Johann Heinrich von Thünen, *Der isoli[e]rte Staat in Beziehung auf Landwirtschaft und Nationalökonomie, oder Untersuchungen über den Einfluß, den die Getreidepreise, der Reichthum des Bodens und die Abgaben auf den Ackerbau ausüben* (Hamburg: Perthes, 1826).

12. Audretsch, *Everything in Its Place*.

13. M. Mareshan, "Europe's Economic Suicide? Editorial," 2014, accessed January 2, 2015, at http://www.nineoclock.ro/europe%E2%80%99s-economic-suicide/.

14. Frederick William I of Prussia (1688 –1740) first introduced and practiced what we today call *Standortpolitik*. He was concerned with virtually every aspect of his small country, Prussia and felt compelled to ensure both planning to defend the country against foreign invaders but also to sustain a flourishing economy. He became widely known as the "Soldier King", even though he never started a war, which enabled him to accumulate a large surplus in the royal treasury. As remarkable it may seem for a political leader to accumulate a surplus in the budget in today's world, it was even more exceptional during King William's era. However, what still holds to this very day for *Standortpolitik*, King William understood that policy to promote the economic and social *Wohlstand*, or standard of living, was more pervasive and affected many aspects of policy and life, and was not restricted to just one or a few aspects. He established primary schools, and installed the first chairs in economics (cameral sciences) at the Prussian universities of Halle and Frankfurt an der Oder in 1727. Cameralism has since then often been viewed as the science of government, dedicated to reforming society and promoting economic development in the 18th-century countries comprising what is today Germany. The Cameralists were the first academics in regional science at universities, pointing out that the state should not solely focus on maintaining the law and promoting collective prosperity but also to mobilize the resources of land and population in service of the common good. See Andre Wakefield, *The Disordered Police State: German Cameralism as Science and Practice* (Chicago: University of Chicago Press, 2009).

15. Hans-Werner Sinn, *Ist Deutschland Noch zu Retten?* (Berlin: Econ Verlag, 2004); Hans-Werner Sinn, *Can Germany Be Saved? The Malaise of the World's First Welfare State* (Cambridge, MA: MIT Press, 2009); Dennis J. Snower, Alesso J. G. Brown, and Christian Merkl, "Globalization and the Welfare State: A Review of Hans-Werner Sinn's *Can Germany Be Saved?" Journal of Economic Literature* 47 (1), 2009, 136–158.

16. Horst Siebert, *The German Economy: Beyond the Social Market* (Princeton, NJ: Princeton University Press, 2005).

17. Hans-Werner Sinn, "Ordnungspolitik Funktioniert Immer," *Der Spiegel*, November 6, 2014, accessed November 13, 2014, at http://www.spiegel.de/wirtschaft/soziales/ökonomie-kritik-hans-werner-sinn-antwortet-wolfgang-muenchau-a-1001214.html.

18. Maris Hubschmid, "Das Ende der Dynamik," *Der Tagesspiegel*, June 1, 1214, 17, accessed July 25, 2014, at http://www.tagesspiegel.de/wirtschaft/arbeitsmarkt-das-ende-der-dynamik/6696496.html.

19. Richard Florida, "The World Is Spiky," *Atlantic*, October 25, 2005, accessed December 26, 2014, at http://www.creativeclass.com/rfcgdb/articles/other-2005-The%20World%20is%20Spiky.pdf.

20. Audretsch, *Everything in Its Place*

21. Robert M. Solow, "A Contribution to the Theory of Economic Growth," *Quarterly Journal of Economics* 70 (1), 1956, 65–94; and Robert M. Solow, "Technical Change and the Aggregate Production Function," *Review of Economics and Statistics* 39 (3), 1957, 312–320.

22. David B. Audretsch, *The Entrepreneurial Society* (New York: Oxford University Press, 2007). P.5

23. "The Death of Distance," *Economist*, September 30, 1995, accessed January 15, 2015, at accessed at http://www.economist.com/node/598895.

24. "The Death of Distance."

25. Edward E. Leamer, "A Flat World, a Level Playing Field, a Small World after All, or None of the Above? A Review of Thomas L Friedman's *The World Is Flat*," *Journal of Economic Literature* 45 (1), 2007, 83–126.

26. http://www.youtube.com/watch?v=jtEErh-wFrc.

27. David B. Audretsch and Maryann P. Feldman, "R&D Spillovers and the Geography of Innovation and Production," *American Economic Review* 86 (3), 1996, 630–640; and Maryann P. Feldman and David B. Audretsch, "Innovation in Cities: Science-Based Diversity, Specialization and Localized Monopoly," *European Economic Review* 43, 1999, 409–429.

28. Audretsch and Feldman, "R&D Spillovers"; Zoltan J. Acs, David B. Audretsch, and Maryann P. Feldman, "Real Effects of Academic Research," *American Economic Review* 82, 1992, 363–367; Adam Jaffe, "The Real Effects of Academic Research," *American Economic Review* 79, 1989, 957–970; and Adam Jaffe, Manuel Trajtenberg, and Rebecca Henderson, "Geographic Localization of Knowledge Spillovers as Evidenced by Patent Citations," *Quarterly Journal of Economics* 63, 1993, 577–598.

29. Thomas Friedman, *The World Is Flat* (London: Lane, 2005).

30. David B. Audretsch, *The Entrepreneurial Society* (New York: Oxford University Press, 2007).

31. Lester Thurow, *Fortune Favors the Bold* (Cambridge: MIT Press, 2002), 11.

32. Friedman, *The World Is Flat.*

33. Audretsch, *Everything in Its Place.*

34. Bruce Katz, *The Metropolitan Revolution: How Cities and Metros Are Fixing Our Broken Politics and Fragile Economy* (Washington, DC: Brookings, 2014); Audretsch, *Everything in Its Place*; Edward Glaeser, *Triumph of the City: How Our Greatest Invention Makes Us Richer, Smarter, Greener, Healthier, and Happier* (New York: Penguin, 2014), and David B. Audretsch, Al Link, and Mary Walshok (eds.), *The Oxford Handbook of Local Competitiveness* (New York: Oxford University Press, 2015).

35. Philip McCann, Dominique Foray, and Raquel Artega-Argiles, "Smart Specialization and Its Application in European Regional Policies," in Audretsch, Link, and Walshok, *Oxford Handbook of Local Competitiveness* (New York: Oxford University Press, 2015).

36. McCann, Foray, and Artega-Argiles, "Smart Specialization"; and Mark Thissen, Frank Van Oort, Dario Diodato, and Arjan Ruijs, *Regional Competitiveness and Smart Specialization in Europe* (London: Edward Elgar, 2013).

37. John Maynard Keynes, *The Economics of the Peace* (New York: Harcourt Brace, 1920).

38. Marcel Hülsbeck and Erik E. Lehmann, "Entrepreneurship Policy in Bavaria: Between Laptop and Lederhosen," in David B. Audretsch, Isabel Grilo, and A. Roy Thurik (eds.), *Handbook of Research on Entrepreneurship Policy* (Cheltenham: Edward Elgar, 2007), 200–212.

39. Audretsch, *Everything in Its Place.*

40. Audretsch, *Everything in Its Place.*

41. The Employment Act of 1946, accessed December 26, 2014, at http://www.encyclopedia.com/topic/Employment_Act_of_1946.aspx.

42. Harry S. Truman, "Statement by the President Upon Signing the Employment Act," accessed December 26, 2014, http://www.presidency.ucsb.edu/ws/index.php?pid=12584.

43. The Employment Act of 1946.

44. Audretsch, *The Entrepreneurial Society.*

45. "Reincarnation Valley (Jena, Germany)," *Economist*, February 11, 2006, accessed February 13, 2015, at http://www.economist.com/node/5465133.

46. The study conducted in 2014 and was accessed at www.ef.com/epi.

47. "Studenten haben Fernweh," Institut der deutschen Wirtschaft Köln, *iwd* 8 (February 20, 2014), 1–2.

48. Accessed at www.ef.com/epi.

49. Bundesministerium für Wirtschafts und Technologie (German Federal Ministry of Economics and Technology), 2000.

50. Bundesministerium fürWirtschafts und Technologie (German Federal Ministry of Economics and Technology), 2000.

51. "Wenn der Profit zur Pleite führt: Mehr Gewinne—und mehr Arbeitslose: Wo bleibt die soziale Verantwortung der Unternehmer?" *Die Zeit*, February 2, 1996, 1.

52. "The Sick Man of the Euro," *Economist*, June 3, 1999, accessed June 5, 2015, at http://www.economist.com/node/209559.

53. Quoted from Peter Watson, *The German Genius* (New York: Harper Perennial, 2011), 2–3.

54. See Richard E. Baldwin and Charles Wyplosz, *The Economics of European Integration*, 5th ed. (New York: McGraw Hill, 2014).

55. Paul Krugman, "On the Inadequacy of the Stimulus," *New York Times*, September 5, 2011.

56. Daniel Mitchell, "The Anti-stimulus Plan," Heritage Foundation, December 20, 2001, accessed August 15, 2014, at http://www.heritage.org/research/commentary/2001/12/the-anti-stimulus-plan.

57. http://www.campusmartinsried.de/eng/izb/index.html.

CHAPTER 5

1. http://dictionary.reference.com/browse/infrastructure, accessed September 30, 2014.

2. http://dictionary.reference.com/browse/infrastructure, accessed September 30, 2014.

3. David Brooks, "The Good Order," *New York Times*, September 26, A27.

4. James M. McPherson, *Battle Cry of Freedom: The Civil War Era* (New York: Oxford University Press, 1988).

5. Monika Herzig, *David Baker: A Legacy of Music* (Bloomington: Indiana University Press, 2011).

6. Mark Twain, "The Awful German Language," appendix D from *A Tramp Abroad*, accessed September 30, 2014 at http://www.crossmyt.com/hc/linghebr/awfgrmlg.

7. Klaus Schubert and Martina Klein, *Das Politiklexikon* (Bonn: Dietz, 2001).

8. Alfred Schüller and Hans-Günter Krüsselberg (eds.), *Grundbegriffe zur Ordnungstheorie und Politischen Ökonomik*, 6th ed. (Marburg: Marburger Ges. f. Ordnungsfragen d. Wirtschaft, 2004).

9. Miahi Hare Shahn, "Europe's Economic Suicide?" *Nine O'Clock*, April 18, 2012, accessed September 22, 2012, at http://www.nineoclock.ro/europe%E2%80%99s-economic-suicide/.

10. There was, for a brief time, a subfield in economics, industrial organization, that made an explicit link between the structure of an industry and its performance. See, for example, Frederic M. Scherer, *Industrial Market Structure and Economic Performance* (Chicago: Rand McNally, 1970). This approach died out by the 1990s and has largely disappeared and remains a historical footnote.

11. Bernd Frick and Erik E. Lehmann, "Corporate Governance in Germany: Ownership, Codetermination and Firm Performance in a Stakeholder Economy," in Howard Gospel and Andrew Pendleton (eds.), *Corporate Governance and Labour Management* (New York: Oxford University Press, 2005), 122–147.

12. Named after the president of the German trade union ÖTV (public service, transport, and traffic) and member of the German Socialist Party (SPD), Heinrich Kluncker.

13. "Streik," *Der Spiegel*, February 2, 1974, accessed January 19, 2015, at http://www.spiegel.de/spiegel/print/d-41784370.html.

14. "Germany's Banking System: Old-Fashioned but in Favour," *Economist*, November 19, 2012, accessed February 2, 2015, at http://www.economist.com/news/finance-and-economics/21566013-defending-three-pillars-old-fashioned-favour.

15. "Germany's Banking System."

16. Empirical evidence shows that the German model of finance was able to mitigate financing constraints on companies in Germany through the mid-1970s. An abundance of relatively inexpensive and accessible credit facilitated firm finance during this era corresponding to the Wirtschaftswunder. See David B. Audretsch and Julie Ann Elston, "Financing the German Mittelstand," *Small Business Economics* 9, 1997, 97–110; and David B. Audretsch and Julie Ann Elston, "Does Firm Size Matter? Evidence on the Impacts of Liquidity Constraints on Firm Investment Behavior in Germany," *International Journal of Industrial Organization* 20, 2001, 1–17.

17. "Germany's Banking System."

18. "Germany's Banking System."

19. Erik E. Lehmann and Doris Neuberger, "Do Lending Relationships Matter? Evidence from Bank Survey Data in Germany," *Journal of Economic Behavior and Organization* 45, 2001, 339–359.

20. See https://www.kfw.de/KfW-Group/About-KfW/Auftrag/Inl%C3%A4ndische-F%C3%B6rderung/, accessed March 20, 2015; and Audretsch and Elston, "Financing the German Mittelstand."

21. Erik E. Lehmann, Doris Neuberger, and Solvig Raethke, "Lending to Small and Medium-Sized Firms: Is There an East-West Gap in Germany?" *Small Business Economics* 23, 2004, 23–39.

22. Erik E. Lehmann and Jürgen Weigand, "Does the Governed Corporation Perform Better? Governance Structures and Corporate Performance in Germany," *European Finance Review* 4, 2000, 157–195.

23. See Alexander Dyck, "Comment on Caroline Fohlin, 'The History of Corporate Ownership and Control in Germany,'" in Randall K. Morck, *A History of Corporate Governance around the World: Family Business Groups to Professional Managers* (Chicago: University of Chicago Press, 2005), 278.

24. See Dyck, "Comment on Caroline Fohlin," 278.

25. Economists typically define a public good as being nonexcludable and nonexhaustive in that no one can be excluded from using that good, and the consumption of the good by one person does not prevent others from also using or consuming that good (Kenneth Arrow, "Economic Welfare and the Allocation of Resources for Invention," in Richard R. Nelson, (ed.), *The Rate and Direction of Inventive Activity* [Princeton: Princeton University Press, 1962]).

26. Michael Hüther, "Infrastruktur zwischen Standortvorteil und Investitionsbedarf: Statement," Press Conference, February 17, 2014, Berlin.

27. Adam Nagourney, "Infrastructure Cracks as Los Angeles Defers Repairs," *New York Times*, September 1, 2014.

28. Nagourney, "Infrastructure Cracks."

29. Fareed Zakaria, "Are America's Best Days behind Us?" http://fareedzakaria.com/2011/03/03/are-americas-best-days-behind-us/.

30. John Nichols, "The Infrastructure of American Democracy Is Dysfunctional," *Nation*, January 22, 2014, accessed September 30, 2014, at http://www.thenation.com/blog/178057/infrastructure-american-democracy-dysfunctional#.

31. Nichols, "Infrastructure of American Democracy."

32. Edward Conrad, "How to Fix America," *Foreign Affairs*, May–June 2013, accessed September 30, 2014, at http://www.foreignaffairs.com/articles/139124/edward-conard-fareed-zakaria/how-to-fix-america.

33. http://www.gtai.de/GTAI/Navigation/EN/Invest/Business-location-germany/Business-climate/infrastructure.html, accessed September 30, 2014.

34. Institut der deutschen Wirtschaft Köln, "Aufs Gleis gesetzt," *Ifw-dienst* 47 (November 11, 2014), 6.

35. Institut der deutschen Wirtschaft Köln, "Infrastruktur zwischen Standortvorteil und Investitionsbedarf"; and IW-Dienst, "Immer noch ein Standortvorteil," 8 (February 20, 2014), 4–5.

36. Institut der deutschen Wirtschaft Köln, "Infrastruktur zwischen Standortvorteil und Investitionsbedarf."

37. "Ailing Infrastructure: Scrimping Threatens Germany's Future," *Der Spiegel International*, July 12, 2013, accessed September 30, 2014, at http://www.spiegel.de/international/germany/diw-weak-infrastructure-investment-threatens-german-future-a-907885.html.

38. "Ailing Infrastructure: Scrimping Threatens Germany's Future," *Der Spiegel International*, July 12, 2013, accessed September 30, 2014, at http://www.spiegel.de/international/germany/diw-weak-infrastructure-investment-threatens-german-future-a-907885.html.

39. "Germany's Ailing Infrastructure: A Nation Slowly Crumbles," *Der Spiegel International*, September 18, 2014, accessed September 30, 2014, at http://www.spiegel.de/international/germany/low-german-infrastructure-investment-worries-experts-a-990903.html.

40. Marcel Fratzscher, *Die Deutschland Illusion* (Berlin: Hanser, 2014).

41. However, this opinion is not shared by all leading economists in Germany. Christoph Schmidt, professor of economics and president of the RWI Essen, or Rheinisch-Westfälisches Institut für Wirtschaftsforschung e.V, and executive of the Advisory Council on the Economic Development, agrees that infrastructure is important to generate competitive advantages, but also criticizes the pessimistic view of Fratzscher. He argues that Fratzscher compares each kind of investment in infrastructure with those of other countries, like Mexico, Turkey, or Spain, without taking into account the average high level of capital stock of the infrastructure in total. See "Unternehmer sind nicht doof," *Wirtschaftswoche* 5 (January 5, 2015), 32–35.

42. Robert R. Solow, "A Contribution to Theory of Economic Growth," *Quarterly Journal of Economics* 70 (1), 1956, 65–94; and Robert R. Solow, "Technical Change and the Aggregate Production Function," *Review of Economics and Statistics* 39 (3), 1957, 312–320.

43. Alfred Chandler, *The Visible Hand: The Managerial Revolution in American Business* (Cambridge: Belknap Press of Harvard University Press, 1977); and Alfred Chandler, *Scale and Scope: The Dynamics of Industrial Capitalism* (Cambridge, MA: Harvard University Press, 1990).

44. Jay Barney, "Strategic Factor Markets: Expectations, Luck and Business Strategy," *Management Science* 32 (10), 1986, 1231–1244; and Birger Wernerfelt, "The Resource-Based View of the Firm," *Strategic Management Journal* 5 (2), 1984, 171–180.

45. David Aschauer, "Is Public Expenditure Productive?" *Journal of Monetary Economics* 23 (2), 1989, 177–200; Catherine J. Morrison Paul and Amy E. Schwartz, "State Infrastructure and Productive Performance," *American Economic Review* 86, 1996, 1095–1111; and Nina Czernich, Oliver Falck, Tobias Kretschmer, and Ludger Wössmann, "Broadband Infrastructure and Economic Growth," *Economic Journal*, 121, 2011, 505–532.

46. Institut der deutschen Wirtschaft Köln, "Infrastruktur zwischen Standortvorteil und Investitionsbedarf."

47. Deloitte, "Human Capital Trends 2013," accessed October 1, 2014 at http://www.deloitte.com/view/en_US/us/Services/consulting/human-capital/268bfb80ddbcd310VgnVCM2000003356f70aRCRD.htm.

48. Richard L. Florida, *The Rise of the Creative Class: And How It's Transforming Work, Leisure, Community and Everyday Life* (New York: Basic Books, 2002).

49. Bundesministerium für Wirtschaft und Energie, *Monitoring zu Kultur- und Kreativwirtschaft* 2013, Berlin, 2013.

50. "Activists in Hamburg Resist Creative Class Policies," 2010, accessed November 3, 2014, at *The Creative Class Struggle*, http://creativeclassstruggle.wordpress.com/2010/01/12/.

51. Jeroen Beekmans, "Hamburg's Manifest against the Creative Class," 2010, accessed November 1, 2014, at *The Pop-Up City*, http://popupcity.net/hamburgs-manifest-against-the-creative-class/.

52. Edward L. Glaeser and Joshua D. Gottlieb, "The Wealth of Cities: Agglomeration Economies and Spatial Equilibrium in the United States," *Journal of Economic Literature* 47 (4), 2009,983–1028.

53. Florida, *Rise of Creative Class*, 292.

54. Nicholas Stang, "Book Review: 'Berlin Now' by Peter Schneider," *Wall Street Journal*, August 15, 2014.

55. Stang, "Book Review."

56. Melanie Fasche, "The Challenges of Turning Potential into Growth," presentation on May 30, 2012, at the Hertie School of Governance, Berlin.

57. "Berlin ist für junge Menschen der attraktivste Standort," *Berliner Morgenpost*, July 4, 2012, accessed September 16, 2014, at http://www.morgenpost.de/lifestyle/article107787948/Berlin-ist-fuer-junge-Menschen-der-attraktivste-Standort.html.

58. Mark Scott, "Start-Ups Take Root in Berlin," *New York Times*, April 30, 2013, B1.

59. https://www.google.de/?gws_rd=ssl#q=Fisher+z+berlin.

60. http://www.vogue.de/fashion-shows/berlin-fashion-week.

61. "Designer in Berlin: Der Traum vom großen Modegeschäft," *Die Zeit*, accessed December 18, 2014, at http://www.zeit.de/lebensart/mode/2011–08/mode-branche-berlin/seite-2.

62. Gordon L. Clark, Maryann P. Feldman, and Meric S. Gertler (eds.), *The Oxford Handbook of Economic Geography* (Oxford: Oxford University Press, 2000).

63. Michael Piore and Charles Sabel, *The Second Industrial Divide: Possibilities for Prosperity* (New York: Basic Books, 1984).

64. Robert Putnam, *Bowling Alone: The Collapse and Revival of American Community* (New York: Simon and Schuster, 2000); and James J. Coleman, "Social Capital in the Creation of Human Capital," *American Journal of Sociology* 94, 1988, 95–121.

65. Putnam, *Bowling Alone*, 19.

66. Steven N. Durlauf, "On the Empirics of Social Capital," *Economic Journal*, November 2002, 459–479; and Joel Sobel, "Can We Trust Social Capital?" *Journal of Economic Literature*, 40, March 2001, 139–154.

67. Anil Rupasingha, Stephan J. Goetz, and David Freshwater, "Social and Institutional Factors as Determinants of Economic Growth: Evidence from the United States Counties," *Papers in Regional Science* 81, 2002, 139–115; and Craig Aubuchon, Barry Rubin, and Trent Engbers, "Reexamining the Economic Impact of Social Capital," paper presented at the Association for Research on Nonprofit Organizations and Voluntary Action Conference, November 2002, Indianapolis, IN.

68. Alfonso Martinez Cearra, "Bilbao: Revitalisation through Culture," accessed January 3, 2015, at http://www.rudi.net/books/10603.

69. AnnaLee Saxenian, *Regional Advantage* (Cambridge, MA: Harvard University Press, 1994), 96–97.

70. http://www.faz.net/aktuell/wirtschaft/menschen-wirtschaft/neuer-rekord-deutschland-hat-so-viele-vereine-wie-nie-zuvor-12288289.html.

71. "Monitoring-Report Digitale Wirtschaft," Bundesministerium für Wirtschaft und Energie, Berlin, accessed November 3, 2014, at www.bmwi.de.

72. David B. Audretsch, *Everything in Its Place: Entrepreneurship and the Strategic Management of Cities, Regions and States* (New York: Oxford University Press, 2015).

73. Tom Peters and Robert H. Waterman, *In Search of Excellence* (New York: Harper and Row, 1984).

74. SAP was founded in June 1972 as Systemanalyse und Programmentwicklung (System Analysis and Program Development).

75. Jennifer L. Woolley, "The Creation and Configuration of Infrastructure for Entrepreneurship in Emerging Domains of Activity," *Entrepreneurship Theory and Practice*, 2013, 38 1042–2587.

76. David B. Audretsch, Diana Heger, and Tobias Veith, "Infrastructure and Entrepreneurship," *Small Business Economics* 44 (2), 2015, 219–230.

77. Brooks, "The Good Order," A27.

78. Brooks, "The Good Order," A27.

CHAPTER 6

1. "Von wem stammt der Slogan 'Laptop und Lederhose'?" *Focus*, accessed October 18, 2015, at http://www.focus.de/politik/deutschland/csu/tid-11102/bayern-von-wem-stammt-der-slogan-laptop-und-lederhose_aid_317314.html.

2. John Hooper, "The Laptop and Lederhosen Formula," *Guardian*, September 1, 2002, accessed October 18, 2014, at http://www.theguardian.com/world/2002/sep/02/germany.eu.

3. Hooper, "Laptop and Lederhosen Formula."

4. The evolution from the managed economy to the entrepreneurial economy is explained by David B. Audretsch and Roy Thurik, "What's New about the New Economy? Sources of Growth in the Managed and Entrepreneurial Economies," *Industrial and Corporate Change* 10 (1), 2001, 267–315; and Roy Thurik, Erik Stam, and David B. Audretsch, "The Rise of the Entrepreneurial Economy and the Future of Dynamic Capitalism," *Technovation*, July 2013, 302–310.

5. William J. Niven, "The Reception of Steven Spielberg's *Schindler's List* in the German Media," *Journal of European Studies*, June 1, 1995, accessed October 21, 2014, at http://www.highbeam.com/doc/1G1-17387557.html.

6. Quoted from "*Schindler's List* Hits Home," *Newsweek*, March 13, 1994, accessed October 21, 2014, at http://www.newsweek.com/schindlers-list-hits-home-186204.

7. Quoted from "Schindler's List Hits Home."

8. Niven, "Reception of *Schindler's List*."

9. Mark Twain, "The Awful German Language," *A Tramp Abroad*, appendix D, 1880, cited from J. R. LeMaster, James Darrell Wilson, and Christie Graves Hamric, "The Awful German Language," in *The Mark Twain Encyclopedia* (London: Routledge, 1993), 57–58.

10. George J. Stigler, "Production and Distribution in the Short Run," *Journal of Political Economy* 47, 1939, 305–327; Zoltan J. Acs, David B. Audretsch, and Bo Carlsson, "Flexible Technology and Plant Size," *International Journal of Industrial Organization* 12 (4), 1994, 359–372; David E. Mills and Laurence Schumann, "Industry Structure with Fluctuating Demand," *American Economic Review* 75, 1985, 758–767; and Zoltan J. Acs and David B. Audretsch, *Innovation and Small Firms* (Cambridge, MA: MIT Press, 1990).

11. The *Reinheitsgebot* or the "German Beer Purity Law" originated on November 30 1487 with the decree by Albert IV, Duke of Bavaria, that only three ingredients – water, malt and hops – can be used for the brewing of beer. On April 1516 Duke Wilhelm IV of Bavaria, endorsed the law as one to be followed in their duchies, adding standards for the process of brewing and sales of beer. See Horst D. Dornbusch, *Prost! The Story of German Beer* (Brewers Publications: United States, 1997).

12. Joseph A. Schumpeter, *Theorie der wirtschaftlichen Entwicklung* (Berlin: Duncker und Humblot, 1911).

13. Thomas K. McCraw, *Prophet of Innovation: Joseph Schumpeter and Creative Destruction* (Cambridge, MA: Belknap Press of Harvard University Press, 2007), 495.

14. McCraw, *Prophet of Innovation*, 6.

15. Joseph A. Schumpeter, *Capitalism, Socialism and Democracy* (New York: Harper, 1942), 13.

16. Paul Carrol, "Die Offene Schlacht," *Die Zeit*, September 24, 1993, 18.

17. Peter Hall and David Soskice, *Varieties of Capitalism: The Institutional Foundations of Comparative Advantage* (New York: Oxford University Press, 2001).

18. Christian Dustmann, Bernd Fitzenberger, Uta Schönberg, and Alexandra Spitz-Oener, "From Sick Man of Europe to Economic Superstar: Germany's Resurgent Economy," *Journal of Economic Perspectives* 28 (1), 2014, 167–188.

19. Michalel C. Burda, "Mehr Arbeitslose—der Preis für die Osterweiterung? Zur Auswirkung der EU-Osterweiterung auf die europäischen Arbeitsmärkte im Osten und Westen," in *Schriften des Vereins fuer Socialpolitik Neue Folge* (Berlin: Duncker und Humblot, 2000), 79–102.

20. Named after Peter Hartz, a human resources executive and board member of the German public company Volkswagen AG, located in Lower Saxony. Hartz became notable as adviser to Gerhard Schröder, German chancellor (1998—2005) and former head of the state of Lower Saxony (1990—1998), with whom Hartz developed the so-called Hartz Reforms of the German labor market and job agencies.

21. Bernd Fitzenberger, "Nach der Reform ist vor der Reform? Eine arbeitsökonomische Analyse ausgewählter Aspekte der Hartz-Reformen," in Günther Schultze (ed.), *Reformen für Deutschland—Die wichtigsten Handlungsfelder aus ökonomischer Sicht* (Munich: Schaeffer-Peschel Verlag, 2009), 21–48; Ulf Rinne and Klaus F. Zimmermann, "Another Economic Miracle? The German Labor Market and the Great Recession," *IZA Journal of Labor Policy* 1, 2012, 401–423; and Ulf Rinne and Klaus F. Zimmermann, "Is Germany the North Star of Labor Market Policy?" *IMF Economic Review* 61 (4), 2013, 702–729.

22. The word "Deutschland" is derived from the indogerman word *teuta*, which simply means "people". With the beginning of the Middle age, the Latin expression *theodiscus* was used describing people not speaking Latin – the prevalent language of scholars. The expression "deutsch" thus simply expresses the language of the people. Germany is called "Deutschland" by the Germans themselves, and thus refers to the land where the people speak "*deutsch*". Germany, the name given by the Anglo-Saxon countries (Germany) and Italy (Germania) however expresses the land where the Germanic people (Teutonic, Suebian, Gothic, Franconian, Alemannic, among others) lived. France and Spain have historical Germanic roots (the Franconia tribes, Charlemagne) and thus name Germany Allemagne, derived from Alemanni (meaning all men between the rivers Rhine and the Danube). See Peter Arens and Stefan Brauburger, *Die Deutschlandsaga* (Munich: Bertelsmann/Random House, 2014).

23. "The Bearable Lightness of Being: How Germans Are Learning to Like Themselves," *Der Spiegel International*, July 17, 2014, accessed December 26, 2014, at http://www.spiegel.de/international/germany/football-championships-help-boost-german-image-at-home-and-abroad-a-981591.html.

24. "Bearable Lightness of Being."

25. "Bearable Lightness of Being." Chancellor Angela Merkel repeated this same phrase publicly in November 2014; see https://www.youtube.com/watch?v=McusC3-49 pA, accessed January 19, 2015.

26. "Skilled Migrants Want to Stay Long-Term," *The Local*, October 16, 2014.

27. Peter Ross Range, "The German Model," *Handelsblatt*, August 5, 2012, accessed October 20, 2014, at http://www.handelsblatt.com/politik/konjunktur/nachrichten/report-the-german-model/6966662.html.

28. Range, "The German Model."

29. Veysel Oezcan, "Germany: Immigration in Transition," Migration Policy Institute, July 1, 2004, accessed October 20, 2014, at http://www.migrationpolicy.org/article/germany-immigration-transition/.

30. Oezcan, "Germany: Immigration in Transition."

31. Kaja Shonick, "Politics, Culture, and Economics: Reassessing the West German Guest Worker Agreement with Yugoslavia," *Journal of Contemporary History* 44 (4), 2009, 719–736.

32. Oezcan, "Germany: Immigration in Transition."

33. Oezcan, "Germany: Immigration in Transition."

34. Oezcan, "Germany: Immigration in Transition."

35. Rita Chin, *The Guest Worker Question in Postwar Germany* (Cambridge: Cambridge University Press, 2007).

36. Range, "The German Model."

37. Fareed Zakaria, "Are America's Best Days Behind Us?" accessed October 15, 2014, at http://fareedzakaria.com/2011/03/03/are-americas-best-days-behind-us/.

38. Range, "The German Model."

39. It started and is mainly concentrated in the East German city of Dresden. They call them "patriotic Europeans against the Islamization of the Occident." Saxony, with Dresden as its capital, is less than 1 percent Muslim. Heinrich August Winkler, historian emeriti from Berlin University, argues that the valley around Dresden was historically an island in the former DDR (the "valley of the innocents"). People were not able to receive TV programs from West Germany and are thus less enlightened and informed. "Eine Geschichte von Kämpfen," interview by Heinrich August Winkler, in *Wirtschaftswoche* 4 (January 19, 2015), 24.

40. "Germany's Anti-Islam Marches: The Uprising of the Decent," *Economist*, accessed January 19, 2015, at http://www.economist.com/news/europe/21638194-xenophobic-marches-continue-parts-germany-others-stand-up-uprising-decent?zid=307&ah=5e80419d1bc9821ebe173f4f0f060a07.

41. "Bearable Lightness of Being."

42. Quoted in "Bearable Lightness of Being."

43. "In Exodus from Israel to Berlin, Young Nation's Fissures Show," *New York Times*, October 17, 2014, A4.

44. "Israelis bringen Unternehmergeist mit," *Der Spiegel*, accessed at http://www.spiegel.de/wirtschaft/soziales/start-ups-berlin-israelis-bringen-unternehmergeist-mit-a-1009223.html. "Israelis in Berliner Start-ups: Willkommen im Land des Feierabends," *Der Spiegel*, December 31, 2014, accessed January 1, 2015, at http://www.spiegel.de/wirtschaft/soziales/start-ups-berlin-israelis-bringen-unternehmergeist-mit-a-1009223.html.

45. "Exodus from Israel," A4.

46. "Exodus from Israel," A4.

47. "Israelis in Berliner Start-ups."

48. Guido Kleinhubbert, "Headhunting in the Euro Crisis: German Provinces Struggle to Lure Skilled Workers," *Der Spiegel*, August 14, 2012, accessed October 7, 2014, at http://www.spiegel.de/international/germany/german-provinces-struggle-to-lure-southern-european-workers-a-849778.html.

49. Kleinhubbert, "Headhunting."

50. Kleinhubbert, "Headhunting."

51. Kleinhubbert, "Headhunting."

52. Peter Schneider, *Berlin Now* (New York: Farrar, Straus and Giroux, 2014), quoted in Nicholas Stang, "Book Review: 'Berlin Now' by Peter Schneider," *Wall Street Journal*, August 15, 2014.

53. Schneider, *Berlin Now*, quoted in Stang, "Book Review."

54. Schneider, *Berlin Now*.

55. Stang, "Book Review."

56. Klaus F. Zimmermann, "Die Zukunft gestalten!" in Klaus F. Zimmermann (ed.) *Deutschland—was nun? Reformen für Wirtschaft und Gesellschaft* (Munich: Verlag Beck, 2006), 1–28.

57. Range, "The German Model."

58. "U.S. Labor Force Participation Rate Has Stalled, While Others' Hasn't," *Family Inequality*, October 29, 2012, accessed October 25, 2014, at http://familyinequality.wordpress.com/2012/10/29/u-s-womens-labor-force-participation-stalled-while-others-havent/.

59. "Bundestag beschliesst Frauenquote ohne Gegenstimmen," *Frankfurter Allgemeine Zeitung*, March 7, 2015, 1.

60. Richard Florida, *The Rise of the Creative Class* (New York: Basic Books, 2002).

61. Jane Jacobs, *The Economy of Cities* (New York: Vintage Books, 1969).

62. Florida, *Rise of Creative Class*.

63. Florida, *Rise of Creative Class*, 131.

64. Carlos Haertel, "Global R&D Strategies," keynote presentation at the Fifteenth TCI Annual Global Conference, Bilbao, Spain, October 17, 2012.

65. Haertel, "Global R&D Strategies."

66. Haertel, "Global R&D Strategies."

67. Haertel, "Global R&D Strategies."

68. Haertel, "Global R&D Strategies."

69. Michael Spence, "Globalization and Unemployment: The Downside of Integrating Markets," *Foreign Affairs*, July–August 2011, accessed October 19, 2014, at http://www.foreignaffairs.com/articles/67874/michael-spence/globalization-and-unemployment.

70. Spence, "Globalization and Unemployment."

71. Spence, "Globalization and Unemployment."

72. Alice Tidy, "France's Specialization? Demonizing Globalization," *CNBC News*, May 5, 2014, accessed October 27, 2014, at http://www.cnbc.com/id/101642549.

CHAPTER 7

1. Don Lochbiler, *Coming of Age in Detroit, 1873–1973* (Detroit: Wayne State University Press, 1973).

2. Lochbiler, *Coming of Age in Detroit*, vii.

3. Ralph Gomory, "On Manufacturing and Innovation," *Huffington Post Business—the Blog*, July 9, 2013, accessed October 27, 2014, at http://www.huffingtonpost.com/ralph-gomory/on-manufacturing-and-inno_b_3567196.html.

4. John R. Pierce and Peter K. Schott, "The Surprisingly Swift Decline of U.S. Manufacturing Employment," December 2012, accessed October 30, 2014, at http://economics.yale.edu/sites/default/files/schott-09-oct-2013.pdf.

5. Economic Research, Federal Reserve of St. Louis, accessed October 30, 2014, at http://research.stlouisfed.org/fred2/series/MANEMP.

6. "Why Manufacturing Doesn't Matter," *Forbes*, June 10, 2013, accessed October 27, 2014, at http://www.forbes.com/sites/sap/2013/06/10/why-manufacturing-doesnt-matter/.

7. "Factory Jobs Are Gone: Get Over It," *Bloomberg Business Week*, January 23, 2014, accessed October 30, 2014, at http://www.businessweek.com/articles/2014-01-23/manufacturing-jobs-may-not-be-cure-for-unemployment-inequality.

8. "Factory Jobs Are Gone."

9. Michael Mandel, "The Myth of American Productivity," *Washington Monthly*, February 2012, accessed October 30, 2014, at http://www.washingtonmonthly.com/magazine/january_february_2012/features/the_myth_of_american_productivo34576.php?page=all.

10. Mandel, "Myth of American Productivity."

11. Mandel, "Myth of American Productivity."

12. Gomory, "On Manufacturing and Innovation."

13. "Peugeot on the Brink: How Paris Is Killing French Industry," *Der Spiegel*, August 17, 2012, accessed October 30, 2014, at http://www.spiegel.de/international/europe/french-industrial-policies-are-aiding-rapid-decline-of-peugeot-a-850348.html.

14. "Why Doesn't Britain Make Things Anymore?" *Guardian*, November 16, 2011, accessed October 27, 2014, at http://www.theguardian.com/business/2011/nov/16/why-britain-doesnt-make-things-manufacturing.

15. Charles W. Wessner, "How Does Germany Do It?" ASME, November 2013, accessed October 30, 2014, at https://www.asme.org/engineering-topics/articles/manufacturing-processing/how-does-germany-do-it.

16. Wessner, "How Does Germany Do It?"

17. Wessner, "How Does Germany Do It?"

18. Thomas L. Friedman, *The World Is Flat* (London: Lane, 2005).

19. Friedman, *The World Is Flat*; "Why Doesn't Britain Make Things Anymore?"

20. Cited from Peter Ross Range, "The German Model," *Handelsblatt*, August 5, 2012, accessed October 15, 2014, at http://www.handelsblatt.com/politik/konjunktur/nachrichten/report-the-german-model/6966662.html.

21. "Why Doesn't Britain Make Things Anymore?"

22. "Why Doesn't Britain Make Things Anymore?"

23. "Peugeot on the Brink."

24. "Peugeot on the Brink."

25. Chase Gummer, "Behind Germany's Success Story in Manufacturing," *Wall Street Journal*, June 1, 2014, accessed November 14, 2014, at http://online.wsj.com/articles/behind-germanys-success-story-in-manufacturing-1401473946.

26. "The MP3 History," Fraunhofer Institute for Integrated Circuits, accessed November 14, 2014, at http://www.mp3-history.com/en/the_mp3_history.html.

27. Gummer, "Behind Germany's Success Story."

28. Gummer, "Behind Germany's Success Story."

29. Wessner, "How Does Germany Do It?"

30. Gummer, "Behind Germany's Success Story."

31. David B. Audretsch and Erik E. Lehmann, „Universitäten als regionale Förderer der Wirtschaft: Jena und die Optoelektronik", *ifo Dresden*, 3, 2004, 8–23.

32. Gummer, "Behind Germany's Success Story."

33. Quoted from Gummer, "Behind Germany's Success Story."

34. Michael Shank and Thorben Albrecht, "Germany's Lesson for U.S.—Keep Faith with Workers," *CNN*, February 24, 2012, accessed November 14, 2014, at http://edition.cnn.com/2012/02/24/opinion/shank-albrecht-manufacturing-jobs/.

35. Range, "The German Model."

36. Range, "The German Model."

37. "Inspiration Dresden," *New European Economy*, accessed November 12, 2014, at http://www.neweuropeaneconomy.com/top-stories/361-inspiration-dresden.

38. "Inspiration Dresden."

39. "Inspiration Dresden."

40. Accessed October 30, 2014, at http://www.tradingeconomics.com/germany/productivity.

41. Accessed November 14, 2014, at http://stats.oecd.org/index.aspx?DataSetCode=ANHRS.

42. Glen Stansbery, "Why Germans Have Longer Vacation Times and More Productivity," Open Forum, September 20, 2010, accessed October 30, 2014, at https://www.americanexpress.com/us/small-business/openforum/articles/why-germans-have-longer-vacation-times-and-more-productivity-1/.

43. "Who Deserves Vacation More?" *New York Times*, April 28, 2011, accessed at http://www.nytimes.com/roomfordebate/2010/8/4/why-dont-americans-have-longer-vacations/who-deserves-vacation-more.

44. "Europe versus America: Do Longer Holidays Translate to Higher Productivity?" *Der Spiegel*, August 20, 2009, accessed October 30, 2014, at http://www.spiegel.de/international/business/europe-versus-america-do-longer-holidays-translate-to-greater-productivity-a-643900.html.

45. Herbert Giersch, Karl-Heinz Paqué, and Holger Schmieding, 1992, *The Fading Miracle* (Cambridge: Cambridge University Press, 1992).

46. Christian Dustmann, Bernd Fitzenberger, Uta Schönberg, and Alexandra Spitz-Oener, "From Sick Man of Europe to Economic Superstar: Germany's Resurgent Economy," *Journal of Economic Perspectives* 28 (1), 2014, 167–188.

47. Increases in the Benelux countries, the Scandinavian countries, and the new Eastern Europe countries all exceed those of Central Europe. The Conference Board, *International Labor Comparisons Program*, December 2014.

48. Dustmann et al., "Sick Man of Europe."

49. Herbert Giersch, Karl-Heinz Paqué, and Holger Schmieding, *The Fading Miracle: Four Decades of Market Economy in Germany* (Cambridge: Cambridge University Press, 1992); and Dustmann et al., "Sick Man of Europe."

50. Dustmann et al., "Sick Man of Europe."

51. Range, "The German Model."

52. Range, "The German Model."

CHAPTER 8

1. Hans-Dietrich Genscher, "Erklärung der Bundesregierung zum Vertrag über die abschließende Regelung in Bezug auf Deutschland durch den Bundesminister des Auswärtigen," Deutscher Bundestag, Plenarprotokoll 11/226, September 20, 1990, 17803B–17807D.

2. Marc Young, "Klinsmann's Real Victory: Germany's New Attitude," *Der Spiegel*, July 5, 2006, accessed December 27, 2014, at http://www.spiegel.de/international/klinsmann-s-real-victory-germany-s-new-attitude-a-425,267.html.

3. "The Bearable Lightness of Being: How Germans Are Learning to Like Themselves," *Der Spiegel International*, July 17, 2014, accessed October 12, 2014, at http://www.spiegel.de/international/germany/football-championships-help-boost-german-image-at-home-and-abroad-a-981,591.html.

4. Young, "Klinsmann's Real Victory."

5. "Wie eine Rede die Deutschen befreite," *Süddeutsche Zeitung*, January 31, 2015, accessed February 5, 2015, at http://www.sueddeutsche.de/politik/alt-bundespräsident-zum-kriegsende-wie-eine-weizsäcker-rede-die-deutschen-befreite-1.2329266.

6. Tom Brokaw, *The Greatest Generation* (New York: Random House, 1998).

7. Erik Kirschbaum, "65 Years after WW2—Should Germans Still Feel Guilty?" *Global News Journal*, May 7, 2010. The original title in German is Hannah Vogt, *Schuld oder Verhängnis: Zwölf Fragen an Deutschlands jüngste Vergangenheit* (Frankfurt am Main: Verlag M. Diesterweg, 1961).

8. "Bearable Lightness of Being."

9. "Germans Reject Their Joyless Image to Become Europe's Optimists," *Guardian*, June 26, 2014, accessed October 14, 2014, at http://dinarvets.com/forums/index.php?/topic/181106-germans-reject-their-joyless-image-to-become-europes-optimists/.

10. "Germans Reject Their Joyless Image."

11. "The Germans: How Germans See Themselves," *Der Spiegel*, May 7, 2005, accessed October 14, 2014, at http://www.spiegel.de/international/spiegel-special-the-germans-how-germans-see-themselves-a-356,216.html.

12. Neil McGregor, *Germany: Memoirs of a Nation* (London: Allen Lane, 2014).

13. Günter Hellman, "Normatively Disarmed, but Self-Confident," *IP Journal*, May 1, 2011, accessed October 11, 2014, at https://ip-journal.dgap.org/en/ip-journal/topics/normatively-disarmed-self-confident-0.

14. "Bearable Lightness of Being."

15. "The Germans: How Germans See Themselves."

16. "Bearable Lightness of Being."

17. "Bearable Lightness of Being."

18. "Bearable Lightness of Being."

19. "Bearable Lightness of Being."

20. Quoted from Hellman, "Normatively Disarmed, but Self-Confident."

21. Hellman, "Normatively Disarmed, but Self-Confident."

22. Kirschbaum, "65 Years after WW2."

23. Yascha Mounk, *Stranger in My Own Country: A Jewish Family in Modern Germany* (New York: Farrar, Straus and Giroux, 2014).

24. "Bearable Lightness of Being."

25. "Bearable Lightness of Being."

26. "The Germans: How Germans See Themselves."

27. Kirschbaum, "65 Years after WW2."

28. "Bearable Lightness of Being."

29. "Germans Reject Their Joyless Image."

30. "Germans Reject Their Joyless Image."

31. "Deutschland—Land der Ideen," report of the IW Consult GmbH, Institut der deutschen Wirtschaft Köln, May 11, 2012, accessed October 12, 2014, at http://www.iwconsult.de/fileadmin/user_upload/downloads/public/pdfs/iw-bericht_land-der-ideen_20,120,809_highq.pdf.

32. "Deutschland—Land der Ideen."

33. "Deutschland—Land der Ideen."

34. "Deutschland—Land der Ideen."

35. "Lasst uns gelassener sein," *Süddeutsche Zeitung*, accessed January 15, 2015, at http://www.sueddeutsche.de/kultur/zur-zdf-doku-die-deutschen-lasst-uns-gelassener-sein-1.555998–2.

36. "Bearable Lightness of Being."

37. Amity Shlaes, *Germany: The Empire Within* (New York: Farrar, Straus and Giroux, 1991)

38. "Polls Apart: What Europeans Think of Each Other," *Economist*, May 15, 2013, accessed October 12, 2014, at http://www.economist.com/blogs/graphicdetail/2013/05/what-europeans-think-each-other.

39. "Germany—Highly Recommended," accessed October 12, 2014, at http://www.land-der-ideen.de/en/news/germany-highly-recommended.

40. "BBC Poll: Germany Most Popular Country in the World," *BBC News Europe*, May 23, 2013, accessed October 15, 2014, at http://www.bbc.com/news/world-europe-22,624,104.

41. Cited from Peter Ross Range, "The German Model," *Handelsblatt*, August 5, 2012, accessed October 15, 2014, at http://www.handelsblatt.com/politik/konjunktur/nachrichten/report-the-german-model/6966662.html.

42. Cited from Range, "The German Model."

43. David B. Audretsch, *Everything in Its Place: Entrepreneurship and the Strategic Management of Cities, Regions and States* (New York: Oxford University Press, 2015).

44. Albert N. Link, *A Generosity of Spirit: The Early History of the Research Triangle Park* (Research Triangle Park: Research Triangle Foundation of North Carolina, 1995).

45. Kenneth Labich, "The Best Cities for Knowledge Workers," *Money Magazine*, November 15, 1993, accessed December 27, 2014, at http://money.cnn.com/magazines/fortune/fortune_archive/1993/11/15/78612/index.htm.

46. Link, *A Generosity of Spirit*.

47. Richard L. Florida, *The Rise of the Creative Class: And How It's Transforming Work, Leisure, Community and Everyday Life*. (New York: Basic Books, 2002) 293.

48. Florida, *Rise of Creative Class*, 299.

49. Joel Kotkin, "The U.S.' Biggest Brain Magnets," *Forbes*, accessed at http://www.forbes.com/2011/02/10/smart-cities-new-orleans-austin-contributors-joel-kotkin.html.

50. Edward L. Glaeser and Joshua D. Gottlieb, "The Wealth of Cities: Agglomeration Economies and Spatial Equilibrium in the United States," *Journal of Economic Literature* 47 (4), 2009, 983–1028.

51. "The Cost of Cool: To Stay Sexy, Must the German Capital Remain Poor?" *Economist*, September 1, 2011, accessed October 20, 2014, at http://www.economist.com/node/21529075.

52. Melanie Fasche, "The Challenges of Turning Potential into Growth," presentation on May 30, 2012, at the Hertie School of Governance, Berlin.

53. Peter Schneider, *Berlin Now* (New York: Farrar, Straus and Giroux, 2014), quoted in Nicholas Stang, "Book Review: 'Berlin Now' by Peter Schneider," *Wall Street Journal*, August 15, 2014, accessed August 20, 2014, at http://www.wsj.com/articles/book-review-berlin-now-by-peter-schneider-1,408,128,756.

54. Stang, "Book Review."

55. Schneider, *Berlin Now*.

56. Stang, "Book Review."

57. "Crisis Migration: Italian Start-Ups Flock to Berlin," *Der Spiegel*, June 14, 2013, accessed December 27, 2014, at http://www.spiegel.de/international/germany/italians-flock-to-berlin-to-join-flourishing-start-up-scene-a-903,908.html.

58. http://www.university-industry.com/index/scientificcommittee and private correspondence.

59. "Berlin ist für junge Menschen der attraktivste Standort," *Berliner Morgenpost*, April 7, 2012, accessed December 27, 2014, at http://www.morgenpost.de/lifestyle/article107787948/Berlin-ist-fuer-junge-Menschen-der-attraktivste-Standort.html.

60. Fasche, "Challenges of Turning Potential into Growth."

61. Caitlin Winner left Amen in 2014 to work for Facebook.

62. Personal communication with Caitlin Winner.

63. Magdalena Räth, "Amen streicht weitere Million ein und startet neu," Gründerszene.de, March 28, 2012, accessed December 27, 2014, at http://www.gruenderszene.de/news/amen-sunstone-capital.

64. Mark Scott, "Start-Ups Take Root in Berlin," *New York Times*, April 30, 2013, B1.

65. "Die neue Gründerszene in Berlin," *Tip-Berlin*, August 11, 2011, accessed December 27, 2014, at http://www.tip-berlin.de/kultur-und-freizeit-stadtleben-und-leute/die-neue-grunderszene-berlin.

66. "Die neue Gründerszene in Berlin."

67. "Die neue Gründerszene in Berlin."

68. "Ashton Kutcher überzeugt sich von 'Amen' in Berlin," *Berliner Morgenpost*, December 11, 2012, accessed September 5, 2014, at http://www.morgenpost.de/vermischtes/stars-und-promis/article1861212/Ashton-Kutcher- über zeugt-sich-von-Amen-in-Berlin.html.

69. Räth, "Amen streicht weitere Million."

70. Young, "Klinsmann's Real Victory."

CHAPTER 9

1. Francis Fukuyama, "The End of History," *National Interest*, Summer 1989, 3–18; and Francis Fukuyama, *The End of History and the Last Man* (New York: Free Press, 1992).

2. "The Sick Man of the Euro," *Economist*, January 3, 1999.

3. "France and Friends: Merkel Increasingly Isolated on Austerity," *Der Spiegel*, September 3, 2014, accessed November 15, 2014, at http://www.spiegel.de/international/europe/the-anti-austerity-camp-is-growing-as-merkel-becomes-more-isolated-a-989357.html.

4. "France and Friends."

5. "France and Friends."

6. William A. Niskanen and Stephen Moore, "Supply-Side Tax Cuts and the Truth about the Reagan Economic Record," Cato Institute, Policy Analysis no. 261, October 22, 1996, accessed November 15, 2014, at http://www.cato.org/publications/policy-analysis/supplyside-tax-cuts-truth-about-reagan-economic-record

7. David Harper, "Understanding Supply Side Economics," *Investopedia*, accessed November 15, 2014, at http://www.investopedia.com/articles/05/011805.asp

8. "German 'Austerity' Obsession Is Wrong: Economist," *CNBC*, September 1, 2014, accessed November 15, 2014, at http://www.cnbc.com/id/101961184#.

9. Alison Smale and Liz Alderman, "Germany's Insistence on Austerity Meets with Revolt in the Eurozone," *New York Times*, October 7, 2014, accessed November 15, 2014, at http://www.nytimes.com/2014/10/08/business/rift-opens-among-eurozone-leaders-over-germanys-insistence-on-austerity.html?_r=0.

10. Bruce Bartlett, "Tax Cuts and 'Starving the Beast,'" *Forbes*, May 7, 2010, accessed November 15, 2014, at http://www.forbes.com/2010/05/06/tax-cuts-republicans-starve-the-beast-columnists-bruce-bartlett.html.

11. Peter Ross Range, "The German Model," *Handelsblatt*, August 5, 2012, accessed October 15, 2014, at http://www.handelsblatt.com/politik/konjunktur/nachrichten/report-the-german-model/6966662.html.

12. Cited from Range, "The German Model."

13. Range, "The German Model."

14. Cited from Range, "The German Model."

15. Cited from Range, "The German Model."

16. Cited from Range, "The German Model."

17. Cited from Range, "The German Model."

18. David B. Audretsch, *Everything in Its Place: Entrepreneurship and the Strategic Management of Cities, Regions and States* (New York: Oxford University Press, 2015).

19. David B. Audretsch, Albert Link, and Mary Walshok (eds.), *The Oxford Handbook of Local Competitiveness* (New York: Oxford University Press, 2015).

20. Audretsch, *Everything in Its Place.*

21. http://www.brainyquote.com/quotes/keywords/secrets.html#qvEH22Hf3sJJmkWp.99.

22. Range, "The German Model."

23. Charles W. Wessner, "How Does Germany Do It?" ASME, November 2013, accessed October 30, 2014, at https://www.asme.org/engineering-topics/articles/manufacturing-processing/how-does-germany-do-it.

Works Cited

Acs, Zoltan J. 2012. *The Philanthropist: Completing the Circle of Prosperity*. Princeton, NJ: Princeton University Press.

Acs, Zoltan J. and David B. Audretsch. 1988. "Innovation in Large and Small Firms: An Empirical Analysis." *American Economic Review* 78 (4), 678–690.

Acs, Zoltan J. and David B. Audretsch. 1990. *Innovation in Small Firms*. Cambridge, MA: MIT Press.

Acs, Zoltan J. and David B. Audretsch (eds.). 1993. *Small Firms and Entrepreneurship: An East-West Perspective*. Cambridge: Cambridge University Press.

Acs, Zoltan J. and David B. Audretsch (eds.). 2010. *Handbook of Entrepreneurship Research: An Interdisciplinary Survey and Introduction*. 2nd ed. New York: Springer.

Acs, Zoltan J., David B. Audretsch, and Bo Carlsson. 1994. "Flexible Technology and Plant Size." *International Journal of Industrial Organization* 12 (4), 355–369.

Acs, Zoltan J., David B. Audretsch, and Maryann P. Feldman. 1992. "Real Effects of University Research." *American Economic Review* 82 (1), 363–367.

Acs, Zoltan J., David B. Audretsch, and Erik E. Lehmann. 2013. "The Knowledge Spillover Theory of Entrepreneurship." *Small Business Economics* 41, 757–774.

Aldridge, T. Taylor and David B. Audretsch. 2011. "The Bayh-Dole Act and Scientist Entrepreneurship." *Research Policy* 40 (8), 1058–1067.

Anderson, R. C. and D. M. Reeb. 2003. "Family Ownership, Corporate Diversification, and Firm Leverage." *Journal of Law and Economics* 46, 653–684.

Arens, Peter and Stefan Brauburger. 2014. *Die Deutschlandsaga*. Munich: Bertelsmann.

Arrow, Kenneth. 1962. "Economic Welfare and the Allocation of Resources for Invention." In Richard R. Nelson (ed.), *The Rate and Direction of Inventive Activity*. Princeton, NJ: Princeton University Press. 609–625.

Aschauer, David. 1989. "Is Public Expenditure Productive?" *Journal of Monetary Economics* 23 (2), 177–200.

Aubuchon, Craig, Barry Rubin, and Trent A. Engbers. 2002. "Reexamining the Economic Impact of Social Capital." Paper presented at the Association for Research on Nonprofit Organizations and Voluntary Action Conference, November, Indianapolis, IN.

Audretsch, David B. 1989. "Legalized Cartels in West Germany." *Antitrust Bulletin* 34 (3), 579–600.

Audretsch, David B. 1991. "New-Firm Survival and the Technological Regime." *Review of Economics and Statistics* 73, 441–450.

Audretsch, David B. 1995. *Innovation and Industry Evolution*. Cambridge, MA: MIT Press.

Audretsch, David B. 1998. "New Firms and Creating Employment." In John T. Addison and Paul J. J. Welfens (eds.), *Labor Markets and Social Security: Wage Costs, Social Security Financing and Labor Market Reforms in Europe*. Heidelberg: Springer. 130–163.

Audretsch, David B. 2000. "Germany, Along with Europe, Is Embracing the New Economy." *European Affairs* 1 (3), 46–51.

Audretsch, David B. 2006. "Innovationen: Aufbruch zur Entrepreneurship-Politik." In Klaus F. Zimmermann (ed.), *Deutschland—was nun? Reformen für Wirtschaft und Gesellschaft*. Munich: Deutscher Taschenbuch Verlag. 237–250.

Audretsch, David B. 2007. *The Entrepreneurial Society*. New York: Oxford University Press.

Audretsch, David B. 2008. "Die Entrepreneurial Society im Zeitalter der Globalisierung." In Beatrice Weder di Mauro (ed.), *Chancen des Wachstums: Globale Perspektiven für den Wohlstand von Morgen*. Frankfurt: Campus Verlag. 91–110.

Audretsch, David B. 2011. Testimony on *Spurring Innovation and Job Creation: The SBIR Program,* Hearing before the Honorable Committee on Small Business, 112th Congress, March 16.

Audretsch, David B. 2014. "Scientific Entrepreneurship: The Stealth Conduit of University Knowledge Spillovers." *George Mason Law Review* 21 (4), 1015–1026.

Audretsch, David B. 2015. *Everything in Its Place: Entrepreneurship and the Strategic Management of Cities, Regions and Countries*. New York: Oxford University Press.

Audretsch, David B., Werner Bönte, and Max Keilbach. 2008. "Entrepreneurship Capital and Its Impact on Knowledge Diffusion and Economic Performance." *Journal of Business Venturing* 23 (6), 687–698.

Audretsch, David B. and Julie Ann Elston. 1997. "Financing the German Mittelstand." *Small Business Economics* 9, 97–110.

Audretsch, David B. and Julie Ann Elston. 2001. "Does Firm Size Matter? Evidence on the Impacts of Liquidity Constraints on Firm Investment Behavior in Germany." *International Journal of Industrial Organization* 20, 1–17.

Audretsch, David B. and Maryann P. Feldman. 1996. "R&D Spillovers and the Geography of Innovation and Production." *American Economic Review* 86 (3), 630–640.

Audretsch, David B. and Michael Fritsch. 1996. "Creative Destruction: Turbulence and Economic Growth." In Ernst Helmstädter and Mark Perlman (eds.), *Behavioral Norms, Technological Progress, and Economic Dynamics: Studies in Schumpeterian Economics*. Ann Arbor: University of Michigan Press. 137–150.

Audretsch, David B. and Michael Fritsch. 2002. "Growth Regimes over Time and Space." *Regional Studies* 36, 113–124.

Audretsch, David B., Diana Heger, and Tobias Veith. 2015. "Infrastructure and Entrepreneurship." *Small Business Economics* 44 (2), 219–230.

Audretsch, David B., Marcel Hülsbeck, and Erik E. Lehmann. 2013. "Families as Active Monitors of Firm Performance." *Journal of Family Business Strategy* 4 (2), 118–130.

Audretsch, David B. and Max Keilbach. 2004. "Does Entrepreneurship Capital Matter?" *Entrepreneurship Theory and Practice* Fall, 419–429.

Audretsch, David B. and Max Keilbach. 2004. "Entrepreneurship Capital and Economic Performance." *Regional Studies* 38, 949–959.

Audretsch, David B. and Max Keilbach. 2007. "The Theory of Knowledge Spillover Entrepreneurship." *Journal of Management Studies* 44 (7), 1242–1254.

Audretsch, David B. and Max Keilbach. 2008. "Resolving the Knowledge Paradox: Knowledge-Spillover Entrepreneurship and Economic Growth." *Research Policy* 37 (1), 1697–1705.

Audretsch, David B., Max Keilbach, and Erik E. Lehmann. 2006. *Entrepreneurship and Economic Growth*. New York: Oxford University Press.

Audretsch, David B. and Erik E. Lehmann. 2004. „Universitäten als regionale Förderer der Wirtschaft: Jena und die Optoelektronik", *ifo Dresden*, 3, 8–2.

Audretsch, David B. and Erik E. Lehmann. 2005. "Does the Knowledge Spillover Theory of Entrepreneurship Hold for Regions?" *Research Policy* 34 (8), 1191–1202.

Audretsch, David B. and Erik E. Lehmann (eds.). 2011. *Corporate Governance in Small and Medium-Sized Firms*. Cheltenham: Edward Elgar.

Audretsch, David B. and Erik E. Lehmann. 2014. "Academic Sources of Knowledge Spillovers in Germany." Working paper, Augsburg University.

Audretsch, David B. and Erik E. Lehmann. 2015. "The Emergence of the Mittelstand Company: A German Perspective." Working paper, University of Augsburg.

Audretsch, David B., Erik E. Lehmann, Albert N. Link and Alexander Starnecker (eds.). 2012. *Technology Transfer in a Globalized Economy*. Heidelberg: Springer.

Audretsch, David B., Al Link, and Mary Walshok (eds.). 2015. *The Oxford Handbook of Local Competitiveness*. New York: Oxford University Press.

Audretsch, David B. and Talat Mahmood. 1995. "New-Firm Survival: New Results Using a Hazard Function." *Review of Economics and Statistics* 77 (1), 97–103.

Audretsch, David B. and Roy Thurik. 2001. "What's New about the New Economy? Sources of Growth in the Managed and Entrepreneurial Economies." *Industrial and Corporate Change* 10 (1), 267–315.

Audretsch, David B. and Hideki Yamawaki. 1988. "R&D, Industrial Policy, and U.S.-Japanese Trade." *Review of Economics and Statistics* 70 (August), 438–447.

Aw, Bee-Yan. 1983. "The Interpretation of Cross-Section Regression Tests of the Hecksher-Ohlin Theorem with Many Goods and Factors." *Journal of International Economics* 14, 163–167.

Baldwin, Richard E. and Philippe Martin. 2004. "Agglomeration and Regional Growth." In J. Vernon Henderson and Jacques-François Thisse (eds.), *Handbook of Regional and Urban Economics*, vol. 4. Amsterdam: Elsevier. 2671–2711.

Baldwin, Richard and Charles Wyplosz. 2014. *The Economics of European Integration*. 5th ed. New York: McGraw Hill.

Barney, Jay. 1986. "Strategic Factor Markets: Expectations, Luck and Business Strategy." *Management Science* 32 (10), 1231–1244.

Becker, Gary S. 1964. *Human Capital: A Theoretical and Empirical Analysis, with Special Reference to Education*. Chicago: University of Chicago Press.

Berghoff, Hartmut. 2006. "The End of Family Business? The Mittelstand and German Capitalism in Transition, 1949–2000." *Business History Review* 80, 263–295.

Berlin, Leslie. 2006. *The Man behind the Microchip: Robert Noyce and the Invention of Silicon Valley*. New York: Oxford University Press.

Bowen, Harry P., Edward Leamer, and Leo Sveikauskas. 1987. "Multicountry, Multifactor Tests of the Factor Abundance Theory." *American Economic Review* 77, 791–809.

Bowen, Harry P. and Leo Sveikauskas. 1989. "Inter-industry Regression Estimates of Factor Abundance." In David B. Audretsch and Michael P. Claudon (eds.), *The Internationalization of U.S. Markets*. New York: New York University Press. 49–72.

Bresnahan, Timothy and Alfonso Gambardella (eds.). 2004. *Building High-Tech Clusters: Silicon Valley and Beyond*. Cambridge: Cambridge University Press.

Brokaw, Tom. 1998. *The Greatest Generation*. New York: Random House.

Bundesministerium für Wirtschaft und Energie. 2012. *Monitoring-Report Digitale Wirtschaft*. Berlin.

Bundesministerium für Wirtschaft und Energie. 2013. *Monitoring zu Kultur- und Kreativwirtschaft*, Berlin.

Burda, Michael C. 2000. "Mehr Arbeitslose—der Preis für die Osterweiterung? Zur Auswirkung der EU-Osterweiterung auf die europäischen Arbeitsmärkte im Osten und Westen ("More Unemployment—the Price of Eastward Expansion? The Impact of the Eastward Expansion of the EU on European Labor Markets in the East and West"). In *Schriften des Vereins für Sozialpolitik Neue Folge*. Berlin: Duncker & Humblot. 79–102.

Burda, Michael C. and Jennifer Hunt. 2011. "What Explains the German Labor Market Miracle in the Great Recession?" Working Paper No. 17187, National Bureau of Economic Research.

Bush, Vannevar. 1945. *Science: The Endless Frontier*. Washington, DC: US Government Printing Office.

Caves, Richard. 1998. "Industrial Organization and New Findings on the Turnover and Mobility of Firms." *Journal of Economic Literature* 3, 1947–1982.

Chandler, Alfred. 1977. *The Visible Hand: The Managerial Revolution in American Business*. Cambridge, MA: Belknap Press of Harvard University Press.

Chandler, Alfred. 1990. *Scale and Scope: The Dynamics of Industrial Capitalism*. Cambridge, MA: Harvard University Press.

Chin, Rita. 2007. *The Guest Worker Question in Postwar Germany*. Cambridge: Cambridge University Press.

Christenson, Clayton M. 1997. *The Innovator's Dilemma: When New Technologies Cause Great Firms to Fail*. Boston: Harvard Business Review Press.

Clark, Gordon L., Maryann P. Feldman, and Meric S. Gertler (eds.). 2000. *The Oxford Handbook of Economic Geography*. Oxford: Oxford University Press.

Coleman, James J. 1988. "Social Capital in the Creation of Human Capital." *American Journal of Sociology* 94, 95–121.

Commission of Experts for Research and Innovation. 2014. *Research, Innovation and Technological Performance in Germany: Report 2014*. Berlin: Commission of Experts for Research and Innovation.

Conrad, Edward. 2014. "How to Fix America." *Foreign Affairs*, May–June 2013.

Cringley, Robert X. 1993. *Accidental Empires: How the Boys of Silicon Valley Make Their Millions, Battle Foreign Competition, and Still Can't Get a Date*. New York: Harper Business.

Czernich, Nina, Oliver Falck, Tobias Kretschmer, and Ludger Wössmann. 2011. "Broadband Infrastructure and Economic Growth." *Economic Journal* 121, 505–532.

Derouzos, Michael L., Richard K. Lester, and Robert M. Solow. 1989. *Made in America: Regaining the Productive Edge*. Cambridge, MA: MIT Press.

Dornbusch, Host D. 1997. *Prost! The Story of German Beer*. Brewers Publications: United States.

Durlauf, Steven N. 2002. "On the Empirics of Social Capital." *Economic Journal*, November, 459–479.

Dustmann, Christian, Bernd Fitzenberger, Uta Schönberg, and Alexandra Spitz-Oener. 2014. "From Sick Man of Europe to Economic Superstar: Germany's Resurgent Economy." *Journal of Economic Perspectives* 28 (1), 167–188.

Eichengreen, Barry. 2008. *The European Economy since 1945: Coordinated Capitalism and Beyond*. Princeton, NJ: Princeton University Press.

Fallon, Daniel. 1980. *The German University: A Heroic Ideal in Conflict with the Modern World*. Boulder: University of Colorado Press.

Feldman, Maryann P. 1994. *The Geography of Innovation*. New York: Springer.

Feldman, Maryann P. and David B. Audretsch. 1999. "Innovation in Cities: Science-Based Diversity, Specialization and Localized Competition." *European Economic Review* 43 (2), 409–429.

Fitzenberger, Bernd. 2009. "Nach der Reform ist vor der Reform? Eine arbeitsökonomische Analyse ausgewählter Aspekte der Hartz-Reformen." In Günther Schultze (ed.), *Reformen für Deutschland: Die wichtigsten Handlungsfelder aus ökonomischer Sicht*. Munich: Schaeffer-Peschel Verlag. 21–48.

Franks, Julian, Colin Mayer, and Hannes F. Wagner. 2006. "The Origins of the German Corporation: Finance, Ownership and Control." *Review of Finance* 10 (4), 537–585.

Fratzscher, Marcel. 2014. *Die Deutschland-Illusion: Warum wir unsere Wirtschaft überschätzen und Europa brauchen*. Hamburg: Hanser Verlag.

Frick, Bernd and Erik E. Lehmann. 2005. "Corporate Governance in Germany: Ownership, Codetermination and Firm Performance in a Stakeholder Economy." In Howard Gospel and Andrew Pendleton (eds.), *Corporate Governance and Labour Management*. New York: Oxford University Press. 122–147.

Friedman, Thomas. 2005. *The World Is Flat*. London: Lane.

Fritsch, Michael. 1997. "New Firms and Regional Employment Change." *Small Business Economics* 9, 437–448.

Fukuyama, Francis. 1989. "The End of History." *National Interest*, Summer, 3–18.

Fukuyama, Francis. 1992. *The End of History and the Last Man*. New York: Free Press.

Giersch, Herbert, Karl-Heinz Paqué, and Holger Schmieding. 1992. *The Fading Miracle: Four Decades of Market Economy in Germany*. New York: Cambridge University Press.

Gilbert, Brett Anitra, Patricia P. McDougall, and David B. Audretsch. 2006. "Clusters, Knowledge Spillovers and New Venture Performance: An Empirical Examination." *Journal of Business Venturing* 23 (4), 405–422.

Gilbert, Brett Anitra, Patricia P. McDougall, and David B. Audretsch. 2006. "New Venture Growth: A Review and Extension." *Journal of Management* 32 (6), 926–950.

Gitlin, Todd. 1993. *The Sixties: Years of Hope, Days of Rage*. New York: Bantam Books.

Glaeser, Edward L. 2014. *Triumph of the City: How Our Greatest Invention Makes Us Richer, Smarter, Greener, Healthier, and Happier*. New York: Penguin.

Glaeser, Edward L. and J. D. Gottlieb. 2009. "The Wealth of Cities: Agglomeration Economies and Spatial Equilibrium in the United States." *Journal of Economic Literature* 47 (4), 983–1028.

Godart, Olivier, Holger Görg, and Aoife Hanley. 2014. "Trust-Based Work-Time and Product Improvements: Evidence from Firm Level Data." Kiel Working Papers No. 1913.

Goodden, Angelica. 2008. *Madame de Staël: the Dangerous Exile*. New York: Oxford University Press.

Griliches, Zvi. 1979. "Issues in Assessing the Contribution of Research and Development to Productivity Growth." *Bell Journal of Economics* 10, 92–116.

Grove, Andy. 1996. *Only the Paranoid Survive*. New York: Crown Books.

Grunenberg, Nina. 2006. *Die Wundertäter, Netzwerke der deutschen Wirtschaft*. Munich: Siedler.

Halberstam, David. 1993. *The Fifties*. New York: Villard Books.

Hall, Sydney G. 1891. "Educational Reforms." *Pedagogical Seminary* (contemporary *Journal of Genetic Psychology*), 1, 1–12.

Hall, Peter and David Soskice. 2001. *Varieties of Capitalism: The Institutional Foundations of Comparative Advantage*. New York: Oxford University Press.

Hannan, Michael T. and John Freeman. 1977. "The Population Ecology of Organizations." *American Journal of Sociology* 82 (5), 929–964.

Hannan, Michael T. and John Freeman. 1989. *Organizational Ecology*. Cambridge, MA: Harvard University Press.

Herzig, Monika. 2011. *David Baker: A Legacy of Music*. Bloomington: Indiana University Press.

Hughes, Kirsty. 1993. "The Role of Technology, Competition and Skills in European Competitiveness." In Kirsty Hughes (ed.), *European Competitiveness*. Cambridge: Cambridge University Press. 133–160.

Hülsbeck, Marcel and Erik E. Lehmann. 2007. "Entrepreneurship Policy in Bavaria: Between Laptop and Lederhosen." In David B. Audretsch, Isabel Grilo, and A. Roy Thurik (eds.), *Handbook of Research on Entrepreneurship Policy*. Cheltenham: Edward Elgar. 200–212.

Hülsbeck, Marcel, Erik E. Lehmann, and Alexander Starnecker. 2013. "Performance of Technology Transfer Offices in Germany." *Journal of Technology Transfer* 38, 199–215.

Institut für Mittelstandsforschung Bonn. 2013. "Der deutsche Mittelstand: Ein Konglomerat verschiedenartigerdchiedenartiger Unternehmen." *IfM Standpunkt* 1.

Jacobs, Jane. 1969. *The Economy of Cities*. New York: Vintage.

Jaffe, Adam. 1989. "The Real Effects of Academic Research." *American Economic Review* 79, 957–970.

Jaffe, Adam, Manuel Trajtenberg, and Rebecca Henderson. 1993. "Geographic Localization of Knowledge Spillovers as Evidenced by Patent Citations." *Quarterly Journal of Economics* 63, 577–598.

Katz, Bruce. 2014. *The Metropolitan Revolution: How Cities and Metros Are Fixing Our Broken Politics and Fragile Economy*. Washington, DC: Brookings.

Keesing, Donald. 1966. "Labor Skills and Comparative Advantage." *American Economic Review* 56, 1249–1258.

Kennedy, Paul. 1989. *The Rise and Decline of Great Powers*. New York: Random House.

Keynes, John Maynard. 1920. *The Economics of the Peace*. New York: Harcourt Brace.

Kulicke, Marianne. 2014. "15 Years of EXIST University-Based Start-Up Programmes." Working paper, Fraunhofer Institute.

Kurz, Heinz D. 2013. *Geschichte des Ökonomischen Denkens*. Munich: C.H. Beck.

Leamer, Edward E. 1995. *The Heckscher-Ohlin Model in Theory and Practice*. Princeton, NJ: Princeton University Press.

Leamer, Edward E. 2007. "A Flat World, a Level Playing Field, a Small World after All, or None of the Above? A Review of Thomas L Friedman's *The World Is Flat*." *Journal of Economic Literature* 45 (1), 83–126.

Lehmann, Erik E., and Doris Neuberger. 2001. "Do Lending Relationships Matter? Evidence from Bank Survey Data in Germany" *Journal of Economic Behavior and Orgnization* 45, 339–359.

Lehmann, Erik E., Doris Neuberger, and Solvig Raethke. 2004. "Lending to Small and Medium-Sized Firms: Is there an East-West Gap in Germany?" *Small Business Economics* 23, 23–39.

Lehmann, Erik E. and Alexander Starnecker. 2012. "Introducing the Universities of Applied Sciences." In David B. Audretsch, Erik E. Lehmann, Albert N. Link, and Alexander Starnecker (eds.), *Technology Transfer in a Global Economy*. Heidelberg: Springer. 99–115.

Lehmann, Erik E. and Jürgen Weigand. 2000. "Does the Governed Corporation Perform Better? Governance Structures and Corporate Performance in Germany." *European Finance Review* 4, 157–195.

LeMaster, J. R., James Darrell Wilson, and Christie Graves Hamric. 1993. "The Awful German Language." In *The Mark Twain Encyclopedia*. London: Routledge. 57–58.

Leontief, Wassily. 1971. "Theoretical Assumptions and Nonobserved Facts." *American Economic Review* 61 (1), 1–7.

Link, Albert N. 1995. *A Generosity of Spirit: The Early History of the Research Triangle Park*. Research Triangle Park: Research Triangle Foundation of North Carolina.

Linss, Vera. 2007. *Die wichtigsten Wirtschaftsdenker*. Wiesbaden: Marix Verlag.

Lochbiler, Don. 1973. *Coming of Age in Detroit, 1873–1973*. Detroit: Wayne State University Press.

Loweinger, T. C. 1971. "The Neo-factor Proportions Theory of International Trade: An Empirical Investigation." *American Economic Review* 61, 675–681.

Maass, F. and B. Fuehrmann. 2012. "Innovationstätigkeit im Mittelstand." Institut für Mittelstandsforschung, *IfM-Materialien*, Bonn.

MacGregor, Neil. 2014. *Germany: Memories of a Nation*. London: Allen Lane.

Magee, Stephen P. 1989. "The Competence Theory of Comparative Advantage." In David B. Audretsch and Michael P. Claudon (eds.), *The Internationalization of U.S. Markets*. New York: New York University Press. 11–23.

Maskus, Keith E., Deborah Battles, and Michael H. Moffett. 1989. "Determinants of the Structure of U.S. Manufacturing Trade with Japan and Korea, 1970–1984." In David B. Audretsch and Michael P. Claudon (eds.), *The Internationalization of U.S. Markets*. New York: New York University Press. 97–121.

McCann, Philip, Dominique Foray and Raquel Artega-Argiles. 2015. "Smart Specialization and its Application in European Regional Policies." In David B. Audretsch, Albert Link, and Mary Walshok (eds.), *The Oxford Handbook of Local Competitiveness*. New York: Oxford University Press.

McCraw, Thomas K. 2007. *Prophet of Innovation: Joseph Schumpeter and Creative Destruction*. Cambridge, MA: Belknap Press of Harvard University Press.

McPherson, James M. 1988. *Battle Cry of Freedom: The Civil War Era*. New York: Oxford University Press.

Mills, David E. and Laurence Schumann. 1985. "Industry Structure with Fluctuating Demand." *American Economic Review* 75, 758–767.

Morrison, Catherine J. and Amy E. Schwartz. 1996. "State Infrastructure and Productive Performance." *American Economic Review* 86, 1095–1111.

Mounk, Yascha. 2014. *Stranger in My Own Country: A Jewish Family in Modern Germany*. New York: Farrar, Straus and Giroux.

Mowery, David, Richard R. Nelson, B. Sampat, and A. Ziedonis. 2004. *Ivory Tower and Industrial Innovation: University-Industry Technology Transfer before and after the Bayh-Dole Act*. Stanford, CA: Stanford University Press.

Nichols, John. 2014. "The Infrastructure of American Democracy Is Dysfunctional." *The Nation*, January 22.

Niven, William J. 1995. "The Reception of Schindler's List in the German Media." *Journal of European Studies*, June 1.

Oezcan, Veysel. 2004. "Germany: Immigration in Transition." Migration Policy Institute, July 1.

Peters, Thomas J. and Robert H. Waterman. 1984. *In Search of Excellence*. New York: Harper and Row.

Piore, Michael M., and Charles Sabel. 1984. *The Second Industrial Divide: Possibilities for Prosperity*. New York: Basic Books.

Putnam, Robert. 2000. *Bowling Alone: The Collapse and Revival of American Community*. New York: Simon and Schuster.

Rinne, Ulf and Klaus F. Zimmermann. 2012. "Another Economic Miracle? The German Labor Market and the Great Recession." *IZA Journal of Labor Policy* 1. 401–423.

Rinne, Ulf and Klaus F. Zimmermann. 2013. "Is Germany the North Star of Labor Market Policy?" *IMF Economic Review* 61 (4), 702–729.

Romer, Paul. 1986. "Increasing Returns and Long-Run Growth." *Journal of Political Economy* 94 (5), 1002–1037.

Romer, Paul. 1990. "Endogenous Technological Change." *Journal of Political Economy* 98, S71–S102.

Romer, Paul. 1994. "The Origins of Endogenous Growth Theory." *Journal of Economic Perspectives* 8, 3–22.

Rose, Frank. 1989. *West of Eden: The End of Innocence at Apple Computer*. New York: Viking Press.

Rupasingha, Anil, Stephan J. Goetz, and David Freshwater. 2002. "Social and Institutional Factors as Determinants of Economic Growth: Evidence from the United States." *Papers in Regional Science* 81, 139–115.

Sarrazin, Thilo. 2010. *Deutschland Schafft Sich Ab: Wie Wir das Land aufs Spiel Setzen*. Berlin: Deutsche Verlags-Anstalt.

Saxenian, AnnaLee. 1994. *Regional Advantage: Culture and Competition in Silicon Valley and Route 128*. Cambridge, MA: Harvard University Press.

Scherer, Frederic M. 1970. *Industrial Market Structure and Economic Performance*. Chicago: Rand McNally.

Schneider, Peter. 2014. *Berlin Now*. New York: Farrar, Straus and Giroux.

Schubert, Klaus and Martina Klein. 2001. *Das Politiklexikon*. Bonn: Dietz.

Schumpeter, Joseph A. 1911. *Theorie der wirtschaftlichen Entwicklung*. Berlin: Duncker und Humblot.

Schumpeter, Joseph A. 1942. *Capitalism, Socialism and Democracy*. New York: Harper.

Schüller, Alfred and Hans-Günter Krüsselberg (eds.). 2004. *Grundbegriffe zur Ordnungstheorie und Politischen Ökonomik*. 6th ed. Marburg: Marburger Ges. f. Ordnungsfragen d. Wirtschaft.

Shlaes, Amity. 1991. *Germany: The Empire Within*. New York: Farrar, Straus and Giroux.

Shonick, Kaja. 2009. "Politics, Culture, and Economics: Reassessing the West German Guest Worker Agreement with Yugoslavia." *Journal of Contemporary History* 44 (4), 719–736.

Siebert, Horst. 2005. *The German Economy: Beyond the Social Market*. Princeton, NJ: Princeton University Press.

Simon, Hermann. 1996. *The Hidden Champions of Germany*. Boston: Harvard Business School Press.

Simon, Hermann. 2009. *Hidden Champions of the Twenty-First Century: The Success Strategies of Unknown World*. Heidelberg: Springer.

Sinn, Gerlinde and Hans-Werner Sinn. 1994. *Jumpstart*. Cambridge, MA: MIT Press.

Sinn, Hans-Werner. 2004. *Ist Deutschland Noch zu Retten?* Berlin: Econ Verlag.

Sinn, Hans-Werner. 2005. *Die Bazar-Ökonomie*. Berlin: Econ Verlag.

Sinn, Hans-Werner. 2009. *Can Germany Be Saved? The Malaise of the World's First Welfare State*. Cambridge, MA: MIT Press.

Snower, Dennis J., Alessio J. G. Brown, and Christian Merkl. 2009. "Globalization and the Welfare State: A Review of Hans-Werner Sinn's *Can Germany Be Saved?*" *Journal of Economic Literature* 47 (1), 136–158.

Sobel, Joel. 2001. "Can We Trust Social Capital?" *Journal of Economic Literature*, March, 40, 139–154.

Solow, Robert. 1956. "A Contribution to the Theory of Economic Growth." *Quarterly Journal of Economics* 39, 312–320.

Solow, Robert. 1957. "Technical Change and the Aggregate Production Function." *Review of Economics and Statistics* 39, 312–320.

Späth, Lothar and Herbert A. Henzler. 1995. *Countdown für Deutschland: Start in der neue Zeit*. Berlin: Siedler.

Spence, Michael. 2011. "Globalization and Unemployment: The Downside of Integrating Markets." *Foreign Affairs*, July–August.

Stigler, George J. 1934. "Production and Distribution in the Short Run." *Journal of Political Economy* 47, 305–327.

Stiglitz, Joseph S. 2004. *The Roaring Nineties: A New History of the World's Most Prosperous Decade*. New York: Norton.

Sutton, John. 1997. "Gibrat's Legacy." *Journal of Economic Literature* 35, 40–59.

Szabo, Steven F. 2015. *German, Russia, and the Rise of Geo-economics*. London: Bloomsbury Academic.

Tent, James F. 1988. *The Free University of Berlin: A Political History*. Bloomington: Indiana University Press.

Thissen, Mark, Fran van Oort, Dario Diodato, and Arjan Ruijs. 2013. *Regional Competitiveness and Smart Specialization in Europe*. London: Edward Elgar.

Thurik, Roy, Erik Stam, and David B. Audretsch. 2013. "The Rise of the Entrepreneurial Economy and the Future of Dynamic Capitalism." *Technovation*, July, 302–310.

Thurow, Lester. 1984. "Losing the Economic Race." *New York Review of Books*, September 27, 29–31.

Thurow, Lester. 1987. "Healing with a Thousand Bandages." *Challenge* 28, 23.

Thurow, Lester. 2002. *Fortune Favors the Bold*. Cambridge, MA: MIT Press.

Turner, Steven R. 1972. "The Prussian Universities and the Research Imperative, 1806–1848." Ph.D. dissertation, Princeton University.

Vogt, Hannah. 1961. *Schuld oder Verhangnis: Zwölf Fragen an Deutschlands jüngste Vergangenheit*. Frankfurt am Main: Verlag M. Diesterweg.

Von Thünen, Johann Heinrich. 1826. *Der isoli[e]rte Staat in Beziehung auf Landwirtschaft und Nationalökonomie, oder Untersuchungen über den Einfluß, den die Getreidepreise, der Reichthum des Bodens und die Abgaben auf den Ackerbau ausüben*. Hamburg: Perthes.

Watson, Peter. 2011. *The German Genius: Europe's Third Renaissance, the Second Scientific Revolution, and the Twentieth Century*. New York: Harper Perennial.

Wernerfelt, Birger 1984. "The Resource-Based View of the Firm." *Strategic Management Journal* 5 (2), 171–180.

Wessel, Maxwell. 2012. "Why Big Companies Can't Innovate." *Harvard Business Review*, September 27.

Wessner, Charles C. (ed.). 2008. *National Research Council: An Assessment of the SBIR Program*. Washington, DC: National Academies Press.

Wakefield, Andres. 2009. *The Disordered Police State: German Cameralism as Science and Practice*. Chicago: University of Chicago Press.

Whyte, William H. 1956. *The Organization Man*. New York: Simon and Schuster.

Wood, Jonathan. 2003. *The Volkswagen Beetle*. Buckinghamshire: Shire Publications.

Woolley, Jennifer L. 2013. "The Creation and Configuration of Infrastructure for Entrepreneurship in Emerging Domains of Activity." *Entrepreneurship Theory and Practice* 38, 1042–2587.

World Economic Forum. 2013. *Human Capital Report*. Geneva: World Economic Forum.

Wurgler, Jeffrey. 2000. "Financial Markets and the Allocation of Capital." *Journal of Financial Economics* 58 (1–2), 187–214.

Yamawaki, Hideki. 1985. "International Trade and Foreign Direct Investment in West German Manufacturing Industries." In Joachim Schwalbach (ed.), *Industry Structure and Performance*. Berlin: Edition Sigma. 247–286.

Zimmerman, Klaus F. 2006. "Vorwort." In Klaus F. Zimmerman (ed.), *Deutschland—was nun? Reformen für Wirtschaft und Gesellschaft*. Munich: Deutscher Taschenbuch Verlag. v–vi.

Zimmermann, Klaus F. 2006. "Die Zukunft gestalten!" In Klaus F. Zimmermann (ed.) *Deutschland—was nun? Reformen für Wirtschaft und Gesellschaft*. Munich: Verlag Beck. 1–28.

Zingales, Luigi. 1998. "Survival of the Fittest or the Fattest? Exit and Financing in the Trucking Industry." *Journal of Finance* 53 (3), 905–938.

Index

Locators followed by n refers to notes.